全国高等院校法律英语专业统编教材
法律英语证书（LEC）全国统一考试指定用书

法律英语写作教程

Legal English Writing Course

张法连　主编

北京大学出版社
PEKING UNIVERSITY PRESS

图书在版编目(CIP)数据

法律英语写作教程/张法连主编. —北京:北京大学出版社,2016.8
(全国高等院校法律英语专业统编教材)
ISBN 978-7-301-27384-5

Ⅰ. ①法… Ⅱ. ①张… Ⅲ. ①法律—英语—写作—高等学校—教材 Ⅳ. ①H315

中国版本图书馆 CIP 数据核字(2016)第 186597 号

书　　　名	法律英语写作教程 FALÜ YINGYU XIEZUO JIAOCHENG
著作责任者	张法连　主编
策 划 编 辑	刘宗彦
责 任 编 辑	刘文静
标 准 书 号	ISBN 978-7-301-27384-5
出 版 发 行	北京大学出版社
地　　　址	北京市海淀区成府路 205 号　100871
网　　　址	http://www.pup.cn
电 子 邮 箱	编辑部 pupwaiwen@pup.cn　总编室 zpup@pup.cn
新 浪 微 博	@北京大学出版社　@北大出版社法律图书
电　　　话	邮购部 62752015　发行部 62750672　编辑部 62754382
印 刷 者	北京溢漾印刷有限公司
经 销 者	新华书店
	787 毫米×1092 毫米　16 开本　21.5 印张　375 千字 2016 年 8 月第 1 版　2024 年 9 月第 6 次印刷
定　　　价	68.00 元

未经许可,不得以任何方式复制或抄袭本书之部分或全部内容。
版权所有,侵权必究
举报电话: 010-62752024　电子信箱: fd@pup.cn
图书如有印装质量问题,请与出版部联系,电话: 010-62756370

前　言

　　法律英语是法律科学与英语语言学有机结合形成的一门实践性很强的交叉学科,是 ESP(English for Specific Purposes)最重要的分支之一。法律英语是以普通英语为基础,在立法和司法等活动中形成和使用的具有法律专业特点的语言,是指表述法律科学概念以及诉讼或非诉讼法律事务时所使用的英语。当今世界的发展日新月异,经济全球化进程突飞猛进,国际交流合作日益加强,涉外法务活动空前频繁。中国共产党十八届四中全会提出要加强涉外法律工作,运用法律手段维护国家的发展利益。经济全球化过程中我们所面临的很多问题其实都是法律问题,而这些法律问题中的绝大多数又都属于涉外法律的工作范畴,所有这些工作都需要法律工作者通过专业外语完成。国家亟需明晰国际法律规则、通晓英语语言的"精英明法"复合型人才,法律英语的重要性日益彰显,掌握专业外语已经成为法律人必备的职业素质。法律英语证书(LEC)全国统一考试的成功推出和中央政法委、教育部"卓越法律人才计划"的顺利启动无疑把法律英语的学习和研究推向了高潮。

　　法律英语是高校英语、法学等专业教学改革的新方向。随着高校英语专业教学改革不断深化,国内许多高校在外语院系开设了法律英语课程或设置了法律英语方向,有些高校甚至尝试设置了法律英语专业,收到了良好的社会效果。2013年高等教育出版社出版发行《法律英语专业教学大纲》,标志着法律英语专业的诞生,给高校外语院系设置法律英语专业指明了方向。本套教材正是以该大纲为重要依据编写而成。

　　美国法是英美法系的典型代表,其法律体系完整、内容丰富,既有传统的普通法,又有新兴的成文法;既有统一的联邦法,又有各州的法律。同时,美国法在世界范围内影响深远,学习研究美国法意义重大,这不仅表现为许多国家都在研究美国的法律规则,借鉴其成熟做法,还表现为许多国际公约也参照美国法的理念、原则、规则制订。因此,本书作为法律英语专业的写作教材,主要介绍美国法学院学生必须掌握的几种法律文书的写作方法,当然这也是国际上通用的,也是我们处理涉外法律事务必须掌握的写作技能。

　　本套教材共包括《法律英语精读教程》(上、下)、《法律英语泛读教程》(上、下)、《法律英语写作教程》《法律英语翻译教程》《法律英语视听说》和《英美法律文化教程》以及配套教学使用的《英美法律术语双解》。

　　涉外法律实践要求我们将谈判、咨询、法律研究以及辩论的能力整合在一起。而有一种能力是以上所有能力的基础，这就是高效的法律英语写作能力。法律文书应当是清楚、精准、全面而且通俗易懂的，但涉外法律文书种类的繁杂给我国涉外法律从业人员的工作带来极大的障碍。为了方便涉外法律从业人员学习法律文书写作，本书详细介绍了几种重要、实用的美国法律文书的写作方法。

　　本书共分为六部分。第一部分简略介绍了法律英语写作的基础知识。第二部分为律师信函，详细介绍了几种常用信函的写法。与当事人的沟通信函的主要目的是与当事人明确沟通，因此一般使用通俗易懂的非法律语言，注重的是语言技巧，这是涉外法律从业人员必须轻松掌握并熟练运用的。与对方当事人或其代理律师的沟通信函多是与诉讼相关的信函，涉及大量法律术语，这是希望在法律英语方面提升自己的读者应当重点学习的内容。律师处理日常事务的信函也很有特点，通过本章的介绍使欲从事涉外法律事务的人士在处理日常事务时有章可循。第三部分介绍了法律分析报告（Law Office Memo）或法律备忘录的写法。在英美法系国家，案件法律分析报告由初级律师撰写，高级律师审阅或最终定稿，其内容是通过对案件的客观分析，预测相关的法律适用将对其当事人产生的影响。本书该部分内容主要介绍了概括事实的方法、提出案件主要争议点的技巧以及案件剖析讨论的写作方式。第四部分案件辩论书（Briefs）在法律英语写作中占有相当重要的地位。尽管案件辩论书在许多方面与法律分析报告相类似，但是两者在本质上是不同的。法律分析报告是客观地分析究竟哪方当事人的抗辩理由更加充分，并且一般要在分析的最后阶段才能得出结论；而案件辩论书的撰写人在写作之前已经知道了基本结论，其主要任务是为结论寻找支持的依据，并极力证明他的当事人的抗辩理由更加充分，应当得到法院的支持。因此，在写作方法上，案件辩论书也有别于法律分析报告。我国从事涉外法律工作人员应当特别注意，向初审法院和向上诉法院提交的案件辩论书等法律文书的要求格式是不同的。本书在第四部分着重介绍向初审法院提交的案件辩论书和向上诉法院提交的案件辩论书的写作方法。法庭上的双方律师口头辩论是庭审过程中的重要环节之一，口头辩论并不是律师信口开河、随意发挥。口头辩论的基础就是案件辩论书。第五部分简单介绍了常用合同文本的起草。第六部分主要介绍法律引用问题，引用的准确与否直接影响到法律文书的质量和说服力。

本书的参考资料全部来自美国知名法学院学生所使用的原版法律英语写作参考用书,我们力求保证所选资料的原汁原味。同时,书中引用了大量的律师信函、法律分析报告、案件辩论书等主要法律文书的原版范文。

参加本书编写工作的还有中国石油大学张建科、徐文彬副教授,甘肃政法大学赵永平、马彦峰副教授,中国政法大学曲欣老师和河南财经政法大学朱洁副教授等。感谢法律英语证书(LEC)全国统一考试指导委员会将该套教材指定为复习应考 LEC 的参考用书。

各位教师或同学在使用本书的过程中有什么问题,欢迎及时与编者联系:zhangbook16@yahoo.com。

编者
2016 年 3 月于中国政法大学

CONTENTS 目录

Chapter 1	Basics of Legal Writing	001
Chapter 2	Writing Letters	040
Chapter 3	Law Office Memo	089
Chapter 4	Writing Briefs	121
Chapter 5	Drafting Contracts	248
Chapter 6	Understanding Legal Citations	281
Appendix		294
References		336

Chapter 1

Basics of Legal Writing

> Lawyers in practice are generally judged by the final product they produce: the written, negotiated text. Clearly, in my firm, the first thing new lawyers will be judged upon is their writing. The fastest way to get ahead as a new lawyer is to be an able writer. The fastest way to fail is to be a poor writer.
> —— Bryn Vaaler, Compositional Practice: A Comment on "A Liberal Education in Law," 1 J. ALWD 148, 149 (2002). [1]

Legal writing is a special type of writing done by attorneys, judges, legislators and others in law. The purpose of this writing is to communicate various legal rights, analysis, and legal duties, etc. Unlike regular writing, legal writing is technical and involves continuous dependence on citations, gives importance to precedent and uses special legalese that sounds very formal. There has been a move to reduce such very formal style of writing and to make legal writing simple enough for the layman to understand. However, one must remember that the purpose of legal writing is to make a precise document and informal style may make a legal document's intentions hazy. [2]

1. English Articles

The use of articles ("a" "an" and "the" or no article) is an area of special significance for multilingual writers, since it is characterized by large variation across languages. In consequence, any error in this area will be very noticeable in an text as a mark of non-native writing. Given this fact, it is important for

---

[1] http://raymondpward.typepad.com/rainman2/2004/12/the_importance_.html
[2] http://ezinearticles.com/? What-is-Legal-Writing? &id=1223274

multilingual writers to master the use and non-use of articles and to learn the meaning their use/non-use conveys in English.

e.g. THE complaint was dismissed.

A new witness changed the course of the trial.

AN accountant was called to testify.

[0] Justice was served.

This section covers the English articles THE, A, AN and their omission. We will also show you a method for deciding which article to use when you are not sure.

Two important concepts are linked to article usage: "countability" and "definiteness." Understanding these concepts will help you decide whether to use an article or not and on which article to use.

Definiteness Articles in English have two types of reference: DEFINITE (referring to a specific member of a group, e.g. THE) and INDEFINITE (referring to any member of a group, e.g. A, AN). A "definite" article is used to give specific reference to a noun and to refer to something known to both the writer/speaker and the reader/listener.

e.g. I welcomed THE visitor today.

(Definite reference: both the writer/speaker and the reader/listener know what visitor you are referring to)

vs.

I received A visitor today.

(Indefinite reference: you are not specifying what visitor you are referring to and you are the only one who knows that)

The definite article THE is used when BOTH the writer/speaker and the reader/listener know what is being referred to. If neither of them or only one of them knows what is being referred to, then the indefinite articles A/AN should be used.

Definiteness	Examples	Does the ___ know what is being referred to?	
		Writer/Speaker	Reader/Listener
Definite	I read THE book yesterday.	yes	yes
Indefinite	I read A book on Criminal Law yesterday.	yes	no
Indefinite	I know you read A book on Criminal Law.	no	yes
Indefinite	I will buy A book on Criminal Law.	no	no

Chapter 1
Basics of Legal Writing

(1) Indefinite Articles: A and AN

A and AN refer to any member of a group; you are not referring to any member in particular.

- **a**+singular noun beginning with a consonant: **a** reaction
- **an**+singular noun beginning with a vowel: **an** act
- **a**+singular noun beginning with a consonant sound (even though it may start with a vowel letter): **a** uniform (same sound as in *young* or *yesterday*)

When an adjective modifies the noun, the use of A or AN is determined by the initial sound of the adjective immediately following the article (and no longer by the noun):

an enemy;	but	**a** furious enemy;
a performance;	but	**an** average performance;
a European criminal;	but	**an** undetectable European criminal;

Unlike other languages, English requires the presence of indefinite articles to indicate membership:

• religion:	Maria Ramirez is **a** Roman Catholic from the NY archdiocese.
• profession:	I am **a** lawyer.
• nation:	Mr. Brown is **an** Englishman who immigrated to this country in 1959.

(2) Definite Article: THE

English requires the use of the definite article THE before singular and plural nouns to indicate specific reference, reference to a particular member of a group.

Compare: A dog bit the plaintiff. (any dog; either you do not need to specify which dog you are referring to or you simply don't know)

vs.

The dog bit the plaintiff. (a specific dog; both you and your reader/listener know which dog you are referring to)

In general, the article THE is used:

- with noncountable nouns that are made more specific by using a modifying phrase or clause (underlined below):

e.g. **the** defense <u>presented at the trial</u> was especially weak

the image he projects does not favor his case

the concept of diversity applies here

• and when a noun has a specific reference to something unique;

e.g. **the** 2001 CUNY budget

the Pentagon

the last State of the Union address

• and it is **not** used with noncountable nouns that refer to something in a general sense;

e.g. [0] Justice is a concept difficult to grasp sometimes. [0]＝No article

The use of THE (Definite Reference) is determined by the following specific instances:

• When something is mentioned for the second time in the text;

e.g. I wrote a letter of complaint [first mention, indefinite].

Instead,

I wrote a letter of complaint. THE letter had an angry tone [second mention, definite]

• With the superlative (because it signals there is only one possible referent);

e.g. THE son was THE most articulate witness in the case.

• When only one entity exists;

e.g. THE Moon is a satellite. [There is only one satellite we refer to as "the Moon."]

• When a phrase modifying the noun provides more information that specifies the reference of the noun;

e.g. THE witness (that) you brought refused to testify.

THE witness from Connecticut refused to testify.

THE witness who refused to testify was arrested in a street incident yesterday.

Note

• I read a book about Criminal Law for the exam. (the phrase about Criminal Law is not specific enough to limit the reference of the noun; it could be ANY book about Criminal Law)

vs.

Chapter 1
Basics of Legal Writing

THE book about Criminal Law that was assigned by the professor was too complicated. (the phrase that was assigned by the professor limits the reference to only ONE entity; it's not ANY book: it's the book assigned by the professor).

• When both the writer/speaker and the reader/listener know what is being referred to (maybe because they are in the same situation);

e.g. Open THE window.

I'm going to THE library.

Countable vs. Uncountable Nouns It is important for multilingual writers to recognize crosslinguistic differences in this area. A noun considered uncountable in one language may be considered countable in another and, consequently, pluralized, e.g. *soap* is an uncountable noun in English and cannot be pluralized except by preposing the phrase *a bar of* to it (*I like to use scented soap* vs. *I bought two bars of soap* **but**: *I bought two soaps* is wrong). However, in Spanish the same form can be pluralized, e.g. *Me gustausarjabón* (singular) *desodorante* vs. *Compré dos jabones* (plural).

Countable nouns refer to people, places or things that can be counted (one contract/two contracts, one witness/two witnesses). A countable noun can always be made plural—usually by adding -s or -es or some other plural marker (e.g. *trial[s]*, *parti[es]*, *child[ren]*).

Some words do not show any variation in form between the singular and plural (e.g. *The sheep is in the field* / *The sheep are in the field*).

Uncountable nouns often refer to drinks and food, other general substances, or concepts (*meat, tea, steel, information, justice*).

Examples of Uncountable Nouns in English:

• <u>Food and Drink</u>: bacon, beef, beer, bread, butter, cabbage, candy, cauliflower, chicken, chocolate, coffee, corn, cream, fish, fruit, juice, lettuce, meat, milk, oil, pasta, rice, salt, spinach, sugar, tea, water, whiskey, wine, yogurt.

• <u>General Substances</u>: air, cement, clay, coal, copper, dirt, dust, foam, gasoline, gold, ice, leather, paper, petroleum, plastic, rain, rubber, silver, soap, steel, wood, wool.

• <u>Abstract Nouns</u>: abandonment, access, adultery, advice, alimony, anger, anguish, arson, authentication, beauty, capacity, conduct, confidence, courage, deprivation, desperation, discretion, employment, empowerment, evidence, extortion, fortune, fun, happiness, health, honesty, housing, information, insurance, intelligence, intent, knowledge, land, love, malice, negligence, poverty, privacy, real estate, sadness, satisfaction, strength, truth, wealth.

- Others: biology, clothing, darkness, equipment, furniture, gossip, homework, jewelry, luggage, machinery, mail, money, music, news, poetry, pollution, research, scenery, traffic, transportation, violence, weather, weight, work.

Some uncountable nouns (except for concepts) can be turned into countable nouns by preposing a phrase to them (*two bottles of wine, a bar of soap, a piece of information, an act of violence, a burst of anger, a piece of evidence*).

e.g. The defendant's lawyer is sure the judge will accept <u>new evidence</u> in this case.

vs. The defendant's lawyer is sure the judge will accept three new pieces of evidence in this case.

Some uncountable nouns can be used in the plural form but their meaning changes.

experience/experiences: e.g. He had to rely on experience. / I lived unforgettable experiences in this house.

light/lights: e.g. The apartment didn't have much light. / The bus did not stop at the (traffic) lights.

paper/papers: e.g. This office is wasting too much paper. / I submitted all my papers yesterday.

How can I distinguish between using a definite or an indefinite article with a common noun when I am not sure which one is correct?

If you are unsure whether to use a definite (THE) or an indefinite article (A, AN) with a common noun, you should ask yourself the following questions:

Chapter 1
Basics of Legal Writing

Is the Noun Singular?	Yes Is the noun definite?	Yes use THE e.g. **The** report he submitted was exhaustive.
		No use A/AN e.g. His fax consisted of **a** letter and **a** flyer.
	No Is the noun definite?	Yes use THE e.g. (Pl.) **The** reports to my office were not clear. e.g. (Unc.) **The** information that the officers got was accurate.
		No 0 (No article) e.g. (Pl.) The police sent detailed reports on the case. e.g. (Unc.) There was a serious leakage of information on the case.

<u>Remember</u>: If the Noun is definite (whether it is singular, plural or uncountable), it takes THE.

Some Common Errors to Avoid

• Sometimes non-native speakers of English use "A" or "AN" with plural or uncountable nouns:

a cases (wrong)	instead of	a case
an information (wrong)	instead of	a piece of information

• Some multilingual writers use no article at all for a singular noun:

I saw accident (wrong)	instead of	I saw an accident
I am lawyer (wrong)	instead of	I am a lawyer

• Sometimes non-native speakers use two determiners together when they are not supposed to:

The some criminals were hurt during the incident. (Wrong)
instead of:
Some criminals were hurt during the incident.
or: The criminals were hurt during the incident.

• Another common error is to pluralize uncountable nouns:

The plaintiff bought a bread at the Waltmann's bakery. (Wrong)
Instead of
The plaintiff bought a loaf of bread at the Waltmann's bakery.
The detainee provided a very useful information. (Wrong)
Instead of
The detainee provided very useful pieces of information

• Sometimes, multilingual writers use the indefinite articles A/AN with count nouns in some prepositional phrases that are idiomatic expressions such as *on vacation*, *by plane*, *by car*, *at home*, *at school*, *in school*, *to bed*, *in bed*, *to college*, *at night*, *in court*.

e.g. The witness testified that he had seen the defendant take the child to school[and NOT to THE school] himself.

The Use of Articles with Proper Nouns

Proper nouns refer to specific people, places and things (Martin Luther King, New York City, St. Patrick's Cathedral). However, even though these nouns are inherently definite, the definite article THE is not used with most SINGULAR proper nouns.

e.g. The Susan Brown was considered a troubled woman. (Wrong)
Instead of
Susan Brown was considered a troubled woman.

(This is also a source of errors, since the use of the definite article with proper nouns is allowed in other languages)

In English, you use the article THE with proper nouns

• to emphasize the uniqueness of that entity;
e.g. It's THE Barbra Streisand.

• to specify what singular entity you were referring to;
e.g. THE Elvis I got to know was a defeated king.

• to accompany PLURAL proper nouns, including the plural form of a family name;
e.g. THE Johnsons will go to court today.
The United States
The United Nations

Chapter 1
Basics of Legal Writing

- with proper nouns containing the word OF or a political word like "kingdom" "union" or "republic" or organizational words like "institute" "foundation" or "corporation."

e.g. The city of New Orleans

The Republic of Korea

the City University of New York

The Fulbright Foundation

the Chase Corporation

The Commonwealth of Virginia

But In phrases that have 2 proper noun names, use THE only if the form contains OF;

e.g. THE School of Law of the City University vs. CUNY Law School

THE University of Oxford vs. Oxford

THE city of New Orleans vs. New Orleans

THE Republic of Korea vs. Korea

- before the names of specific geographic regions of most bodies of water;

e.g. The Mississippi River

The Atlantic Ocean

the Middle East

In English you DO NOT use the definite article THE:

- before nouns in the possessive case ('s) if the noun does not take THE;

e.g. The plaintiff learned of THE Mary Brown's responsibility in the theft by reading the defendant's diary. (Wrong)

Instead of

The plaintiff learned of Mary Brown's responsibility in the theft by reading the defendant's diary.

- before most singular proper nouns, including names of most countries, cities, states, continents, streets, parks and persons;

e.g. The corpse was found in Yosemite National Park.

He was part of an expedition to Argentina, Brazil and Peru.

The Use of Articles with Proper Nouns

Do's	Don'ts
• geographical areas (the South, the Middle East, the Far West) • names of seas, oceans and rivers (the Mediterranean, the Atlantic, the Hudson) • gulfs, peninsulas, forests, and deserts (the Persian Gulf, the Valdez Peninsula, the Black Forest, the Sahara) • points on the globe (the Capricorn, the South Pole)	• names of countries (Argentina, Ireland, Iraq), but the US and the Netherlands • names of continents (America, Africa) • names of states, towns or cities (Illinois, Edison, Philadelphia) • names of streets (Main St., Astoria Blvd., Jewel Ave.) • names of islands (Fire Island) but: the Hebrides, the Faroe Islands (island chains) • names of mountains (Mount Sinai, Mount Fuji) but: the Andes or the Alps (ranges of mountains) • names of lakes and bays (Lake Ontario, San Francisco Bay) but: the Great Lakes (a group of lakes)

2. Active/Passive Voice

In a sentence using active voice, the subject of the sentence performs the action expressed in the verb. In a sentence using passive voice, the subject is acted upon. Here are some examples.

a. *active voice*: The police officer arrested the man.

(*The police officer is the subject of the sentence and is performing the action of arresting.*)

b. *passive voice*: The man was arrested by the police officer.

(*The man is the subject of the sentence but he is not performing the action of arresting.*)

A shortcut to try and identify passive construction in your writing is to look for an extra "be" verb (is, are, was, were) and the word "by."

a. *active voice*: The police officer arrested the man.

b. *passive voice*: The man was arrested by the police officer. The man was arrested.

Why should I use the active voice?

(1) The active voice is more concise. For example,

a. active voice: The dog chased the cat. (five words)

b. passive voice: The cat was chased by the dog. (seven words)

(2) The active voice is often stronger than the passive voice. For example,

a. active voice: Judges must explain the reasons behind their decisions.

Chapter 1
Basics of Legal Writing

b. passive voice: The reasons behind their decisions must be explained by judges.

(3) The passive voice tempts the writer to omit the identity of the actor, thus producing a fuzzy truncated passive.

truncated passive: A copy of every Action Letter shall be sent to the Clerk of the Administrative Office for entry and filing, and a memorandum briefly describing the Action Letter shall be distributed to each Commissioner within three days thereafter.

(*Using passive voice here leaves a lot of questions: Who is supposed to send the copy to the Clerk? Who is supposed to write the memorandum? Who is supposed to distribute the memorandum? We can't tell, because the writer used the truncated passive to hide the actor.*)

Tip: In general, use the active voice in your writing.

Is there ever a good reason to use passive voice?

Yes. Here are the four most common good reasons.

(1) Sometimes you may not want to name the actor because you want to play down the actor's role in the event. (For instance, maybe the actor is your client.) *Example*: When the lights went out, several punches were thrown.

(2) Sometimes it's the action that's important, not who does it. *Example*: This Act may be cited as the Unlawful Detention Act of 2002.

(3) Sometimes you may not know who did the acting. *Example*: During the following six months, the fence wire was cut on nine separate occasions.

(4) Sometimes you need the passive in order to connect this sentence smoothly with the preceding sentence or sentences. *Example*: The key question is, therefore, when did the defendant actually receive the summons and complaint? The summons and complaint were not served on the defendant in person until May 18th.

Tip: Be consistent.

Whether you are using active or passive voice, be consistent within a sentence.

a. He *tried* to act cool when he slipped in the puddle, but he was still *laughed at* by the other students. (*Uses active voice in the first clause, passive voice in the second clause*)

b. He tried to act cool when he slipped in the puddle, but the other students still laughed at him. (*Uses active voice in both parts of the sentence.*)

3. Run-on Sentences

Run-on sentences are among the most common sentence-level errors. Although many people think of run-ons as sentences that are just "too long," the problem has little to do with sentence length.

Simply put, run-on sentences are created when two (or more) independent clauses are improperly joined. (An independent clause is a clause that contains a subject and a verb and can stand alone as a complete sentence.)

In a run-on, independent clauses may be run together, with no punctuation or transitional words between them.

e.g. The attorney encouraged her client to settle the case out of court the client refused because he wanted to go to trial.

Or they may be insufficiently connected with just a comma.

e.g. The lawyer handed the judge a memo, it fell on the floor.

(This type of run-on is often called a *comma splice*.)

Once you've identified them, run-ons can be easily corrected in several ways.

(1) Make the run-on two separate sentences. This is often the best choice when the original sentence is very long.

e.g. The attorney encouraged her client to settle the case out of court. The client refused because he wanted to go to trial.

(2) Use a semicolon, or a semicolon plus a transitional word, to link the clauses.

e.g. The lawyer handed the judge a memo; *however*, it fell on the floor.

(3) Use a conjunction (and a comma) to join the clauses.

e.g. The lawyer handed the judge a memo, *but* it fell on the floor.

(4) Reword the sentence to turn one of the independent clauses into a dependent clause using a subordinating conjunction.

e.g. *When* the lawyer handed the judge a memo, it fell on the floor.

Examples of common subordinating conjunctions are *when*, *because*, *before*, *after*, *whereas*, *while*, and *unless*.

4. Sentence Fragments

Sentence fragments, along with run-on sentences, are among the most frequently made sentence errors. A fragment can be defined as a sentence that does not express a complete thought — most often because it is missing a key element, such as a subject or verb, or begins with a subordinating word.

The following examples are all fragments, for different reasons.

Example 1: The attorney objecting to the line of questioning.

The problem with this so-called sentence is that it's missing a verb. Although "objecting" looks like a verb, in this case it's not. Look closely: The phrase "objecting to the line of questioning" is really being used as an adjective to describe "attorney." Which attorney is being discussed? The one who's objecting to the line of questioning.

To make this into a complete sentence, you need to add a verb. If you want to relate a simple, straightforward action, try:

The attorney objected to the line of questioning.

If, however, you wanted to say something more about that attorney, you could write:

The attorney objecting to the line of questioning rose to her feet.

Here, the word "rose" functions as a verb, making this a complete sentence.

Example 2: The jurors remained in the hotel for three days. Bickering the whole time.

While the first sentence here is complete, the second is not — it is missing a subject. The second sentence seems to be an afterthought to the first, so you could link them together:

The jurors remained in the hotel for three days, bickering the whole time.

Or you could add a subject to the second sentence to make it complete:

The jurors remained in the hotel for three days. They were bickering the whole time.

Example 3: Unless the witness testifies.

This sentence is really a dependent (or subordinate) clause that can't stand on its own. If you read it aloud, you're probably thinking, "Unless the witness testifies — WHAT?" The writer here probably meant to attach this clause to the sentence before or after it. The problem could be corrected either way:

This case will be dismissed unless the witness testifies;

or

Unless the witness testifies, we will surely lose this case.

You can prevent fragments of this sort by making sure that whenever you begin with a subordinating word (such as *unless*, *because*, *when*, *if*, etc.), you include enough information in the sentence to create a complete thought.

As a general rule, the best way to avoid creating sentence fragments is to ask yourself, when writing a sentence: "Does this sentence, standing on its own, express a complete thought?" If not, check to see what elements are missing.

Subject/Verb Agreement

Subject/verb agreement can seem straightforward for native speakers and others comfortable with English; we know to write "the attorney argues" and "the attorneys argue." However, some special circumstances can make it more difficult to tell whether a subject and verb really do agree. These complications can arise from the words themselves, or from their order in a particular sentence.

Recognizing Plural and Singular Nouns

Again, the basics are straightforward — we usually add an "s" to the end of a noun to form a plural (a group of more than one "defendant" constitutes "defendants") and know the most common irregular plurals (a group of more than one "child" is a group of "children"). But here are a few to watch out for.

Some words you might not realize are singular

(1) Words that seem to refer to a group but must be treated like individuals because they are grammatically singular. They are:

another	anybody	anyone	anything
each	either	every	everybody
everyone	less	little	much
neither	nobody	none	no one
nothing	somebody	someone	something

For some words, it may help to think of the word split into its parts, so that "everyone" becomes "every one," "none" becomes "not one," and so on. This strategy emphasizes that the subject is "one" ("every" indicates which "one" is under consideration) and "one" is obviously singular.

Wrong: "Of all the students in the class, none have taken Latin."

Right: "Of all the students in the class, none has taken Latin."

(2) Words that end in "s" but represent a concept as a whole. Some examples: news, politics, statistics, economics.

Wrong: "Gymnastics are more dangerous than football."

Right: "Gymnastics is more dangerous than football."

(3) Collective nouns that represent a group of individuals acting as a body. Consider the following.

Right: "The Sons of the Revolution has an intertwined relationship with the state."

Although under ordinary circumstances, "sons" would take a plural verb, in this case the writer has correctly understood that "Sons of the Revolution" is a proper noun referring to one organization as a whole, rather than several particular sons.

Similarly, some common nouns that may represent a group of people acting as one are:

board (of directors)	committee	corporation	couple
court	family	government	jury
majority	panel (of judges)		

Note that some of these words should be handled differently if they are used to represent a group of individuals acting separately (see "Some words you might not realize are plural," below), but that some are always singular; for example, whether it consists of one individual, as in a trial court, or of a body of people, "the court" is regarded as an institution, and therefore takes a singular verb.

Wrong: "The court stated that they were ill-equipped to second-guess the trial court judge's determination."

Right: "The court stated that it was ill-equipped to second-guess the trial court judge's determination."

This is also true of expressions dealing with time, money, and weight.

Wrong: "Five thousand dollars were awarded to the plaintiff."

Right: "Five thousand dollars was awarded to the plaintiff."

Consider such amounts as lump sums rather than individual dollars (pounds, hours, etc.).

Some words you might not realize are plural

(1) Words that come from Latin. "Data" and "agenda" are both plural; although they are often treated as singular in informal conversation, for the purpose of professional writing they should be treated with technical accuracy as plural.

Wrong: "The data does not support this conclusion."

Right: "The data do not support this conclusion."

Or,

Right: "The datum does not support this conclusion."

Some singular/plural pairs that follow this model: agendum/agenda, criterion/criteria, datum/data, dictum/dicta.

(2) Collective nouns that represent a group of individuals who are acting independently. Whereas, for example, the word "jury" would take a singular verb when the jurors act in concert ("the jury decided that ..."), it would take a plural verb when differences between the group are emphasized.

Wrong: "The jury disagrees [among themselves] on this issue."

Right: "The jury disagree on this issue."

If this construction sounds awkward to you, you might rebuild the sentence with a different subject.

Right: "The members of the jury disagree on this issue."

Note that some collective nouns always take plural verbs. Some examples: Elderly, police, poor, young.

Right: "The elderly receive special protection under the law."

Recognizing Subjects and Verbs in Unusual Places

In many sentences, the verb immediately follows the subject: "The police officer frisked the suspect." This form is both common and effective because the close proximity of subject and verb allows the whole sentence to be comprehended quickly. However, variations occur and you cannot necessarily depend on the subject of the sentence to be the noun just left of the verb. Here are some instances of slightly less common structures.

Intervening Words

Sometimes a group of words that modify the subject will come before the verb. This situation can be tricky, because it will put a noun closely related to the subject right next to the verb. Here's an example.

Wrong: "The criminal nature of these incidents do not divest Family Court of jurisdiction."

The writer has tried to create agreement, matching a plural noun, "incidents," with a plural verb, "do not divest." This mistake is natural because "incidents" appears where we often expect the subject, right before the verb. However, "incidents" actually belongs to a prepositional phrase that modifies an earlier word, "nature," and the word should agree with that verb.

Right: "The criminal nature of these incidents does not divest Family Court of jurisdiction."

A test: Try saying the sentence without the intervening words — "The criminal nature do not," or "The criminal nature does not"?

Verbs Preceding Subjects

While verbs usually come after subjects, in a few instances you will find them reversed. This is most common in questions ("What is the standard governing municipal tort liability, and which elements must be met to satisfy the special relationship exception to that rule?") and in sentences beginning with "there."

Right: "There is a long history of judicial intervention in public schools since *Brown v. Board of Education*."

Right: "There are several criteria that courts use in deciding whether or not to intervene in public schools."

Note that "there" is not the subject of the sentence; look after the verb to find the subject and check for agreement. In the first example, the subject, "history," is singular, and should be paired with "is." In the second, the subject, "criteria," is plural, and should be paired with "are."

Compound Subjects

Subjects made up of several individual components joined with "and" take plural verbs: "Both New Horizons and Queens Rising have contracts with the state to provide twenty-four-hour care for youth." However, a couple of special cases exist. Keep an eye out for introductory words such as "each" "every" "either" and "neither."

Subjects joined with "and" are plural, but subjects joined with "or" or "nor" are not (necessarily). Consider the following.

Right: "Neither the Office for Civil Rights nor the Human Rights Commission in Vermont is likely to file a court claim against Bennington."

Although the subject has two elements, "Office for Civil Rights" and "Human Rights Commission," they do not have an additive quality; see "some words you might not realize are singular," above, for a discussion of words like "neither." However, a plural verb is appropriate if the part of the compound subject nearest to the verb is plural. A pair of examples will clarify this.

Right: "Neither the plaintiffs nor the defendant wants to suggest settlement first."

Right: "Neither the plaintiff nor the defendants want to suggest settlement first."

The verb in such cases may be singular or plural, but should agree with the nearest part of the subject. Your ear can guide you here; both "defendant want" and "defendants wants" sound wrong, regardless of any subjects they might be paired with.

Finally, when a compound subject involves the word "each" or "every," use a singular verb. (See "some words you might not realize are singular," above.)

Right: "Every pleading, written motion, and other paper is required to bear the signature of at least one attorney of record."

5. Pronouns

Pronouns are words such as "I" "it" "they" "who" and "this" that stand in for nouns, noun phrases, and other pronouns. This is not a comprehensive introduction to pronouns, but a guide to some of the stickier pronoun situations you might encounter, with examples from legal writing.

(1) Subject vs. Object

Personal pronouns come in pairs, one for use as a subject and one for use as

Chapter 1
Basics of Legal Writing

an object. Most of the time, fluent speakers can hear the difference between "I" and "me," "we" and "us," "he" and "him," "she" and "her," "they" and "them" when used in a sentence; "I went to the movies with them."; "He bought her a present."; Here are some instances that are more likely to be confusing.

In compounds

Wrong: "Her concern for Jeffries increased when John Jeffries threw a glass bottle from the top of the stairs at Mr. Jeffries and she."

Pronouns that are part of compounds should be used in the same form that would be used if the pronouns stood alone. One way to test this is to take out every part of the compound but the pronoun. Which sounds better, "threw a glass bottle ... at she" or "threw a glass bottle ... at her"?

Right: "Her concern for Jeffries increased when John Jeffries threw a glass bottle from the top of the stairs at Mr. Jeffries and her."

After a linking verb

Although pronouns toward the ends of sentences will tend to be objects ("We went with them" "He gave it to me," etc.), those following forms of the verb "to be"; — am, is, are, was, were — are technically restatements of the subject, and therefore require subject form.

Wrong: "It was him who initiated the phone call."

Right: "It was he who initiated the phone call."

Although this phrasing is correct, it may sound archaic to you. If so, you might rewrite the sentence.

Right: "He was the one who initiated the phone call."

Who vs. Whom

Contrary to common usage, "whom" is not just a fancy word for "who" that you should use when you want to sound important. The difference between "who" and "whom" is the same as the difference between "I" and "me"; "I" and "who" are subjects, while "me" and "whom" are objects. Look at the following sentence:

Wrong: "As long as parties are voluntarily participating in mediation and given a choice as to whom their mediator will be, they should be allowed to choose anyone they see fit."

This writer does have a right idea, that "whom" follows a preposition, which generally is followed by an object form. However, the phrase "given a choice as to" introduces a clause, or a dependent part of the sentence that has both a subject and a verb, that might be rewritten to stand alone: "Who will be their mediator?" Here, the clause involves a linking verb, so the subject form of the pronoun is necessary.

Right: "As long as parties are voluntarily participating in mediation and given a choice as to who their mediator will be, they should be allowed to choose anyone they see fit."

Here's a sentence where "whom" is correct.

Right: "The claimed constitutional deprivation must result from the exercise of a right or privilege created either by the state, by a rule of conduct imposed by the state, or by a person for whom the state is responsible."

In this instance, the clause would read: "the state is responsible for ..." Clearly, the object form is called for.

If, in correcting for who/whom and similar pronouns, you find that the technically correct version sounds strange to you, you might want to try rewriting the sentence so that it is both correct and appealing.

Right: "As long as parties are voluntarily participating in mediation and given a choice of mediators, they should be allowed to choose anyone that they see fit."

(2) Singular/Plural Agreement

Pronouns should agree in number with the nouns they refer to ("The students agreed that they would form a study group"). Writers are probably most likely to slip up in agreement when they are unsure whether the pronoun antecedent is singular or plural, or when they are trying to avoid gender bias by using "they."

Some singulars and plurals to watch for

Some nouns, such as collective nouns and words from Latin, may not be instantly recognizable as singular or plural. For example, a court is considered to be an institution, and requires a singular pronoun regardless of whether the court you are writing about consists of one individual or a group of people.

Wrong: "The court stated that they were ill-equipped to second-guess the trial court judge's determination."

Right: "The court stated that it was ill-equipped to second-guess the trial court judge's determination."

Noun/pronoun disagreement and gender bias

You have probably read (or even written) many sentences like this one.

Wrong: "Given that New York State does not currently have a single set of court rules for all non-adjudicative mediators, a private practitioner interested in implementing mediation services in their solo practice may be unsure about what standards to aspire to."

The sentence first discusses "a private practitioner," then refers to "their solo practice." But since there is only one practitioner in the subject, any pronouns referring to that practitioner should be singular: "her solo practice" "his solo practice."

A problem arises when this hypothetical practitioner is potentially either male or female. Thus, "their" has become a common dodge for escaping gender bias, because it does not indicate gender.

Not Really Right: "In order for a child to be classified as requiring special education, he needs to be provided with the necessary evaluations."

Formerly, "he" was assumed to include both male and female individuals, but this practice is no longer widely accepted.

Right but Cumbersome: "In order for a child to be classified as requiring special education, he or she needs to be provided with the necessary evaluations."

No wonder people have reached for "they." The trick for making the technique work is to change the initial noun from singular to plural, so that it matches "they."

Right: "In order for children to be classified as requiring special education, they need to be provided with the necessary evaluations."

(3) Unclear Reference

When they are not handled carefully, pronouns can introduce ambiguity into your writing. When several male persons have been named, which one does "he" indicate? Will your reader see immediately which previously described concept or situation your use of "this" refers to?

With Personal Pronouns

Wrong: "When Rodriguez entered the precinct, she told the officer at the front desk about Jeffries's condition, but rather than taking her report, she was asked to speak directly with Officer Frazier."

Does the second "she" in this sentence refer to Rodriguez, to the officer at the front desk, or even possibly to Jeffries? The phrase "rather than taking her report" leads the reader to expect the next pronoun to refer to the officer at the desk, but "was asked to speak directly with Officer Frazier" sounds like advice to Rodriguez. This sentence could be rewritten in a number of ways; here are two options.

Right: "When Rodriguez entered the precinct, she told the officer at the front desk about Jeffries's condition, but her report was not taken and she was asked instead to speak directly with Officer Frazier."

Right: "When Rodriguez entered the precinct, she told the officer at the front desk about Jeffries's condition, but rather than taking her report, the officer asked her to speak directly with Officer Frazier."

With "This" "That" and "Which"

Wrong: "Mediation may resolve an issue quickly and not allow for parties to heal which may be accomplished by delays in the court system."

What may be accomplished here, resolution or healing?

Wrong: "Perhaps if Tuparo decided that he would not sign the contract until these matters were cleared up or his propositions were considered an argument could be made that this was a counteroffer. Yet this was not the circumstances of this case."

These two sentences use three "this"es and a "these." The agreement problem in the second sentence also makes comprehension more difficult. When instances of the word "this" create a problem in your writing, replace them with something concrete. Here's a way to replace one here:

Right: "... an argument could be made that the additional writing he appended to the contract was a counteroffer."

(4) Other Potential Problems

Here are a few more pronoun issues to look out for.

Who vs. That

Wrong: "Whether a relationship between the mediator and non-English speaking parties can be established when a translator is present that is not part of the procedure."

Right: "Whether a relationship between the mediator and non-English speaking parties can be established when a translator is present who is not part of the procedure."

"Who" is used for people; "that" is used for other nouns.

Consistency

Wrong: "Prison life requires that one give up their liberty and other rights, but not his fundamental right of due process."

In this sentence, "one" "their" and "his" are all meant to refer to the same person, but do so in varying ways. It is better to be consistent; choose one way of referring to the subject and use it throughout the sentence. Here's one option.

Right: "Prison life requires that people give up their liberty and other rights, but not their fundamental right of due process."

Personal Pronouns

Wrong: "We urge the court to deny the motion to dismiss."

In formal legal writing, it is not customary to identify yourself, the writer. In the conventions of this discourse, words like "I" "we" and "our" are avoided.

6. Punctuation

Punctuation is one component of writing that people seldom think about or notice — except when it is wrong. At their worst, misused punctuation marks — commas, semicolons, quotation marks, and the rest — may muddle the meaning of your sentences, leaving your reader confused and frustrated. Even less egregious errors — say, a missing or misplaced apostrophe — can give your written work an appearance of carelessness and lack of attention.

(1) Quotation Marks

Quotation marks are required whenever you are giving the exact words spoken or written by another person. In American English, double quotation marks are used for indicating quotations. Single quotation marks indicate a quote within a quote.

e.g. Prof. McArdle said, "The briefs will be due on Tuesday."

Loucas said, "Prof. McArdle said, 'The briefs will be due on Tuesday.'"

(For those of you familiar with British English conventions, this is a change in style.)

The rules for using other punctuation with quotation marks are fairly straightforward. If you are introducing a quote with a phrase such as "He said" "The record states" or "As Justice Scalia wrote," you must use a comma before the quotation marks.

e.g. The defense attorney shouted, "I object to that question!"

If you want to introduce a quote with an independent clause (a phrase that could stand alone as its own sentence), you must use a colon before the quotation marks.

e.g. The defense attorney raised an objection: "That question is not relevant!"

If, however, you are integrating quoted material within your own sentence, you do not need any introductory punctuation.

e.g. Evelyn described her father as a "stubborn old man."

You must also be careful about the placement of other punctuation marks at the end of quotations. Commas and periods always go inside quotation marks.

e.g. Lou said, "This class is way too noisy."

"This class is way too noisy," said Lou.

Question marks and exclamation points go inside the quotation marks if they are part of the original quotation.

e.g. The security guard asked, "Whose car is this?"

but remain outside the quotation marks if they are part of your own sentence.

e.g. Did the nurse say, "Dr. Adler will be coming soon?"

(In this case, the nurse is not asking the question; the writer of the sentence is.)

Semicolons and colons at the end of a quotation should be placed outside the quotation marks.

e.g. A certain novel begins with the words, "Call me Ishmael"; do you know which novel it is?

Chapter 1
Basics of Legal Writing

(2) Apostrophes

The two main functions of the apostrophe are to form the possessive case of nouns (indicating ownership) and to indicate a missing letter or letters in a contraction.

Possessives

When forming the possessive of a singular subject, 's is generally needed.

e.g. The student's locker was filled with textbooks.

Margie's bagels are delicious.

If a singular noun ends in s, you should still use 's to form the possessive.

e.g. Luis's car is parked on Main Street.

Her boss's office is very large.

However, some writers use an apostrophe alone when the noun is long and contains multiple s sounds. This is not incorrect.

e.g. Officer Gonzales' gun was stolen.

When forming the possessive of plural nouns, you should add only an apostrophe if the noun ends in s.

e.g. The students' grades were posted on the board.

But the occasional plural nouns that don't end in s need 's to form the possessive.

e.g. The children's center opens at 9 a.m.

In two unusual cases, 's is used to form a plural noun. This occurs when you want the plural form of a single letter or of a word referred to as the word itself, as in the following examples.

e.g. Patrick got straight A's throughout four years of college.

This brief contains too many whether's.

Never use an apostrophe to form the plural of a proper name.

e.g. The Blochs came over for dinner.

(3) Contractions

The apostrophe is also used to replace missing letters in a contraction. For example, in the following sentence:

The clerk said the office wouldn't be open on Saturday.

"wouldn't" is a contraction for "would not" — the apostrophe replaces the missing *o*.

Similarly, in the sentence:

We're tired from studying too much.

"we're" stands for "we are," so the apostrophe replaces the missing *a*.

Your/You're & Its/It's

The two instances that cause the most confusion — and the most mistakes — in apostrophe usage are *your/you're* and *its/it's*.

Remember the contraction rule, and your choice should be clear. "You're" stands for "you are," while "your" is the possessive form of "you".

e.g. "*You're* the top student in *your* class," said the dean.

Likewise, "it's" stands for "it is" or "it has," while "its" is the possessive form of "it".

e.g. *It's* time for the orchestra to begin *its* rehearsal.

If you are confused about which word to use in a sentence, pause and ask yourself which meaning you want — a contraction or a possessive noun.

(4) Semicolons

A semicolon can be used to connect two independent clauses that are closely linked in meaning.

e.g. The professor began class at exactly 10 o'clock; students who arrived late missed some of the lecture.

In this example, the two clauses could stand alone as separate sentences, but joining them with a semicolon stresses the relationship between them. Using a comma alone to connect these clauses would not be sufficient and would create a run-on sentence.

A semicolon would also be used to connect independent clauses when a transitional word or phrase is used.

e.g. The small airplane had a smooth flight; *however*, a sudden gust of wind made its landing a little rough.

(5) Commas

Comma placement can dramatically alter the meaning of a sentence. Comma placement determines the grammatical, and therefore logical, structure of the sentence.

When should I use commas?

a) Use commas to separate independent clauses when they are joined by

Chapter 1
Basics of Legal Writing

coordinating conjunctions: and, but, for, or, nor, yet.

Example: Tuparo began his new job, <u>and</u> Burstyn made changes to the personnel policy. (*Note that this could have been expressed in two sentences: Tuparo began his new job. Burstyn made changes to the personnel policy.*)

b) Introductory expressions should be followed by a comma.

e.g. <u>After leaving Weber and Orange</u>, Tuparo took a job at LSRA.

<u>Therefore</u>, he did not make a counteroffer.

c) Use commas to separate three or more words, phrases, or clauses written in a series.

e.g. I bought eggs, milk, and cheese at the store.

Yesterday I read a book, took a walk, and wrote a paper.

d) Use a pair of commas in the middle of a sentence to set off clauses, phrases, and words that are not essential to the meaning of the sentence.

Example: His neighbor, <u>with whom he had had several serious disagreements</u>, removed a section of the fence. (*Note that the clause "with whom he had had several serious disagreements" is not essential to the meaning of the sentence. One way to check this is to see if we could rewrite the sentence to make two complete sentences. Example: His neighbor removed a section of the fence. They had had several serious disagreements.*)

When should I not use commas?

a) Don't use commas to set off parts of the sentence that are essential to the meaning, such as clauses beginning with "that."

e.g. The book that I borrowed from you is excellent.

The last person who saw the victim alive claimed to have seen nothing unusual.

b) Tip: "Which" is generally used with a comma, "that" without.

e.g. Mr. O'Malley's apartment, which is on the seventh floor, is unsuitable for someone with mobility problems. (*Non-essential to the meaning*)

The bill that Ms. Perez received contained several errors. (*Essential to the meaning*)

c) Commas should not separate subjects from their corresponding verbs.

e.g. The new chief operating officer, changed the company's personnel and benefits policies. (*incorrect*)

 d) Commas should not separate verbs from their objects.

 e.g. The new chief operating officer changed, the company's personnel and benefits policies. (*incorrect*)

 e) Commas should not split a double (or compound) predicate.

 e.g. Tuparo finished his Masters, and got a new job. (*incorrect*)

(6) Dash Versus Hyphen

 Rule of thumb, dashes separate, hyphens connect. When typing on word, a dash is made up of two hyphens (—). Newer versions of word will generally connect them into one dash (—).

 a) *Dashes* offer separation but with added drama.

 e.g. Everyone in the group left the scene-even her brother. (*correct*)

 b) Dashes can also be used to set off a clause, parenthetical expression, or list.

 e.g. His neighbor — with whom he had had several serious disagreements — removed a section of the fence. (*you could use commas here instead, but dashes change the emphasis*)

 Our clients — Singh, Lafrance, and Ivanoff — have sent us the documents we requested. (*you could use commas here but it would be more confusing to the reader*)

 c) Use a *hyphen* to connect two parts of a compound noun. e.g. U-turn, stand-in.

 d) A hyphen is used to join two parts of a hyphenated adjective. *Examples*: once-in-a-lifetime opportunity, state-run clinic. (*This often makes the meaning clearer. Consider the possible meaning of the following: working class president, dirty blonde hair, versus working-class president, dirty-blonde hair.*)

 e) Many prefixes are hyphenated, especially if there may be awkwardness or confusion with the spelling. e.g. ex-husband, pre-1968, semi-integrated, non-nuclear. (*Some works are acceptable hyphenated and not. Example: pre-war, prewar.*)

(7) Punctuation with Citations

 Here are a few basic rules regarding punctuation placement with citations.

A citation that appears after a complete sentence should be treated as a complete sentence itself, beginning with a capital letter and ending with a period. This holds true whether the citation is a long or short form. If a cite is given in the middle of a sentence, it must be set off by commas. Notice the punctuation of the citations in the following example:

In New York, the rule is well settled that an advertisement is merely an invitation to enter into negotiations, and is not an offer that may be turned into a contract by a person who communicates an intention to purchase the advertised item. *Geismar v. Abraham & Strauss*, 439 N.Y.S. 2d 1005 (Dist. Ct. Suffolk Co. 1981); *Lovett v. Frederick Loeser & Co.*, 207 N.Y.S. 753 (Manhattan Mun. Ct. 1924). The only general test is the inquiry whether the facts show that some performance was promised in positive terms in return for something requested. *Lovett*, 207 N.Y.S. 2d at 755. However, a purchaser may not make a valid contract by mere acceptance of a "proposition," *Schenectady Stove Co.*, 101 N.Y. at 48, nor does the purchaser have the right to select an item which the seller does not have in stock or is not willing to sell at a reduced price. *Lovett*, 207 N.Y.S. at 757.

As illustrated in the first citation, when two or more cases are named, they must be separated by a semicolon. Also, be careful not to italicize the comma following the name of the case.

7. Editing

Now you've finished your draft and it's time to edit and proofread your paper. You need to review your work for organization and connection of ideas, and for clarity, including correcting errors in grammar and vocabulary. You also need to correct any errors related to punctuation, or mechanics, such as spelling or capitalization.

What Is "Editing"?

Very often we are advised to edit our papers before submitting them, but what does "editing" mean? What do we need to do during that stage of the writing process to improve the quality of our written work?

D. Ferris (2002) describes "editing" as "looking over a paper you have already written to find and correct any errors in grammar, vocabulary, punctuation, or mechanics (spelling or capitalization)." Some other scholars consider "editing" a much broader activity that also refers to issues of organization and coherence.

In this section we offer some strategies that will help you develop self-editing skills.

Self-Editing Strategies

We suggest the following tips to help you edit and proofread your work.

(1) Search for the occurrence of similar errors.

Ask yourself these questions:

- What problems appear repeatedly in my writing?
- What generalizations can I draw about my writing from these errors?
- Do my ideas frequently appear disorganized in the text?
- Do my paragraphs lack a topic sentence?
- Do I tend to repeat the same idea throughout the text, unnecessarily?
- Do I always write the same kind of sentence structure, e.g. subject-verb-object?
- <u>Multilingual students</u>: in what grammar areas do I make most of my errors? e.g., are my errors related to the use of prepositions, verb tenses, articles, connectors, etc.?

(2) Build up a personalized editing checklist.

Once you've identified your patterns of errors, then you should create a checklist for yourself. The next time you edit a paper, you may want to focus exclusively on those errors, or pay more attention to them, and perhaps tackle them first.

(3) Make time for the editing phase.

Remember writing is not over when you have finished your first draft, but after you have revised and edited it. Setting aside time for editing is essential for all of your writing, including in-class exams.

(4) Work on a hard copy.

This creates some distance between you and the final product and allows you to manipulate the paper copy in a more controlled way (you can go back or move forward to previous portions of the text as many times as you want). It also allows you to take down notes directly on the text in an easy way.

(5) Make focused passes through a text to look at a specific issue.

For example, search the text for errors in subject/verb agreement (-s missing from a 3rd person singular verb). Don't try to look at everything at the same time, because you will miss a lot!

Self-editing looks impossible when you think of it in general. However, when you break down the task in pieces and prioritize types of errors, then self-editing becomes more manageable. If you have difficulties with the use of prepositions, but do not have much problem with verb tenses, then, focus on prepositions exclusively. One or two errors in verbs in your paper will not be as problematic as multiple errors in preposition usage. Then use the same procedure with different editing categories, one pass through for each one.

(6) When proofreading, read the paper from back to front.

Breaking the flow of ideas sometimes helps to focus on language issues rather than on the content itself.

(7) Use the dictionary (a lexicon or a thesaurus) in order to make an accurate and varied choice of words.

This way you will have access not only to meanings but also to synonyms, antonyms, shades of meaning, etc. A dictionary is a useful tool both for multilingual students and native speakers.

Editing Under Time Pressure

If you haven't set aside enough time to edit your paper carefully, you can take a shortcut (but never skip this phase!).

(1) Read the question in the assignment and highlight key words and instructions.

(2) Plan your essay.

- Preferably, do so in a loud voice, by asking questions to yourself.
- Write down what you say (main points and points derived from that one).
- Assign paragraphs to your text. Remember: one paragraph=one idea.

(3) Write your paper and check your outline as you go along.

(4) Read the paper nonstop from the beginning to the end at least once.

When you work on different sections separately and then paste them to the general text, there may be problems of connection between those sections that you'll fail to detect unless you read the whole text.

(5) Proofread and edit your paper.

- Are there any spelling errors?
- Are there any words missing from the sentences?
- Are there any words used incorrectly?
- Can you suggest a better word or word form?
- Look at the nouns. Do they have the appropriate singular or plural endings? Is an article needed? Has the appropriate article been used?
- Look at the verbs. Do the verb endings agree (in person -first, second, third-, or in number -singular or plural) with the subjects? Are the verbs in the appropriate tense?
- Look at punctuation. Do you see any problems with commas, periods, semicolons, quotation marks, etc.?
- Are there words that occur repeatedly but unnecessarily in the text?

Checklist

Here's a short general checklist that you may use when editing your papers (but remember: it is better to customize this list so that it considers the characteristics of your own writing.). We provide an example of a problem, and its edited version.

(1) Search for phrase and sentence fragments.

Phrase Fragment:

e.g. *The Court dismissed the charges of aggravated harassment. The charges of aggravated harassment in the second and in the third degree.*

↓

e.g. *The Court dismissed the charges of aggravated harassment in the second and in the third degrees.*

Clause Fragment:

e.g. *The Court dismissed the charge of aggravated harassment. Because the defendant did not initiate the telephone call.*

↓

e.g. *The Court dismissed the charge of aggravated harassment because the defendant did not initiate the telephone call.*

Chapter 1
Basics of Legal Writing

(2) Search for run-on sentences and comma splices.

e.g. *Mary mentioned two previous incidents when John Meyers abused her, she should include those in the petition for the order of protection as well.*

↓

Mary mentioned two previous incidents when John Meyers abused her; she should include those in the petition for the order of protection as well.

Or use two separate sentences, as in:

Mary mentioned two previous incidents when John Meyers abused her. She should include those in the petition for the order of protection as well.

(3) Use the passive voice only when you want to subordinate the subject or source of agency.

e.g. *Joseph was assaulted brutally (by John).* (Passive)

↓

John assaulted Joseph brutally. (Active)

It is appropriate to use the active version if you are prosecuting John for assault. However, the passive version is appropriate for his defense, because John appears less prominently portrayed as the source of the assault. As you can see, syntax is also a tool for persuasion.

(4) Do not overuse the verb "to be" and its conjugated forms.

e.g. *Nora Clements **IS** a prospective client who **IS** seeking an order of protection in Family Court against John Meyers, who **IS** her former boyfriend. To determine if Mary can get the order that she **IS** seeking, we must address both procedural and substantive issues.*

↓

Nora Clements is a prospective client seeking an order of protection in Family Court against John Meyers, her former boyfriend. To determine if Mary can get this order, we must address both procedural and substantive issues.

(5) Use nominalization. (But careful: do not overuse it.)

Nominalization is the transformation of verbs or adjectives into nouns, as in

John is exhausted. (adjective to noun)

↓

John's exhaustion

John's generous behavior (adjective to noun)

↓

John's generosity

John apologized to his friend. (verb to noun)

↓

John's apology to his friend

John published the novel without authorization. (verb to noun)

↓

John's unauthorized publication of the novel.

[The highlighted words have undergone nominalization.]

Though nominalization is useful sometimes, its overuse can really make your writing dense, monotonous, or incomprehensible. This is what happens in:

e.g. *The suggestion was that an immediate intervention to solve the uncomfortable situation would ensure the protection of the members of the organization.*

See how much clearer this sounds when we do not overuse nominalization:

e.g. *They [or somebody] suggested that an immediate intervention to solve the uncomfortable situation would protect the members of the organization.*

e.g. *They [or somebody] suggested that the members of the organization would be more protected if there were an immediate intervention to solve the uncomfortable problem [or conflict, etc.].*

(6) Avoid overly embedded sentences.

Embedded sentences contain many clauses introduced by elements such as *who, that, which*. A sentence with multiple clauses inside or the succession of many sentences containing one embedded clause each makes the text more difficult to read and more confusing.

e.g. *Nora Clements*, **who** is a prospective client **who** seeks an order of protection in Family Court against John Meyers, **who** is her former boyfriend, is requesting our legal advice. To determine if Mary can get the order **that** she

seeks, we must address issues **that** are both procedural and substantive.
↓

Nora Clements is a prospective client seeking an order of protection in Family Court against John Meyers, her former boyfriend. To determine if Mary can get the order she seeks, we must address both procedural and substantive issues.

Or: *Nora Clements, a prospective client, seeks an order of protection in Family Court against her former boyfriend John Meyers. To determine if Mary can get this order, we must address both procedural and substantive issues.*

Or: *Nora Clements seeks an order of protection in Family Court against her former boyfriend John Meyers. To determine if Mary can get this order, we must address both procedural and substantive issues.*

(7) Avoid repetition in sentence structure.

A text that repeats the same sentence structure (e.g. subject-verb-object-rest) over and over again may sound extremely tedious to the reader. Whenever possible, vary the internal structure of your sentences.

e.g. <u>Clements and Meyers</u> were not married. <u>They</u> both had children outside of their relationship. <u>Meyers</u> has lived apart from Clements for approximately a year. <u>Meyers</u> punched Clements in the face repeatedly seven months ago and badly bruised her. <u>Meyers</u> was arrested but Clements refrained from pressing charges. Then <u>Meyers</u> cursed at Clements and attacked her one week ago.

[We have underlined the subjects in this text in order to show that all the sentences and clauses in this text keep the same structure, namely Subject-Verb-Object-Rest.]

Now observe how the text improves when we just change the position of some adverbials (e.g. "Seven months ago" "One week ago") in the sentence, and by using the active voice (*Meyers was arrested by the police.* → *The police arrested Meyers.*).
↓

e.g. <u>Clements and Meyers</u>, who were not married and had children outside of their relationship, have lived apart from each other for approximately a year. Seven months ago *Meyers* badly bruised Clements by punching *her in the face repeatedly*. *The police* arrested Meyers, but *Clements* refrained from pressing charges. One week ago *Meyers* cursed at Clements and attacked her.

[The underlined subjects in this sentence show that subjects no longer occupy the initial position in the sentence; that position varies.]

(8) Avoid tautological definitions. (i.e. avoid defining a term by using it in the definition itself.)

e.g. *John's harassment* constitutes *harassment* in the second degree.

↓

John's behavior constitutes *harassment* in the second degree. [Edited version]

Exercises

1. Fill in the blanks with the correct article: THE, A, AN, or 0 ("zero") (if no article applies).

Just to confirm (1) _____ rushed phone conversation we had today, I've been served with (2) _____ complaint from (3) _____ Small Claims Part of (4) _____ Civil Court brought by (5) _____ shopper against Loman's for (6) _____ breach of (7) _____ contract on (8) _____ theory that she came to our main branch last month in (9) _____ response to (10) _____ ad for (11) _____ leather coats and that we "failed to have (12) _____ merchandise to sell at (13) _____ advertised price." We had advertised these coats in one of our recent circulars. (14) _____ text of (15) _____ advertisement is part of (16) _____ FAX I sent previously to your office.

2. Break each of the following long sentences into at least three separate sentences.

• Appellee Allied Indemnity of New York respectfully suggests that oral argument would be of little benefit because the dispositive issue has been recently authoritatively decided by the Texas Supreme Court in *National Union Fire Insurance Co. v. CBI Industries, Inc.*, 907 S.W.2d 517 (Tex. 1995), and by this Court in *Constitution State Insurance Co. v. Iso-Tex, Inc.*, 61 F. 3d 405 (5th Cir. 1995), because the facts and legal arguments are adequately presented in the briefs and record, and because the decisional process would not be significantly aided by oral argument. [91 words]

• Although no Kansas cases were found that explicitly hold that Kansas requires a corporation to have a valid business purpose in order to engage in certain specified corporate transactions, either for mergers or consolidations, or for a sale of assets followed by a dissolution and liquidation, in a 1994 Supreme Court of Kansas case involving a cash-out merger where the dissenters claimed the defendant's board of directors breached its fiduciary duties to the dissenters, the court cited as one of the trial court's pertinent conclusions of law that it is not necessary for a corporation to show a valid corporate purpose for eliminating stockholders. [105 words]

• The court of appeals noted that the Environmental Protection Agency (EPA) had already issued the applicant a National Pollution Elimination System permit for the actual discharge of wastewater, which would occur from the outfall pipe, and that the issuance and conditions of such permits were generally exempt under the Clean Water Act from compliance with the Environmental Impact Statement (EIS) requirement, and accordingly the court concluded that the Corps had properly excluded the environmental implications of the discharges from the outfall pipe from its analysis and instead considered only the construction and maintenance of the pipeline itself in determining that the issuance of the permit did not constitute a major federal action. [112 words]

3. Edit the following sentences to eliminate the passive voice.

• Testimony was heard from the plaintiff and from three witnesses on behalf of the corporation.

• This is a purely legal question to be determined by the court.

• McCormick's motion for partial summary judgment on the duty to defend should be denied.

• Plaintiff's opposition violates Rule 313 of the California Rules of Court and may be disregarded by the court.

4. Delete at least four consecutive words in the following sentences, replace those words with just one word. You may rephrase ideas and rearrange sentences, but don't change the meaning.

• Even assuming that the fog caused injury to Roelke, Amskills had no duty to prevent that injury because it was idiosyncratic and Amskills could not have been expected to foresee such injury.

• At no time prior to the initial public offering did the underwriters or any officers, directors, or employees have knowledge of any facts that would suggest that "Palm Harbor" could not be completed on schedule and in accordance with specifications.

• Beale has wholly failed to allege facts that, if true, would establish that competition among the nation's law schools would be reduced or that the public has been in any way injured, and this failure to allege facts that would establish an injury to competition warrants the dismissal of her restraint-of-trade claim.

• The Business Corporation Law does not address the ability of a New York corporation to indemnify individuals who are not its employees.

• The court examined a number of cases and stated that there appeared to be only a limited number of instances in which there would exist a duty to disclose the illegal conduct of persons who, through political campaigns, seek election to a public office.

5. Correct the usage errors in the following sentences.

• When Margot arrived, Rodney told her that David had laid down because of his pain.

• Mrs. Clements testified that Kenneth was waving the gun wildly and pointing it at Bill.

• Counsel testified that because the testimony would have harmed her case, she opted to forego it for reasons of trial strategy.

• Since the *Oneida* line of cases are now binding federal law in California, this Court is bound to follow them.

• The cost of any arbitration proceedings will be born by the party designated by the arbitrators.

• The gas would likely be inventory under the Idaho statutes defining the term, but these provisions might not apply since they do not effect Idaho taxable income.

• Texas law prohibits the unjustified interference with a parties' existing or prospective contractual relations.

• For the reasons stated in Jones's initial motion, Jones maintains that the Court's August 27 order precludes Fillmore from preceding on count six in this action.

• The laws of the State of Massachusetts (irrespective of its choice-of-law principals) govern the validity of this Agreement, the construction of its terms, and the interpretation and enforcement of the parties' rights and duties.

• Neither Mr. Robinson's affidavit nor Plaintiffs' deposition testimony carry the force of law.

Chapter 2
Writing Letters

Lawyers use letters, notes and memoranda to communicate information to clients, to request information from government agencies and other lawyers. There are, of course, many other purposes for letters and many styles of writing them. For example, you may want information about a graduate school program, you may need to thank a person who has helped you, or you may want to find temporary or permanent employment.

Lawyers write many letters. These letters serve different purposes, such as advising clients, seeking compliance, sending documents, obtaining information etc.. All letters benefit from clear writing and simple organization. Lawyers who write direct and concise letters to non-lawyers are more likely to achieve successful results. All of these letters have one thing in common: They are not great literature. They will not be read in a hundred years and analyzed for their wit, charm or flowery words. With any luck they will be read just once by a few people, followed quickly by their intended result, whether that be compliance, understanding or agreement. [1]

1. Classification of the Letters

There are mainly three types of legal letters to be covered in this chapter:

(1) Attorney-Client Correspondence

The Attorney-Client Correspondence refers to the letters sending from the attorney to their clients or prospective clients. The attorney may give his client some advice, ask for information, make sure of the attorney's fees, and so on.

---

[1] http://www.jamesmartinpa.com/letters.htm

Chapter 2 Writing Letters

(2) Attorney-Adverse Party Correspondence

The Attorney-Adverse Party Correspondence means the letters sending from the attorney to the adverse party or the attorney representing the adverse party to negotiate, ask the adverse party to take action, and so on.

(3) Daily Correspondence

The Daily Correspondence is the letters attorneys dealing with the routine works concerning law, such as asking for the information of a law school or a legal newsletter.

(4) Letters of Intent

A letter of intent is a preliminary transactional document, generally prepared by lawyers, which captures some or all of the key deal points that the parties have agreed upon. It is usually not the final document that will govern the transaction, and the final transactional documents will generally supercede the letter of intent, usually expressly through integration or merger clauses.

(5) Opinion Letters

Opinion letters or opinions of counsel used in transactional practice form a very important part of modern law firm practice. The opinion letters discussed here are typical of sophisticated transactional practice, and are gradually becoming part of ever more basic transactions.

2. Steps to Write a Letter

There are many factors to be considered in legal letter writing. Please follow the following steps to write a complete legal letter.

(1) Find a letter form.

Find a similar letter you have sent in the past, or see the sample letters in this Chapter.

(2) Do not send a letter to another lawyer's client without that lawyer's consent.

Before sending the letter, find out if the non-lawyer is represented by someone else. Start by asking your client.

(3) Outline your thoughts in a checklist.

Before turning on your computer or dictating machine, pull out a yellow pad and jot down the main points for your letter. List what you want the letter to say. Write the points in any order; write them as they come into your mind.

(4) Start your letter carefully.

Letters begin with boring things like the date and recipient's name and address, but if any of these are missing or wrong, the letter writer will look pretty careless, to say the least. So be careful when starting the letter.

(5) Date your letter.

Date your letter the day you write it, and send it the same day. Consider using the international dating convention of day-month-year rather than the U.S. convention of month-day-year.

(6) Indicate the time of your letter.

If you are sending a fax or email, then type the time next to the date. While letters "cross in the mail" in days, faxes and emails "cross in the wires" in hours and minutes.

(7) Remind your client to preserve attorney-client confidentiality.

Sometimes clients show your letters to others without realizing they can lose the attorney-client privilege of that communication. Add this phrase at the top of the letter to remind them not to do this:

CONFIDENTIAL ATTORNEY-CLIENT COMMUNICATION
DO NOT COPY OR DISCLOSE TO ANYONE ELSE

If the letter is written during or in anticipation of litigation, the following phrase can be used:

CONFIDENTIAL ATTORNEY-CLIENT COMMUNICATION AND WORK PRODUCT
DO NOT COPY OR DISCLOSE TO ANYONE ELSE

(8) Be sure to use the recipient's correct legal name and address.

Your letter may be relied upon for its accuracy, so be accurate. Verification of names can be obtained from the public records, the phone book, or the websites. And when it comes to middle initials, never rely on your memory or guess at it because most of the time you'll be wrong.

(9) Indicate the method of delivery if other than mail.

If being faxed, include the fax number and telephone number. If being sent by FedEx, state whether it is by overnight or second day. If being sent by email, state the email address. This will make it easy for your staff person to send it to the correct place, and it will document for your file how it was sent.

(10) Include a fax notice.

When sending by fax, include a notice in case it is sent to the wrong number. Here is the notice when sending a fax:

> NOTICE: This is privileged and confidential and intended only for the person named below. If you are not that person, then any use, dissemination, distribution or copying of this is strictly prohibited, and you are requested to notify us immediately by calling or faxing us collect at the numbers above.
> Date Sent _____ Time Sent _____
> Number of Pages _____ Receipt _____

(11) Putting more emphasis on body of the letter.

The body of the letter is why you are writing it. You succeed by leaving the reader with full knowledge of why you wrote the letter and what it means. Following these suggestions will keep your letters on the successful end of the scale.

(12) Identify your client.

It is important to let others know who your client is at the earliest opportunity. This accomplishes a great deal. First, it tells the reader that your client has a lawyer. This makes your client happy because most clients want the world to know they have a lawyer. Second, it tells the reader that you are not the reader's lawyer. This makes your malpractice carrier happy because it's one less person who's going to sue you claiming they thought you were representing them when, in fact, you were not.

(13) State the purpose of the letter.

Why leave the reader guessing? Go ahead and say right up front why you are writing the letter. Here are some opening sentences:

> "The purpose of this letter is to _____."
> "I am writing to let you know that _____."

> "This letter is to inform you that _____."
> "My client has instructed me to _____."
> "This is to confirm that _____."
> "This confirms our phone conversation today in which _____."

(14) If there are any enclosures, list them first.

Listing enclosures at the beginning of the letter will make it easier for your staff to assemble them and for the reader to check to be sure all was received. The enclosures should be described with specificity so that there is later no question as to what was enclosed. At a minimum, the title and date of each document should be listed.

(15) Outline the letter as separately numbered paragraphs.

Each paragraph of the letter should state a separate thought, comment, point or concept. No paragraph should be longer than four or five short sentences. If the paragraph is longer, then separate it into subparagraphs. The paragraphs should flow in logical, organized fashion. It is not necessary to write them all at once; you can write them as you think of them. Try to group related concepts in the same paragraphs or in adjacent paragraphs. Give each paragraph a title and underline that title. Think of this as the headline for a newspaper article. This makes it easy for the reader to scan the letter and choose how to more fully read and digest its contents. This also makes it easier for you later when you see the letter in your file and try to remember why you wrote it.

3. Cleaning up

Now that you have the letter written, it's time to do some cleanup work before you hit the sending button or put it in a mailbox.

(1) Let your secretary or paralegal read it.

Not only will your staff frequently find spelling and grammar errors missed by your word processor's spell checker, but they will find inconsistencies and confusing areas that you missed when drafting.

(2) Number every page of the letter, and staple the letter.

If the letter is more than one page long, then it is important to number the pages because they will invariably get out of order. Place the following at the

Chapter 2
Writing Letters

top left corner of each page after the first:

| Recipient's name _____ | Date _____ | Page _____ |

(3) Sign the letter in blue ink, not black ink.

This will make it easier to differentiate the signed original letter from photocopies, and it will make it more difficult for someone to change your letter after you send it.

4. Techniques to Write Efficiently

Why does it take lawyers so long to write letters? Because they must be careful with the choice of words and the style. Lawyers write, rewrite, move around, delete, cut and paste the words over and over again until they are happy with the way it sounds. That's the art of legal writing. That's why writing is an art. Follow the following tips:

(1) Write in short sentences.

Short sentences are easier to understand than long ones. "Short, crisp sentences in a language are accessible to lay people."

(2) Use the jargon when necessary, but explain it when you use it.

(3) Repeat yourself only when repetition is necessary to improve clarity or to emphasize a point.

Ambiguity can be created by saying the same thing more than once; it is almost impossible to say it twice without creating ambiguity.

(4) When explaining a difficult concept, describe it from different directions.

The only time repetition is helpful is when explaining a difficult concept. Each time you explain it you can make it a little clearer if you describe it from a different direction, perspective or point of view.

(5) Write in active tense, rather than passive.

Active tense is interesting; passive is boring. Active tense sentences are shorter and use words more efficiently, and their meaning is more apparent.

(6) Watch where you place modifiers.

When adding a modifier before a compound of nouns, be sure to clarify whether you intend the modifier to apply to both nouns or just the first one. If you intend it to apply to both, use parallel construction and write the modifier in front of each noun, otherwise, place one noun at the end of the list and the modifier directly in front of it.

(7) Write numbers carefully.

Write numbers as both words and numerals: ten (10). This will reduce the chance for errors.

(8) Don't be creative with words.

Legal letter writing is not creative writing and is not meant to provoke reflective thoughts or controversies about nuances of meaning. Legal writing is clear, direct and precise. Therefore, use common words and common meanings.

(9) Be consistent in using words.

If you refer to the subject matter of a sales contract as "goods", use that term throughout the letter; do not alternately call them "goods" and "items."

(10) Be consistent in grammar and punctuation.

Write the letter so that no matter what rules they learned the letter is clear and unambiguous.

(11) Eliminate needless words.

Avoid flowery words. That's what good writing is all about. A letter written for the lowest common denominator is understood by every reader.

(12) Be direct and frank.

There is no sense beating around the bush in legal letter writing. Just say what you mean. If you leave the reader wondering what you mean, your letter will only stir the imagination instead of prompting some action.

5. Examples of Drafting a Client Letter

We have compiled the following sample letters to help you become competent with letter drafting. Each section has an annotated description underneath, highlighting important information you will need to remember whilst drafting your letter.

Ref: PD/01932/Intro

Always include a reference providing a mutual point for all parties, ensuring clarity of the document being discussed

01/10/08

Chapter 2
Writing Letters

Ensure the letter is dated particularly if it is to refer to deadlines, for example for the return of information by a prescribed time.

MrA Somebody

21 Whereabouts Close

Anytown

Anyshire

AN7 4RH

Ensure the addressee and address are correct.

Dear Sir

Letters beginning with "Dear Sir/Madam" end in "Yours faithfully," those referring to a name with "Yours sincerely." Where possible try to ascertain how a female addressee prefers to be addressed, for example "Miss" "Mrs" or "Ms."

Re: Road traffic Accident Claim PD/01932

Use an initial heading to identify clearly the matter being discussed in the correspondence. Complex letters can be easier to read and understand if they have sub-headings where necessary. If the letter is part of a complex case that includes many different kinds of documents care must be taken to accurately identify these documents if they are made reference to.

Following your initial meeting with Miss Somebody on 28/12/99 we would pleased to act for you in this matter. Mr Everyman, senior partner, will primarily be responsible for handling your case. Miss Somebody, who is an experienced paralegal and who will be your first point of contact, will assist him. I would like to take this opportunity to refer you to the enclosed document titled "Terms of Business" which I would be grateful if you would read. If you have any questions about any of the information in this letter or the enclosed documents please contact Miss Somebody who will be happy to explain.

It is important that any requisite response is forwarded promptly. You must identify the individuals who will be handling the matter. This must be by name and an explanation as to their position. Ensure that personnel are identified accurately, for example it is both illegal and unethical to hold a person out to be a solicitor if they are not so. It is important to remember that the responsibilities of both the legal personnel and the client are set out from the outset and throughout the conduct of the matter.

Note that the client in this scenario and the paralegal handling the case share the same surname. Always ensure you are aware who the client is, such matters as conflicts of interest must always be borne in mind. Reference must be made to the terms of business of the practice.

From the particulars taken at the initial meeting the incident occurred on the 23/11/99 on Someplace Lane, Anytown, Anyshire at approximately 13.15, where another vehicle collided with the rear of your vehicle whilst you were stationary, waiting to turn out of Someplace Lane onto Anywhere Road. The vehicle was being driven by Mrs Anyone and was travelling at some speed at the time of impact. As a result of the collision your vehicle was extensively damaged to the rear and you where taken to Anytown District Infirmary where it was confirmed that you had suffered whiplash and injuries to your spine.

It is important to clarify any particulars taken at the initial meeting regarding matters that led to your services being required. This enables all parties to be clear of the details. If writing to a lay person it is important to keep the language simple and avoid using "legalese." Be mindful of matters that may determine what is or is not included in the letter for example, if it is going to the other party in a case, confidentiality, disclosure or tactical issues. However care should be taken not to mislead anyone and that statutory requirements are met, for example in respect of disclosure rules.

You expressed that you wished us to conduct a case for you in which you wish to sue for the value of your vehicle that has been assessed by Fixem Garages as a write-off. You also wish to sue for personal injury in respect of the injuries you sustained to your neck and spine. Having examined the information you have provided in this matter we feel that you may have grounds to do so. In order to proceed with the matter we would be grateful if you would provide us with the details of your insurance company and complete the authority to act forms enclosed, once you have read through them, and signed them where indicated.

Make clear any intentions, agreements or requirements so that all parties know exactly what their position is and what is expected of them.

Once we have received the forms from you we will be able to contact your

Insurers, the Infirmary for any medical reports and we will be able to contact the police officers who attended the incident to acquire a police report. When we have this information we will be in a position to draft the appropriate documents using the information provided to commence proceedings against Mrs Anyone.

Plans for future action should be clearly set out so that the client is made aware exactly of the intentions and clear instructions provided if there are any requests for information, documents or other such items. A clear date for when these should be provided by should also be given particularly where there are deadlines to be met. If necessary or where appropriate forms of mediation or Alternative Dispute Resolution should be discussed and offered if not already done so at the initial meeting.

We will, at a later date, need you to provide further details such as any time that you have had to be absent from work and/or any financial loss you have incurred. It would be advisable that you ensure that you keep any receipts for such items as prescriptions or travelling expenses so that we can include them in the case. We will assess and calculate the amount of the claim to be submitted and advise you of such in due course.

All details of intended actions should be provided so that the client is fully aware of what is to happen and they should be kept informed of any changes as promptly as possible. Both your requirements and/or proposals and those of the client must be clearly set out to ensure that all parties are aware of their obligations. Identify and explain any conditions or limitations where any third parties may be involved, for example fee sharers.

Enclosed is a comprehensive document that sets out the firm's costs and expenses that may be incurred during the time we are acting for you. The case will be conducted on a no win no fee basis but a breakdown of costing for your information will be sent to you on a regular basis for information purposes.

Fee, billing and payment method information must be provided. This can be done in the body of the letter, if the matter allows, but if the case is likely to be lengthy or complicated then clarity would suggest that it be enclosed as a separate document. Any information regarding fees or costs must be clear, itemized and available for assessment and/or scrutiny if required.

Should there be any changes to costs or funding through the course of the matter this must be communicated to the client as soon as possible and again must be clear. Any liability for charges or requirements for payments during the conduct of the matter must be communicated to ensure that the client has all the costing information from the outset. Fees should also be agreed from the outset. Sometimes an exact figure may not be possible therefore a practical forecast or range should be provided. In addition, in this instance, an explanation as to the reasons should also be provided. If the client is eligible for public funding this should have been discussed and matters can be clarified in writing at this point.

You should, however, be aware that in the event that the other party wins the case you will become liable for the costs incurred by us and by the other party. The court fees and any other monies that would become chargeable are listed with the billing information. Please feel free to contact the firm should you require an assessment of these costings and we will arrange this for you.

Any financial liabilities that may affect the client must be communicated as early as possible and enquiries into whether the client has any form of protection, for example insurance, explored. The most important point is that costs are made as clear and as transparent as possible in all instances.

We will, of course, keep you informed of progress throughout the course of the matter but should you feel at any time that you are unhappy with any aspect please see the enclosed document which sets out our complaints procedure. We would also wish to draw your attention to the options available to you should you wish to take the complaint beyond our internal procedures.

Information regarding both the in-house complaints procedure and where complaints can be progressed to must be given to the client. As with the fees information, this must be clearly laid out, and again, may be included in a separate document if necessary.

We are happy to be acting for you in this matter and wish to assure you that we will act at all time with the requisite due diligence and in your best interests. Please feel free to contact Miss Somebody on 01234 565656 for any reason.

Chapter 2
Writing Letters

The highlighted phrase need not be included in the letter but it is possibly the most important point to remember and failure to do so in any way can render you or the firm liable to disciplinary action being taken.

In order to ensure that the client is clear about who is dealing with the matter and how they can contact them it is prudent to reiterate the name and provide clear contact details, for example a telephone number or e-mail details.

Please sign where indicated the enclosed copy of this letter and the information sheets and complete the enclosed forms and return both as promptly as possible in order for us to proceed with matter should you wish to continue.

Finally ensure that the client is clear about any instructions included in the text of the letter and emphasize any date deadlines for instructions to be carried out by. Remember you are there to ensure that the client is guided through the legal process as well as ensuring that you do the best possible for them in the circumstances.

A client may well be confused and upset whilst undergoing the process so it is important that they are treated with respect and an appropriate amount of empathy. Even a small action shows that thought has been given to their welfare or needs and will clearly demonstrate that the firm is professional and diligent in all aspects of service.

It is prudent to enclose a copy of the letter and documents explaining cost, complaints procedure and terms of business and ask the client to sign and return them. This will ensure that should a complaint arise there is clear evidence that all the provisions of the Solicitors' Code of Conduct and accompanying requirements have been met as far as required.

Yours faithfully

Remember if a letter has begun with "Dear Sir" it should close with "Yours faithfully" and if it has begun with the client's name with "Yours sincerely."

E Everyman

Senior Partner

Everyman Solicitors

The signature block should contain the name and status of the senior person dealing with the matter or the person for whom you are writing the letter.

There may be times when you will be asked to sign the letter on their behalf and this should be done with a "pp" before your signature to indicate that the signature is not theirs but another person's on behalf of the person named.

Suwyn, Siska & King

Attorneys at Law

65-21 Main Street

Flushing, New York 11367

(718) 340-4200

October 23, 2006

Willi Loman

Loman's Fashions

885 Seventh Avenue

New York, New York 10017

Dear Ms. Loman:

I hope you've been well. Recently you wrote to us that Loman's Fashions had been sued by a shopper in Small Claims Court for a breach of contract. As you've described it, the shopper claims that she responded to an ad for a "manufacturer's closeout" of designer leather coats; the ad stated that the "early" shopper would "catch the savings." The shopper complains that Loman's failed to have the merchandise to sell at the advertised price. Specifically, you have asked for advice on the question whether Loman's breached a contract with the shopper under the circumstances. After researching the issue, and based on the facts set out below, I believe that a court would likely conclude that Loman's did not enter into a contract with this shopper because the advertisement was not an offer to sell the coats; thus, there was no contract that Loman's could breach. I will explain this conclusion more fully below after first setting out the facts as I understand them.[1]

Loman's Fashions, a retailer of women's and men's outerwear, distributed a circular last July advertising a manufacturer's closeout of designer women's leather coats for $59.99, coats that regularly sold for $300.00. The ad announced that the store would open at 7 a.m. on Friday, July 21, and stated that the "early bird catches the savings!" After about fifteen minutes, all the advertised coats had been sold. At 7:30 a.m., a shopper inquired about the coats and was told that there was none left. She then complained that Loman's was obligated to sell her a comparably valued designer leather coat at the advertised price. The store manager declined, and the shopper filed a complaint in Small Claims Court, claiming that Loman's had breached a contract by failing to sell the advertised leather coats at the advertised price.

You mentioned to me that the store occasionally gives rain checks when it is possible to replenish supplies of an item that Loman's can purchase at a discount. In this case, the manufacturer had discontinued the line of coats and Loman's was not willing to sell other, designer leather coats at such a drastic markdown. You are concerned that, if the shopper's interpretation were to be honored, Loman's would have to reconsider its marketing strategies. Although you had assumed that the advertised terms applied only while supplies lasted, your ad had not included language to that effect.[2] You have asked for this law firm's opinion whether this shopper could succeed on her breach of contract claim.

Under these facts, a court would likely apply the well-settled law that a general advertisement that merely lists items for sale is at best an invitation to negotiate, not an offer to form a contract.[3] The courts that have considered this question focus on two related considerations.[4] The first is whether the advertisement is complete and definite in its terms. For example, where an advertisement containing terms for sale was missing the amount of goods available for sale, a court held that the seller had not made an offer that was complete and definite in all material terms. Thus, no contract was ever made between the seller and a person who submitted a purchase order.[5]

The second consideration is whether an advertisement promises to sell an item in return for something requested, for example, if a storeowner promised to sell an item for a specified price to anyone who came to the store ready to pay that amount.[6] Where such a promise was lacking, a court held that an advertisement by a department store was not an offer but an invitation to all persons that the advertiser was ready to receive offers for the goods upon the stated terms.[7] Even if a person's willingness to purchase the advertised item could be thought to turn the offer into a contract, that court ruled that a purchaser did not have the right to select the item that a seller did not have in stock or was not willing to sell at a reduced price.[8]

Applying these legal rules to Loman's advertisement supports the conclusion that the ad was not an offer to enter into a contract of sale and created no contractual duty in Loman's.[9] Here, the advertisement did not specify the amount of coats to sell, but rather described the leather coats as a "manufacturer's closeout" selling at a substantially reduced price.[10] In addition, the advertisement did not contain a promise to sell the leather coats in exchange for some requested act or promise.[11] Furthermore, the ad did not give the public the right to choose any comparably priced leather coat if the advertised coats were no longer available.[12] Although the shopper here might argue that the advertisement did not contain limiting language, for example, that the coats were for sale while supplies lasted,[13] the ad did state that the store, opening for business on the day of the sale at 7 a.m., was catering to early morning shoppers. By announcing that "the early bird catches the savings," the ad implied that the supplies would run out.[14]

To sum up, based on the facts as I have recited them in this letter, I believe that a court would conclude that Loman's ad did not make an offer to sell leather coats that a purchaser could accept, but that it was at best an invitation to negotiate. Thus, no contract came into existence from this transaction.[15] To avoid the possibility that Loman's will face future claims on this same point, I would recommend that, going forward, Loman's ads include language such as "while supplies last" "first come, first served" or "quantities limited — no substitutes permitted." In this way, Loman's would communicate to shoppers that there were no guarantees that they could purchase an advertised item, or a substitute. Although the additional text might increase the cost of advertising, in the long run inserting this additional language in the ads could save you time and the costs involved in defending claims such as this one.[16]

I hope this is helpful, and would be happy to discuss this matter with you further. Please feel free to call my office at (718) 340-4200 if you have questions, or would like to set up a time to meet.[17]

Very truly yours,

Chapter 2
Writing Letters

Madala Suwyn, Esq.

Note

(**1**) Opening paragraph states the client's problem, specifies the legal issue on which the client seeks advice, and states the writer's conclusion.

(**2**) This paragraph and the preceding paragraph set out legally significant facts — facts upon which the writer will base her analysis. The factual criteria of the rule for offers under contract law, discussed in the following paragraph of the letter, are the source of the legally significant facts.

(**3**) The writer here restates her conclusion.

(**4**) The writer begins translating the law into relatively straightforward language, without naming specific cases.

(**5**) The writer here offers an example of how the rule would operate and then explains the implication of this analysis: that no contract was formed.

(**6**) The writer explains part of the rule by providing an example.

(**7**) The writer illustrates the point of law by discussing the facts and ruling in a similar case.

(**8**) The writer refers to an alternative holding in the case.

(**9**) The writer restates her conclusion as she moves to an analysis of her client's facts.

(**10**) The writer applies the first part of the rule — relating to definiteness and completeness of material terms — to Loman's facts.

(**11**) The writer now turns to the second part of the rule, requiring a promise in exchange for a requested act or promise, and applies it to Loman's facts.

(**12**) The writer points to facts (specifically, the absence of facts) in Loman's that provide an alternative basis for the writer's conclusion.

(**13**) The writer introduces a possible counterargument.

(**14**) The writer resolves the counterargument in favor of her original conclusion.

(**15**) The writer summarizes and restates her conclusion.

(**16**) The writer offers some preventive advice that addresses the possibility of future legal claims and also addresses extra-legal factors — cost and time.

(**17**) The writer invites a follow-up conversation with the client.

6. Samples

The following samples illustrate a range of letters and writing styles. These are only samples and not models.

(1) Attorney-Client Correspondence

① Letter Declining Client[①]

SHICHENG LAW FIRM,
BEIJING, CHINA

April 21, 2015

Sarah Smith

IGR Corporation

711 Golden Terrace, Suite 1313

Chicago, IL 60613

Dear Ms. Smith,

We have discussed, investigated and reviewed your potential legal claim. After a cost/benefits and legal analysis, we have decided not to pursue your case. Due to the problems we perceive with taking your case, we are declining to be your attorneys and will take no further action in regard to this matter.

I would urge you, however, that if you wish to pursue your legal rights, you should contact an attorney as soon as possible, since there is a statute of limitations on your potential claim. Also be advised that failure to pursue your claim before the statute runs will result in a complete loss of your rights.

Thank you for considering this law office for legal representation.

Sincerely,

Sun Li

Partner

---

① http://forms.lawguru.com/letter-declining-client_p.html

② Letter Withdrawing from Representation①

SHICHENG LAW FIRM,
BEIJING, CHINA

April 26, 2015

David Sherlock
455W. Wellington Avenue
Chicago, IL 60657

Dear Mr. Sherlock,

This correspondence is to inform you that we intend to move to withdraw from your case. We are doing so for the following reasons: breach of the fee agreement, and lack of merits to the case.

If you want to retain another attorney to substitute in for us, we will cooperate in transferring your file.

We are not making judgment with respect to the merits of your case. However, if you intend to pursue your claim you must move quickly to meet the court deadlines for the trial date.

Sincerely,

Sun Li
Partner

---

① http://forms.lawguru.com/letter-withdrawing-from-representation_p.html

③ Letter Requesting Case Update from Client[①]

SHICHENG LAW FIRM,
BEIJING, CHINA

April 29, 2015

Timothy Tyler
IGR Corporation
711 Golden Terrace, Suite 1313
Chicago, IL 60613

Dear Mr. Tyler,

In the matter of *Timothy Tyler vs. Eastern Pacific University*, I have not received any update regarding the status of the case since March 28, 2009. I would greatly appreciate it if you would provide me with a brief update at your earliest convenience.

Thank you for your continuing assistance in this matter. I look forward to hearing from you soon.

Sincerely,

Sun Li
Partner

[①] http://media.findlegalforms.com/files/admin/Samples/pdf/master/LTR/LTR-LGL-UPDCSE-SAMP.pdf.swf

Chapter 2
Writing Letters

④ Attorney Opinion Letter[①]

June 13, 2014

Joe Black
10 East Doty Street, Suite 701
Madison, WI 53703
(608) 284-1200

Dear Mr. Black,

After our initial meeting, I reviewed the papers you sent me regarding the Sophia Loker matter. As I understand the situation, Ms. Loker signed a written employment agreement with your company. The agreement stated that in the event of termination or resignation from her job as your sales associate, Ms. Loker would not call upon or sell goods to any of your customers for a period of one year.

You have asked me to advise you about your rights, the chance of success, the amount of damages that may be recoverable, the costs involved, and my ability to represent you in this matter.

RIGHTS OF CONFIDENTIALITY AGAINST MS. LOKER

When Ms. Loker signed a written contract with your company, she agreed not to call upon any of your customers for a period of one year. This is called a restrictive covenant. To enforce your covenant against Ms. Loker, you must bring an action against her and prove your case. You have a choice of forums in which to bring the action: federal district court or a state court. Since it is easier to obtain an injunction (an action to immediately stop her from selling to your customers) in a state court rather than a federal court, I would suggest the state court.

I must advise you that injunctions are largely discretionary with the court, and there are several factors here that might lead it not to grant one on your behalf. Since you have waited for eight months before threatening to sue Ms. Loker, my guess is that you have about a twenty percent (20%) chance of obtaining an injunction.

RIGHTS TO AND AMOUNT OF DAMAGES

Your chances of obtaining money damages against Ms. Loker are much greater than your chances for an injunction. From our discussion and the facts and evidence suggested in your papers, it appears that the amount of recoverable damages would be measured by the profits you have lost since the time Ms.

---

① http://www.eduzhai.net/yingyu/615/764/yingyu_247409.html

Loker began selling competitive products to your customers. It should be understood that if we win our case, however, Ms. Loker may not voluntarily pay the judgment. Thus, it may be necessary to enforce the judgment by having a sheriff or marshal seize and sell assets not exempt from execution.

However, if Ms. Loker does not own assets, such as real estate, money in bank accounts, stocks, etc., but owns only personal items exempt from execution under the laws of our state, then any judgment you obtain may not be worth much.

NEGATIVES TO LAWSUIT

Besides the fact that you may lose a lawsuit against Ms. Loker or that any judgment obtained may be uncollectible, there are other negative factors you should consider before bringing a lawsuit. These include court costs and attorney fees. Court costs are recoverable, but other costs, such as travel, the time lost when you are called to testify (or required to help us develop the case), and attorney fees, are not recoverable.

MY SERVICES

I am familiar with the nature of your manufacturing business and I am qualified to represent you in this matter if you choose to proceed. My fee would be based on my normal hourly charge of $250 for myself and $150 for associates. Trial time is billed at $1,000 per day. The initial services of preparing a complaint and serving same would cost approximately $300. Preparing a request for an injunction and attending a hearing on the injunction would cost approximately $2,500.

It is quite possible that Ms. Loker would not retain her own counsel and not answer the complaint. This means that a default judgment could be taken without the necessity of a trial. Here attorney fees would probably amount to no more than $1,000. I require a $1,000 retainer to open a file and commence an action. If you wish to proceed with this matter, I will need to know the full names and addresses of your customers to whom Ms. Loker is presently selling and the estimated sales volume which you have lost.

If you have any questions, please call me.

Very truly yours,
Li Jun
Partner with Shicheng Law Firm
Beijing, China

⑤ Letter to a Prospective Client

SHICHENG LAW FIRM,
BEIJING, CHINA

September 17, 2014

David Trace
JGR Corporation
711 Golden Terrace, Suite1316
Chicago, IL60613

Dear David,

I enjoyed seeing you at the International Trade Association meeting at the World Trade Center in Chicago. I hope you found the meeting as rewarding as I did. I have been a member of that association for several years.

Enclosed are the materials you requested. They explain the legal services that our firm provides to clients. I call your attention to page four (4) of our firm brochure, which describes our work in international business transactions for companies such as yours.

I will call you next week to answer any question you might have.

Sincerely,

Li Hui
Partner

⑥ Follow-up Letter to a Client (After Initial Meeting)

SHICHENG LAW FIRM,
BEIJING, CHINA

David Trace
JGR Corporation
711 Golden Terrace, Suite 1316
Chicago, IL 60613

Dear David,

I enjoyed meeting with you last week in my office. Thank you for giving me the opportunity to talk with you about the legal services that our firm offers.

The information that I promised to forward to you about international intellectual property law is enclosed. You may also be interested in the materials on revolving letters of credit as a tool to finance international business transactions.

I will call you next week to follow up. Please call me if you have any questions.

Sincerely,

Li Hui
Partner

⑦ Letter of a Contract Advice

[Date _____]

[Client _____]
[Address _____]
Re: [Client/Matter _____]

Dear _____,

Enclosed are copies of the following that I received yesterday:

Letter from [Name _____] dated _____ draft of [Title _____] Contract

Schedule A to Contract   Schedule B to Contract

The following are my comments concerning these documents:

Read the Documents. I strongly advise that you read each of these documents. I have read them, and this letter sets forth my thoughts, but you may think of other questions when you read them. You have special knowledge about your business that I do not have, and your special knowledge may lead you to see potential problems in these documents that I could not see. So, please read these documents, jot down questions while you read them, and then call me to discuss them.

Term. The Term seems to me to be rather short. Perhaps the Term should be longer.

Price. The Price is not clearly defined. The Contract refers to unit price but does not define what a unit is.

Please call me after you read this letter and its enclosures.

Very truly yours,

[Lawyer _____]
Enclosures

⑧ An Engagement Letter

SHICHENG LAW FIRM,
BEIJING, CHINA

[Date _____]

CONFIDENTIAL ATTORNEY-CLIENT COMMUNICATION
DO NOT COPY OR DISCLOSE TO ANYONE ELSE

[Client's name _____]
[Address _____]
Re: Legal Representation
Dear _____,

This will confirm that you have retained me to represent your interest in connection with _____. The scope of representation is as follows: _____.

You are going to furnish me copies of the following documents before I start working: _____. I will begin to work as soon as I receive a fee retainer of $ _____ from you. The retainer will be deposited to my trust account and will be applied toward fees and costs as earned and incurred. As that retainer is used up, additional retainers will be billed to continue the work.

Fees are based on the amount of time spent at hourly rates of $ _____ for me and $ _____ for my paralegal. You will also pay for such costs as copies, postage, fax, long distance, recording, FedEx, courier, etc. Enclosed is my resume, which I gave you at the initial conference and which explains how I bill for my services. If you have any questions, please do not hesitate to call.

The range of fees for this work will vary with the amount of time it takes. I estimate that fees will be a minimum of $ _____.

Please note that the scope of my representation does not include advice or services regarding the following: accounting, tax, financial, business, management, and related non-legal matters and advice (I advise that you engage a CPA, tax attorney or business consultant to advise you regarding these

Chapter 2
Writing Letters

matters); title searches, surveys, inspections and other non-legal work relating to real estate (I advise that you engage a title insurance company, abstractor, surveyor or other licensed professional to provide you these services); securities, labor, and other legal matters not handled by this firm (I advise that you engage a lawyer who specializes in these matters if you need such advice). I would be happy to refer you to others who may provide you with these services.

I appreciate your trust and confidence in asking me to assist you. I will endeavor to do my best for you at all times.

Very truly yours,
[Lawyer _____]

(2) Attorney-Adverse Party Correspondence
⑨ Attorney Response to Former Employee[①]

SHICHENG LAW FIRM,
BEIJING, CHINA

March 16, 2015

Manger of Personnel Department
PINGAN Insurance Company
25 Zhongguancun Street
Beijing, China

Dear Sir or Madam,

This law firm represents Jennifer White. Please direct any further correspondence regarding that company to the undersigned. I have had an opportunity to review your letter of February 13, 2008 and the February 25, 2008 written offer letter, signed by my client and accepting the position of manager assistant of Sales Department.

The clear language of the written offer provided that Jennifer White was an "at will" employee. Her employment was not for any specified length of time and could not be terminated with or without cause. However, Jennifer White was terminated for legitimate, non-discriminatory business reasons.

In light of the foregoing, PINGAN Insurance Company has paid Jennifer White for all amounts owned her as a result of her employment. Should you wish to discuss this issue further? Please contact me at your earliest convenience.

Sincerely,

Lin Ping
Partner

[①] http://media. findlegalforms. com/files/admin/Samples/pdf/lhoda/28200/ATTY-LTR-FETC-US-SAMP. pdf. swf

⑩ Letter to Adverse Insurance Company①

SHICHENG LAW FIRM,
BEIJING, CHINA

March 12, 2015

PINGAN Insurance Company
25 Zhongguancun Street
Beijing, China

Attn: Wu Di

Re: Your Insured: Jennifer White
    Our Client: Zhang Bin
    Your Claim No.: 123456

Dear Mr. Wu,

As you know, this office has been retained by the above-mentioned with references to personal injuries sustained as a result of a traffic collision caused by your insured. Enclosed with the copy of this letter sent by mail are the police report and medical records and bills. Please inform us what your insured's liability policy limits are. Additional medical records and billing statements as well as a HIPPA release will be forwarded in the near future.

At this time our client is unable to rent a car on his own. If you are unwilling to provide a rental at this time, our client will rent a car through a rental agency that takes liens. This would most likely be an expensive rental. Please advice as to your position on this matter as soon as possible.

We want to assure our client that you are willing to entertain his claim in good faith. To that end, please acknowledge in writing that you accept liability for the incident and PINGAN Insurance Company is ready, willing and able to review our settlement package on the issue of damages only. This letter will be calendared for a response in 10 days from its date. Thank you for your courtesy in responding as soon as possible.

Sincerely,

Lin Ping
Partner

---

① http://forms.lawguru.com/letter-to-adverse-insurance-company_p.html

⑪ Letter Warning the Adverse Party①

August 16, 2014

Herbert Smith
23# Guilin Road
Changchun Jilin, China

Dear Mr. Smith,

Mr. Winer has retained our firm and asked us to contact you about two related matters. If an attorney is representing you, please provide this letter to your attorney and have him or her contact me.

First, we request that you return the $5,000 deposit that Mr. Winer paid to you in October, 2005 in connection with certain work that you were supposed to perform for Mr. Winer in revising and maintaining Mr. Winer's website, "feeds.scripting.com". Mr. Winer had previously sent you a consulting agreement regarding this work and made it clear to you that he would not hire you to perform this work without a written agreement signed by each of you. It is our understanding that neither you nor Mr. Winer signed such an agreement, that the redesigned site was never completed and launched, and that Mr. Winer has advised you that he no longer wishes to use your services for this project.

Second, Mr. Winer has recently learned that you have used the contents of his website "feeds.scripting.com" as well as a computer application authored by him and certain third-party information, to launch a public web site known as the "OPML Factory", presently located at "opml.cadenhead.org." The contents of "feeds.scripting.com" and the computer program are Mr. Winer's property and are protected by federal copyright law as well as by state law. Mr. Winer has not authorized you to use his property to launch the "OPML Factory" and your use of his property for such a purpose constitutes a willful infringement of Mr. Winer's copyrights under 17 U.S.C. 101, et seq., for which you can be liable for statutory damages as high as $150,000 for each unauthorized use, pursuant to 17 U.S.C. 504(c)(2), and liable for Mr. Winer's attorneys' fees if he were to bring an action against you in the United States District Court to enforce his rights, pursuant to 17 U.S.C. 505. Accordingly, on behalf of Mr.

---

① http://workbench.cadenhead.org/news/2881/letter-dave-winers-attorney

Winer, we demand that you immediately cease using or distributing all materials that Mr. Winer provided to you in connection with the "feeds.scripting.com" project, that you return to Mr. Winer all such materials, that you cease operating the "OPML Factory" and any other websites or portions of websites derived from his property, that you destroy any works derived from Mr. Winer's computer program, and that you desist from these uses and from any other infringement of Mr. Winer's property in the future.

Specifically, we must insist that, by no later than next Wednesday, March 15, you:

(1) return the $5,000 deposit to Mr. Winer;

(2) return all materials, third-party data and applications that Mr. Winer provided to you in connection with the "feeds.scripting.com" project;

(3) destroy all works derived from such materials, data and applications, and provide us a sworn statement, signed under penalty of perjury of the laws of the State of California, attesting that you:

a) have destroyed all such derivative works and

b) no longer possess copies of any the materials, data and applications obtained from Mr. Winer; and

(4) take down the "OPML Factory" website (presently located at "opml.cadenhead.org") and any other websites or pages that you derived from "feeds.scripting.com".

If you do not take these actions by next Wednesday, March 15, we shall assume that you will not be complying with Mr. Winer's demands and we will take all appropriate actions to enforce Mr. Winer's rights.

Sincerely,

Zhang Li

Partner

⑫ Letter Negotiating with the Adverse Party①

July 16, 2014

Dear Mr. Stewart,

It has come to our attention that you have created and are operating a website which you have labeled "The Bill O'Reilly Sucks. com Web Site." We are hereby advising you that the unauthorized use of Mr. O'Reilly's name for commercial purposes is clearly a violation of O'Reilly's rights. Section 43 (a) of the Lanham act (15 U. S. C. & 1125 (a)) states that it is violation of a person's rights to use that person's name in commercial advertising or promotion which misrepresents the nature, characteristics, or qualities of that person's services. You have clearly traded on the goodwill and name of Bill O'Reilly in using his name in the title of your website. There is no doubt that Mr. O'Reilly's name has acquired distinctiveness and secondary meaning with the general public. His nightly program "The O'Reilly Factor" is the highest rated cable television news program in the country. He has personally authored two books, both of which have been on *The New York Times* bestseller list.

You also have violated Mr. O'Reilly's right under Section 51 of the New York Civil Rights Law. That provision bars the use of a living person's name, portrait, picture or voice for trade or advertising purposes without the written consent from that person. It is also obvious that you have been using Mr. O'Reilly's name in connection with your commercial attempt to sell advertising. Indeed, immediately under the greeting on the website is a solicitation for viewers to purchase advertising on your website. Although the use of Mr. O'Reilly's name in the body of the copy on the website may be protected usage, the recurring use of his name as the title of your website is not protected under the first amendment.

Mr. O'Reilly and Fox News Network, LLC insist that you immediately discontinue using Mr. O'Reilly's name in any way as a designation for your website and that you provide us with written confirmation that you have done

---

① http://www.oreilly-sucks.com/images/foxletter.jpg

so. To the extent that you ignore this request, you do so at your own peril. All of the rights and remedies of Mr. O'Reilly and Fox News Network LLC are expressly reserved.

Very truly yours,

Dianne Brandi
[Law Firm]

⑬ Letter to Negotiate with the Attorney of the Adverse Party①

June 26, 2014

Mike Atkins
[ADRESS]

Dear Mike,

I write this letter in an attempt to bring closure to the disputes between Dr. Gallegos and the ECISD. As you know Dr. Gallegos has sued the ECISD to prevent the release of certain confidential, educational records to the public. Furthermore, it is my understanding that certain members of the ECISD board have voiced disputes and concerns about Dr. Gallegos; particularly a concern about whether Dr. Gallegos' criticism of the ECISD District plan and its authors was warranted. In defending the ECISD District plan and its authors, certain board members publicly lashed out at Dr. Gallegos, arguably defaming him in the process. Furthermore, the ECISD District plan authors filed an employment grievance against Dr. Gallegos, asking that he be fired. As you know, Dr. Gallegos' assertions were proven correct in that that ECISD District plan was shown to have been plagiarized from the Georgetown ISD District plan, and one of the authors of the ECISD District plan has now resigned because of this fact. Certain members of the ECISD board have publicly accused Dr. Gallegos of passing a fraudulent plan, in order to provide unwarranted political cover for the true perpetrators of the fraudulent plan. But for Dr. Gallegos, ECISD would not be aware today that it had passed a copy of a plan developed specifically for Georgetown ISD. Although certain board members publicly criticized Dr. Gallegos, it remains uncertain whether the general public is aware that Dr. Gallegos is responsible for shining light on this unseemly transaction, and that he should be commended, not criticized. Dr. Gallegos is anxious for the general public to understand his role in these events and to clear his name.

Also, earlier this year, the ECISD board passed a motion to evaluate Dr. Gallegos this September. This motion is out of order, in that the board cannot evaluate staff other than the superintendent, and it changes an evaluation

---

① http://www.accessmylibrary.com/coms2/summary_0286-31740664_ITM? email=sarahnenu@163.com&library=

document without seeking staff input. Dr. Gallegos has charged me with investigating the possibility of filing a declaratory judgment action against the ECISD to determine whether the actions of the board are in contravention of other board policy and or state law.

Dr. Gallegos has also charged me with investigating the merits of a potential defamation action against one or more ECISD board members, and investigating other ways to enable him to tell his story to the greater public in order to restore his good name and professional reputation.

However, in an attempt to avoid more litigation and to resolve existing litigation, Dr. Gallegos would be willing to sign a release and waiver of all claims, in exchange for a buy-out of his existing contact of employment with ECISD, with good references. Such an agreement would allow Dr. Gallegos to land in a better employment position and would allow the ECISD to be free and clear of any potential claims he may pursue. It seems that such a deal would be in the mutual best interests of both parties.

Because the early summer is the best time for an educator to make a transition, I respectfully request a response to this offer at your earliest convenience.

As always, if you would like to discuss these matters, please give me a call.

Very truly yours,

Kevin F. Lungwitz
[Law Firm]

⑭ Letter of a Contract Negotiation

[Date _____]

[Name _____]
[Address _____]
Re: [Client/Matter _____]

Dear _____,

This confirms that I received your [Date _____] letter and its enclosed draft of the [Title _____] Contract. I have read the draft, discussed it with my client [Client _____], and have the following initial comments that we will need to resolve before we can move ahead with negotiating the finer points of the Contract:

Term. The Term would need to be at least _____ years before my client could seriously consider entering into the Contract.

Unit Price. The Unit Price would need to be at least $ _____ before my client could consider the Contract financially feasible.

Controlling Law. My client does business only in the State of Florida and does not desire to engage a lawyer in [State _____], so the Contract will need to provide that Florida law controls.

Publicity. My client requests that the last sentence of paragraph 3 on page 2 of the Contract be changed to read as follows: _____.

Please discuss these points with your client and let me know if your client is willing to pursue negotiation of a contract along these lines.

Very truly yours,

[Lawyer _____]
[Law Firm]
cc: [Client _____]

Chapter 2
Writing Letters

⑮ A Demand Letter

[Date _____]

[Name _____]

[Address _____]

By fax to [Fax # _____]; phone [Phone # _____]/And by FedEx Priority Overnight/And by email to [Email address _____]/Or by U.S. Registered Mail Return Receipt Requested

Re: [Client _____]

Dear _____,

This office represents [Client _____]. It has come to our attention that you are building and operating stores having trade dress confusingly similar to the stores of our client. You have copied the following elements of our client's trade dress, among others: _____.

This letter is formal notice that your use is an infringement of our client's trade dress rights under Section 43(a) of the Lanham Act, 15 U.S.C. §125(a). *Two Pesos, Inc. v. Taco Cabana, Inc.*, 60 U.S.L.W. 4762 (1992 WL 141119 (U.S.)). Our client also claims copyright in its store design, which copyright you have also infringed. We have reason to believe that your infringement is intentional and deliberate and that you are attempting to copy our client's business by copying its trade dress and store design.

Our client hereby demands that you immediately do the following:

Cease and desist building and operating stores having trade dress similar to [Client _____] stores; Cease and desist any and all other violations of the Lanham Act and the copyright laws; and remove and destroy all elements of our client's trade dress and store design from your stores.

If you fail to comply with this demand, our client may seek relief in court for an injunction and damages. Judicial relief includes, but is not limited to: destruction of the infringing articles under 15 U.S.C. §118; treble damages, your profits, any damages sustained by our client, court costs and attorneys fees under 15 U.S.C. §117; injunction under 15 U.S.C. §116; injunction and damages under the copyright laws. Our client reserves all rights it may have.

Our client neither waives nor abandons its right by sending you this demand letter prior to filing suit.

Please confirm in writing to this office that you will comply with this letter within one week of its receipt.

Very truly yours,

[Lawyer _____]

[Law Firm]

(3) Daily Correspondence

⑯ Letter Requesting a Copy of a Publication

August 16, 2014

Professor Zhang Li
China Law Institute
Zhongguancun Road
Beijing 1000860
P. R. China

Dear Professor Zhang,

I would like to order a copy of the book, *An Introduction to Chinese Environmental Law*, Please advise me of the current cost (in U.S. or Canadian dollars, if possible) to purchase the book and to have it sent by airmail. If it is convenient for you, you may fax this information to me at (fax number).
Thank you.

Sincerely,

[Lawyer _____]
[Law Firm]

⑰ Letter to Thanks to a Speaker

July 25, 2014

Mr. Richard P. Bruno
Supervisory Import Specialist
United States Customs Service
610 S. Canal Street, Room 450A
Chicago, IL 60607

Dear Mr. Bruno,

I enjoyed your presentation yesterday on customs law and procedure in the United States. Thank you for coming to speak at the law school and for staying after class to answer additional questions about how the United States Customs Service enforces trademarks and other intellectual property rights. I was especially interested in your explanation of how the Customs Service has no authority to prevent the importation of goods that violate a patent unless directed to do so by an exclusion order issued by the U. S. International Trade Commission. I confess that I am often confused about which governmental agencies have responsibilities over these matters. Your explanation of the exclusion orders issued by the Commission made this easier for me to understand.

Thank you also for bringing the brochures discussing import quotas, foreign trade zones, and customs duty drawback. I look forward to reading these brochures and learning more about these issues.

Thank you again for coming to the school. You were very gracious with your time.

Sincerely,
[NAME]

⑱ Letter Requesting Information about a Law School Program

July 16, 2014

Professor William B. T. Mock
Director, International and Comparative Law Program
The John Marshall Law School
315 S. Plymouth Court
Chicago, IL 60604 USA

Dear Professor Mock,

Thank you for speaking with me today about the number and variety of LL. M. programs available in the United States. As I mentioned to you on the phone, I graduated from the Liaocheng University in 1999, with specializations in corporate and copyright law. Soon after graduation, I obtained a position as in-house counsel with a large government bank, where I worked on a number of financial, corporate, and real estate matters.

I am interested in eventually moving to the private sector, but I would first like to obtain some additional legal education in the United States. Your school's program in International and Comparative Law seems to fit my needs exactly. I would be very grateful to receive further information about the specific courses offered in the program, the academic requirements for admission, and, if possible, information about housing options near the school.

Sincerely,

Zhang Lei

⑲ Letter Requesting Information about the Legal English and Orientation Course

Jan. 16, 2015

Ms. Keri Lawhead
International Law Institute
1615 New Hampshire Ave., N.W.
Washington, D.C. 20009-2520 U.S.A.

Dear Ms. Lawhead,

I have been accepted into an LL.M. program at U.S. law school for the fall semester. I have heard that your summer training programs in *Introduction to Legal English and Orientation in the U.S. Legal System* are helpful for lawyers who want a good overview of U.S. law, and that these courses are especially helpful for persons who, like me, will be enrolled in full time studies at an American law school.

I would greatly appreciate it if you could please send me further information about the courses and how to register for them.

Sincerely yours,

[Name]

㉑ Letter Requesting an Invitation

**The Supreme People's Court of the
People's Republic of China**

Feb. 16, 2014

The Honorable Chief Judge Gregory Carman
U. S. Court of International Trade
One Federal Plaza
New York, NY 10007 USA

Dear Judge Carman,

I am a judge on the Supreme People's Court of the People's Republic of China. I will be visiting New York in July, in connection with a meeting at the United Nations Headquarters. I would be most grateful if I could stop by your court when I am in New York. I would like to learn more about the advantages and disadvantages of establishing a special court for international trade and customs law issues. As you may know, the national legislature in my country is presently considering the merits of establishing a special commercial law court with an emphasis on matters related to international trade and foreign investment disputes. I am certain that my visit to your court would be very enlightening.

I look forward to your reply.

Very truly yours,

ZHOU, Qiang
Chief Justice

P. S. I would also like to see the library facilities at your court, especially the collections on international trade and customs law issues.

㉑ Letter to Confirm a Meeting

SHICHENG LAW FIRM,
BEIJING, CHINA

Oct. 16. 2014

David Trace

JGR Corporation

711 Golden Terrace, Suite 1316

Chicago, IL 60613

Dear David,

I enjoyed talking with you yesterday. Our firm welcomes the opportunity to discuss how we can assist you in building an international business.

I look forward to meeting with you at 3:00 p.m. on October 19th at my office. I have enclosed the latest issue of our client newsletter for your review. You may be particularly interested in the information on establishing joint ventures in China.

If you have any questions before our meeting, please feel free to call me. I look forward to seeing you on October 19th.

Sincerely,

Song Lianhui

Partner

(4) Letter of Intent.

㉒ Letter of Acquisition of Assets

LETTER OF INTENT
(ASSET PURCHASE /SALE)
[LETTERHEAD OF PURCHASER]

[date]

CONFIDENTIAL

[Addressee]

[Address]

Re: Acquisition of Assets from [Company name],
   a [type of entity & jurisdiction of formation]

Dear [Addressee]:

This letter confirms our understanding of the mutual present intentions of [Full, Formal Name of Purchaser] (the "Purchaser") and [Full, Formal Name of Seller], (the "Seller") with respect to the principal terms and conditions under which the Purchaser will acquire substantially all of the Seller's assets (the "Assets"). This transaction is referred to as the "Acquisition" and the Seller and Purchaser are referred to, collectively, as the "Parties."

This letter is written with the understanding that the Seller is, among other things, [disclose any material information that, if left undisclosed, could constitute such a material discovery that one or both parties could back out of their deal claiming surprise, misrepresentation, material omission, frustration of purpose, or impossibility, e.g. bankruptcy or conservancy of a party, the need for board, regulator or other approval, and the like.]

[If non-binding: The Parties acknowledge that this letter does not contain all matters upon which an agreement must be reached in order for the Acquisition to be consummated. Further, among other conditions specified herein or otherwise agreed to by the parties, the obligations of the Parties hereto consummate the Acquisition are subject to the negotiation and execution of the Purchase Agreement and Loan Documents referred to below. Accordingly, this letter is intended solely as a basis for further discussion and is not intended to be and does not constitute a legally binding agreement; provided, however, that the provisions set forth in paragraphs 6, 7, 9, 10, 11, and 12 below and this paragraph shall be binding upon the Parties and, only with respect to paragraphs 9, 10, 11, and 12, shall survive termination.]

i. Purchase of Assets. At the closing (the "Closing"), subject to the satisfaction of all conditions precedent contained in the Purchase Agreement, the Purchaser will purchase from the Seller, and the Seller will sell to the Purchaser, all of the Seller's Assets except those listed on Exhibit A hereto, if any. The Purchaser may assign some or all of its rights hereunder prior to the Closing to one or more of its subsidiaries.

ii. Purchase Price. The purchase price for the Assets will be $ _____, payable to the Seller, in cash, when [specify time, condition, or event triggering closing].

iii. Definitive Agreement. The Purchaser and the Seller shall use reasonable diligence to commence good faith negotiations in order to execute and deliver a definitive agreement relating to the Acquisition (the "Purchase Agreement") acceptable to the parties hereto on or prior to [date certain]. [Specify what happens if this does not occur including whether or not there are legal, binding obligations.] All terms and conditions concerning the acquisition shall be stated in the Purchase Agreement, including representations, warranties, covenants, and indemnities that are usual and customary in a transaction of this nature and as may be mutually agreed upon between the parties. Subject to the satisfaction of all conditions precedent contained in the Purchase Agreement, the Closing will take place no later than [date certain] or as soon thereafter as possible.

iv. Representations and Warranties. The Agreement will contain representations and warranties customary to transactions of this type, including without limitation, representations and warranties by the Seller as to (a) the accuracy and completeness of the Company's financial statements; (b) disclosure of all the Seller's contracts, commitments, and liabilities, direct or contingent; (c) the physical condition, suitability, ownership and status of liens, claims, and other adverse interest with respect to the Seller's assets; (d) the Seller's ownership of the Assets; (e) the absence of a material adverse change in the condition (financial or otherwise), business, properties, assets of the Seller;

and (f) the organization, valid existence, good standing, and capitalization of the Seller.

v. Conditions to Consummation of the Acquisition. The respective obligations of the parties with respect to the Acquisition shall be subject to satisfaction of conditions customary to transactions of this type, including without limitation, (a) execution of the Purchase Agreement by all parties; (b) the obtaining of all requisite regulatory, administrative, or governmental authorizations and consents; (c) approval of the Acquisition by the Board of Directors of the Purchaser; (d) absence of a material adverse change in the condition (financial or otherwise) of the Assets; (e) satisfactory completion by the Purchaser of due diligence investigation of the Company as provided in paragraph 2(b)(ii) above; and (f) confirmation that the representations and warranties of the Seller are true and accurate in all respects.

vi. Access to Company. The Seller shall give the Purchaser and its representatives full access to any personnel and all properties, documents, contracts, books, records, and operations of the Seller relating to is business. The Seller shall furnish the Purchaser with copies of documents and with such other information as the Purchaser may request.

vii. Other Offers. The Seller (or the Seller's directors, officers, employees, agents, or representatives) may solicit, encourage or entertain proposals from or eider into negotiations with or furnish any nonpublic information to any other person or entity regarding the possible sale of the Seller's business, assets or stock so long as such activities do not unreasonably interfere with the ability of the Purchaser to enter into and perform under the Purchase Agreement. The Seller shall notify the Purchaser of any proposals by third parties with respect to the acquisition of all or any portion of the Seller's business, assets, or stock and furnish the Purchaser the material terms thereof.

viii. Conduct of Business. The Seller shall conduct its business in the ordinary course, consistent with the present conduct of its business and previous practices. Prior to the closing, and for a reasonable time subsequent thereto, the Seller will render management and consulting services to the Purchaser so as to allow the Seller to utilize the Assets to continue business in the normal course. The Seller will render such management and consulting services to the Purchaser on terms and conditions to be agreed upon by the Seller and the Purchaser prior to [date certain].

ix. Expenses. Each of the parties shall pay all of its expenses incident to this letter, the Purchase Agreement and consummation of the transactions contemplated hereby and thereby. The Seller and the Purchaser each represent and warrant that there are no brokerage or finder's fees which are or will be payable in connection with the Acquisition.

x. Confidentiality. Each of the parties hereto agrees that it will not use, or permit the use of, any of the information relating to the Seller or the Purchaser respectively furnished to each other in connection with this letter, the Purchase Agreement or the Acquisition ("Confidential Information"), except publicly available or freely usable material as otherwise obtained from another source, in a manner or for a purpose detrimental to the Seller, the Seller or the Purchaser or otherwise than in connection with this letter, the Agreement, and the transactions contemplated hereby and thereby.

xi. Disclosure. Neither party will issue any public announcement concerning the transaction without the approval of the other party, except as may be required by law.

xii. Termination. Termination of negotiations by the Purchaser on the one hand and the Seller on the other prior to the execution and delivery of the Purchase Agreement shall be without liability and no party hereto shall be entitled to any form of relief whatsoever, including, without limitation, injunctive relief or damages. Upon the earlier of (a) the mutual written agreement of the parties hereto or (b) the failure by the parties here to execute and deliver the Purchase Agreement on or prior to [date certain], this letter shall terminate and the parties shall be released from all liabilities and obligations with respect to the subject matter hereof, except as provided in the second paragraph of page 1 of this letter.

xiii. Counterparts. This letter may be executed in one or more counterparts, each of which shall be deemed an original, and all of which together shall constitute one and the same instrument.

If the foregoing correctly sets forth our mutual understanding, please so indicate by signing two copies of this letter in the spaces provided below and returning one copy to us no later than 5:00 p.m. on _____, 2001.

Very truly yours,

_____

[Signature of Purchaser]

Accepted and agreed as of the date first written above.

[Seller]

Signed: _____

By: _____

    Typed Name

Its: _____

    Title

Exercises

1. Suppose you are David Hesler, a law clerk with ABC Law Firm in Minnesota. Ben Lee, a successful businessman in Minneapolis came to your office to seek legal advice. Ben complained that his former business partner John Smith is building and operating stores having trade dress confusingly similar to his stores in a neighbor city St. Paul. You did some research and found that this is really an infringement of Ben's trade dress rights under Section 43(a) of the Lanham Act, 15 U.S.C. 125(a). Please write a 300-400 words demand letter representing Ben Lee to John Smith to ask him to stop the infringement immediately.

2. Suppose you were Marie Lin, a lawyer of ABC Law Firm. You have answered a call from Loren Tyler, who wanted to establish a joint venture in China. Please write a follow-up letter to recommend your law firm. You send your law firm brochure with the letter as well.

Loren Tyler's address:

ABC Corporation, 414 Arbor Creek Drive, Indianapolis, IN 46254, U.S.A.

Your law firm address:

ABC Law Firm, Room 602 Cyber Tower Building, Beijing, 100086, P.R. China

3. Supposed you are Li Jun, a law clerk with ABC Law Firm in China. Joseph Harrison, a personnel manager, came to your office to seek legal advice. Joseph complained that the former employee Jennifer White disclosed some confidential information to his competing company. He asked the chance of success of suing Jennifer White. You did some research and found that he probably win the case. Please write a 300-400 words letter to your client to tell the detailed information.

4. Suppose you are Wang Lu, a law clerk with ABC Law Firm in China. Catherine Dinuba, the manager assistant of Royal Residence Company Limited, asked the advice of building an international business. You did some research on building joint ventures and wanted to range a meeting with Ms. Dinuba. Please write 300-400 words to her to confirm the time and place to meet. At the same time, enclose the newsletter of your law firm.

Chapter 3

Law Office Memo

A law office memo, more often called a legal memorandum, is a vital tool to everyone in the law firm, from paralegals to lawyers. This document presents information about a case or law in a few pages, consolidating your research. Many people find writing legal memos helps strengthen their understanding of their cases. The most obvious function of the memorandum is to inform others of the results of your research. Almost all the legal documents in the United States are required to be written or typed in double-spaced format.

A lawyer's most important job is advising a client how to approach a particular situation in light of the relevant law. Sound legal advice may permit a client to benefit from some situations and avoid exposure to liability in others. When a client seeks advice too late, proper counseling can minimize the damage. Even if litigation occurs — for whatever reason — good legal advice can help bring about a fruitful conclusion. For every case that goes to court, however, there are dozens of others that were never litigated, and did not have to be, because someone followed a lawyer's advice.

Legal advice to a client is often based on a formal memorandum of law, which is a basic document of legal writing. It is usually written by a clerk or junior attorney for a more experienced attorney to predict what effect application of the relevant law will have on the client's situation. Senior attorneys use memoranda to determine what advice to give a client. Three fundamental principles should guide you in researching, drafting, and writing an office memorandum:

Be objective. The hallmark of a memo is objectivity. Scrupulously examine your own arguments as well as those you anticipate from your opponent. Only then can you honestly assess the strengths and weaknesses of our client's case. Above all, you must be honest about what the law permits and what it does not; you cannot afford to mislead the senior attorney or your client with wishful thinking or advocacy.

Be thorough. Office memos form the basis for major decisions people make. Consequently, you should make every effort to ensure that these decisions can be made on the basis of sound analysis. You can do this only if your knowledge of the relevant law is solid and your thinking is clear.

Communicate. The memo must be organized and written so that your thoughts are clearly presented and precisely stated. All of your effort is for nothing unless the readers understands what you are saying. People do not usually read legal writing for fun, so make the readers' job as easy as you can. Remember, too, that your readers may not be familiar with the relevant law.

1. Office Memo Format and Explanation

This chapter sets out a short description of one way to put together an office memorandum. The format and structure may differ somewhat from law office to law office (and, here in law school, from professor to professor). Once you are in practice, you can adjust the format to your office's requirements.

You are writing this for the benefit of another lawyer who has asked you to address a specific question, and expects an answer to that question. Your reader may have a general familiarity with the law you are discussing but may not be familiar with specific cases (or, if applicable, statutory provisions) that you have found to be relevant to the analysis. Therefore, as you write, keep asking yourself: will the reader be able to follow my analysis? Have I organized my analysis to track all the steps in the "CRRACC" paradigm (conclusion-rule statement-rule explanation-application-counterargument-conclusion)? If your organization plan skips any steps of your thought process (for example, if you move directly from a bare statement of the rule to an application to your facts, without first discussing in greater depth the cases from which the rule is derived), your reader will not be able to follow your analysis and ultimately will not find your work to be useful. Remember to keep the needs and expectations of your audience (here, a legally-trained reader) in mind.

One final but important reminder: an office memorandum is a predictive statement of the law. You are not writing to persuade a court but to predict how a court would apply the law to the facts of your situation. Therefore, you need to maintain an objective tone, and remember to address any counterarguments.

The standard office memorandum usually contains the following sections:

(1) Heading or Caption

(2) Question Presented

(3) Brief Answer

(4) Facts

(5) Discussion

(6) Conclusion

Heading or Caption

Begin the first page as follows:

MEMORANDUM

TO: Name of person who assigned the research project

FROM: Your name

DATE: Date memo is turned in

RE: Name of client, and a short description of the subject matter of the memorandum

Put the title of each subsequent section of your memo at the beginning of that section, in all caps, and centered.

Question Presented

The subject of the memo is a question: How does the relevant law apply to the key facts of the research problem? Thus, the question presented is analogous to the issue or question presented in a case brief. The question presented should be sufficiently narrow and should be objective. It is usually one sentence, and often begins: "Whether..." or "Does..." The question incorporates legally relevant facts as well as the rule involved. Although questions are usually framed so that they can be answered yes or no (or probably yes or probably no), sometimes they cannot (such as "Under New York law, has a retailer made a binding offer when...?"). Always include the name of the jurisdiction involved, e.g. New York, the Second Circuit.

Brief Answer

The brief answer should clearly and fully respond to the question presented. Begin with your conclusion: yes, no, probably yes, etc., if the question can be answered that way. Then give a brief (usually no more than four or five sentences long) self-contained explanation of the reasons for your conclusion. Summarize for your reader how the relevant law applies to your significant facts. As a general rule, include no citations.

Facts

Provide a formal and objective description of the legally significant facts in your research problem. The legally significant facts are the facts that are relevant to answering the legal question presented. For example, in an issue involving whether a minor can disaffirm a contract, a legally significant fact would include the nature of the item or service contracted for (was it clothing, food, shelter, related to health care, etc.) and whether the minor had access to the item in any case, without having to become contractually obligated to pay for it. The description should be accurate and complete. Present the facts in a logically coherent fashion, which may entail a chronological order. Include legally significant facts — facts upon which the resolution of the legal question presented will turn, whether they are favorable or unfavorable to the client for whom you are writing — and include background facts that will make the context of the problem clear. In this section, do not comment upon the facts or discuss how the law will apply to the facts. All factual information that later appears in the discussion section of the memorandum should be described in the facts section.

Discussion

This is the heart of the memo. Here, you need to educate the reader about the applicable legal principles, illustrate how those principles apply to the relevant facts, and explore any likely counterarguments to the primary line of analysis you present.

Many law offices will expect you to begin with a short thesis paragraph that briefly identifies the issue and the applicable rule (without elaboration), and restates the short answer. Follow with an introductory section, which provides a map or framework for the discussion as a whole. The introductory section should summarize and synthesize the rule, setting out all subparts of the rule and clarifying how they relate to one another. When the synthesized rule is derived from case law, the discussion of the cases should focus on general principles, on the criteria that courts use to describe the rule, rather than on the specific facts and reasoning of the cases. The introductory section is also where you would mention, if applicable, information about the procedural posture of a case, about burdens and standards of proof, and about rules of interpretation pertinent to the law you are applying. You should identify any undisputed issues, and explain why they are not in dispute. Then state the order in which the remaining issues or subparts of an issue will be discussed. For a useful discussion of an introductory section, please see pp. 111-114 in Linda H. Edwards, *Legal Writing and Analysis* (Aspen 2003).

You should use "CRRACC" as a guide to constructing the discussion section. Use a separate "CRRACC" for each issue or sub-issue.

After setting forth the conclusion and the rule, you should explain the rule by providing an in-depth discussion of the cases from which the rule is derived. Your discussion of the cases should be specific as to their facts and reasoning.

In your application section, you should compare the facts and the reasoning of the cases to the facts of your client's situation. You need to analogize and distinguish the cases — show why they are similar to or different from your client's circumstances. Be sure to address any counterarguments that could be raised, but show why you believe they would not prevail.

Ultimately for each issue or sub-issue you should conclude as to how you think a court would likely rule on your facts.

The basic structure of the **discussion** section might look like this:

Short thesis paragraph: = C

Briefly restate the question and your answer

Introductory paragraph: = R

Provide a map or framework for the discussion as a whole, including statement of the synthesized rule

Provide background regarding the general rule

Explain policy reasons underlying the rule

Explain any exceptions to the rule

Explain policy reasons underlying the exception(s)

In-depth explanation of the rule = R

Illustrate how rule has been applied in other cases

Application of law to facts = A

Analogize and distinguish other cases to your case

Counterargument = C

Discuss and resolve any counterarguments in favor of your principal line of analysis

Conclusion = C

Answer the question presented

Conclusion

Summarize your analysis and conclusion to the question presented. Identify the level of certainty with which you render a conclusion for each issue or sub-issue, but be sure to draw a conclusion even for closer questions. Do not provide citations. The conclusion should be limited to one paragraph, and in some cases involving just one short issue, the conclusion might not be necessary at all.

2. The Discussion

The Discussion is a core part in a memorandum. This section identifies additional principles concerning objectivity that are important in a memorandum.

(1) State your conclusion on each issue or sub-issue objectively and candidly.

Legal memos are written to predict outcomes. Clients rely on memos to make choices about their lives and businesses. Senior lawyers rely on memos to advise clients and make decisions concerning strategy or procedure. Just as your description of the law and your analysis must be scrupulously objective, so your prediction of the outcome of the issue must be under consideration.

Your prediction is reflected in your conclusion. Properly stating your conclusion requires you to balance adverse interests. On one hand, you must take a position. Clients and senior attorneys do not want a set of competing considerations. They want you to tell them how the issue will likely be resolved. They want you to make a judgment, to predict the outcome. They do not want waffling statements such as "our client might prevail" or "our client has a chance of successfully defending the claim."

On the other hand, your obligation to be objective requires you to point out the weaknesses in your client's position. Accordingly, statements such as "our client will prevail" or "our client definitely will lose," while stating a position, might be misleading in their confidence. Some legal positions are sufficiently one-sided to merit such confidence. If they are, such as when you have one or a series of "givens," you should make an unequivocal statement. Often, however, your analysis will lead you to conclude that your client's chances of success are best measured in degrees of probability, rather than absolutes. Your task then is to frame your conclusion candidly to reflect these degrees of probability.

Each case is different, and the possible ways to describe your conclusion are limited only by your creativity. Strong conclusions can be expressed as "most likely," somewhat certain conclusions can be expressed as "probably," even less certain conclusions can begin with "on balance," and so forth. The point is that you must balance competing considerations in your statement. Let's look at this example.

You represent Herbert Pearson, the owner of a 52-foot sports fishing yacht that was transported by ship from Florida to Colombo, Sri Lanka. As the yacht was being unloaded at Colombo, the ship's crane malfunctioned, causing the yacht to fall into the water and sink. The yacht, worth $750,000, is now a total loss. Pearson wants to sue the ship owner for damages, and you have been asked to write a memo on his chances of success.

The United States Carriage of Goods by Sea Act ordinarily would limit Pearson's recoverable damages to $500. Your research has revealed, however, cases holding that the ship owner would not be entitled to limit its liability of it failed to advise Pearson properly in the bill of lading that the limitation was applicable and that the limitation could be avoided by paying a greater freight rate. The language in the bill of lading issued to Pearson is ambiguous. You nonetheless believe that the reasoning of the authorities supports Pearson's position, that a decision in Pearson's favor would be fair, and that the arguments supporting Pearson's position are significantly stronger than opposing arguments. Consider the following statements of your conclusion.

> ANSWER A: Pearson will prevail in recovering full damages for loss of his yacht.
>
> ANSWER B: Pearson may prevail in recovering full damages for loss of his yacht, but there are strong arguments to the contrary.
>
> ANSWER C: Pearson will most likely prevail in recovering full damages for loss of his yacht.

Answer C is the best because it honestly and candidly conveys the writer's views on Pearson's chances of success. It gives the writer's best judgment while letting the reader know that there is some room for doubt.

Answer A is too bold; it leads the reader to believe that there is no doubt that a court will decide the case in favor of Pearson. Answer A is not objective.

Answer B gives the reader a mixed message. It says that Pearson may succeed but, then again, he may not. This is not a prediction; it is merely a statement that the case could go either way. Conclusions such as this are confusing and do not satisfy the writer's obligation to assess the client's chances of success candidly and objectively.

(2) Describe the law objectively.

Although there are many legitimate ways to describe the law, you must describe it objectively. Avoid the temptation to oversimplify or slant your explanation so that it favors your client's position. Objectivity in describing the applicable law is essential to your credibility. In any subsequent litigation, your client will not want to learn for the first time that there is a case or statutory provision hostile to his position. Because memos predict likely outcomes in actual or potential legal disputes, the importance of maintaining objectivity in describing the law cannot be overemphasized.

Objectivity may differ from accuracy. It is possible to explain the supportive cases of statutory provisions accurately but fail to explain other cases or provisions that are relevant but damaging. Sometimes these omissions are stark, but they can also be subtle.

Example: The new State Recycling Act requires each municipality with more than 5,000 people to set up a recycling program. Your client, the village of Elk Crossing, is interested in obtaining a grant to finance a recycling program

Chapter 3
Law Office Memo

for its population of 700. The village seeks your opinion on whether it can obtain a grant under the Act to pay for its recycling program. The Elk Crossing recycling program is one of the oldest and most successful in the State and has been featured in several national magazines. Consider these descriptions of the Act's grant provision.

> ANSWER A: Section 902 of the Recycling Act provides that "the Department of Environmental Quality shall award grants for the development and implementation of municipal recycling programs, upon application from any municipality."
>
> ANSWER B: Section 902 of the Recycling Act provides that "the Department of Environmental Quality shall award grants for the development and implementation of municipal recycling programs, upon application from any municipality. In awarding these grants, the Department shall give priority to municipalities that are required to establish a recycling program under this Act."

Answer B is better because it contains both the good news and the bad news. The good news is that grants are available to municipalities that are not required to set up a recycling program. The bad news is that these municipalities are given a lower priority than other municipalities. A description like this gives your client a much better sense of its chances than Answer A. By stating only the good news, Answer A sets up your client to learn the bad news later—probably after a lot of wasted time and expense.

(3) Explain the analysis objectively.

Objectivity in memorandum writing is important because the weaknesses of your position will come to light sooner or later, and it is better for that to happen sooner. An objective analysis is one that a reasonable attorney, reading dispassionately, would find to be an accurate and fair explanation of the strengths and weaknesses of your position, even if your description of the law is objective, which does not necessarily mean your analysis will be objective. You must avoid putting a "spin" on your analysis to favor your client's position.

Consider these analyzes (the analysis) of the recycling grant problem.

> ANSWER A: The village will be able to obtain a grant only of funds remained after the Department has awarded grants to municipalities required to establish a recycling

program. Section 902 of the Recycling Act provides that "the Department of Environmental Quality shall award grants for the development and implementation of municipal recycling programs, upon application from any municipality. In awarding these grants, the Department shall give priority to municipalities that are required to establish a recycling program under this Act." The village of Elk Crossing qualifies for a grant because "any municipality" may be awarded a grant under section 902. Municipalities required to implement recycling programs are given first priority for this grant, and Elk Crossing is not one of those municipalities. Therefore, it will be able to obtain a grant only of funds remain after the other grants have been awarded.

ANSWER B: The village will be able to obtain a grant. Section 902 of the Recycling Act provides that "the Department of Environmental Quality shall award grants for the development and implementation of municipal recycling programs, upon application from any municipality. In awarding these grants, the Department shall give priority to municipalities that are required to establish a recycling program under this Act." The village of Elk Crossing qualifies for a grant because "any municipality" may be awarded a grant under section 902. The Department will ensure the availability of funds for Elk crossing because it is required to encourage recycling under the Act. It would be absurd and inappropriate for the Department to award grants only to larger municipalities and deny a grant to a nationally prominent program with a long and successful history.

ANSWER C: The village will be able to obtain a grant only if funds remain after the Department has awarded grants to municipalities required to establish a recycling program. Section 902 of the Recycling Act provides that "the Department of Environmental Quality shall award grants for the development and implementation of municipal recycling programs, upon application from any municipality. In awarding these grants, the Department shall give priority to municipalities that are required to establish a recycling program under this Act." The village of Elk Crossing qualifies for a grant because "any municipality" may be awarded a grant under section 902. Municipalities required to implement recycling programs are given first priority for this grant, and Elk Crossing is not one of those municipalities. Therefore, it will be able to obtain a grant only if funds remain after the other grants have been awarded. The national prominence of the Elk Crossing recycling program, however, coupled with its long and successful history, may make it difficult for the Department to deny the village a grant.

Chapter 3
Law Office Memo

Answer C is the best. Answer C concludes that Elk Crossing may be able to obtain a grant if funds are available after the high-priority municipalities have received their grants. Answer C then states that the national prominence and success to the Elk Crossing program may make it difficult for the Department to deny a grant. The Department may award larger municipalities slightly smaller grants, ensuring there is enough money for Elk Crossing, for example, or it may give Elk Crossing high priority among the smaller municipalities. Answer C explains the law and the facts and then discusses the possible effect of the program's success in objective terms.

Answer B is wrong because it is not objective. First, it omits the legal analysis showing that Elk Crossing is a low-priority municipality. Second, it indulges in editorial commentary that effectively contradicts part of the statute. Answer B provides much the same basic legal analysis as Answer A, but then adds several sentences to show why the grant will be awarded. Answer B states that the Act requires the Department to encourage recycling and then, using that premise, states that money will be available to smaller municipalities. The statute, however, specifically gives priority to larger municipalities. The writer is advocating when she ought to be assessing his client's chances of success.

Answer A is wrong for a different reason. Although it concludes that the Department may be able to award Elk Crossing a grant, it does not discuss factors that may affect how the Department exercises its discretion. The national prominence and success of the Elk Crossing program are surely among these factors. Simply ignoring these factors makes it seem as if Elk Crossing is just another small municipality. By being "too objective," in other words, Answer A is biased against the village.

3. Statement of Facts for a Memorandum

An office memo structured according to the traditional pattern has a separate section for the Statement of Facts. This statement gives the reader a context for the legal problem at issue and shows what facts are important to its resolution.

Every legal problem involves the interplay of numerous facts, only some of which are relevant to its analysis. Whether you acquire these facts from interviews with clients or witnesses, from examination of documents, or from a senior attorney, you will invariably accumulate more facts than work with only those necessary to understand and resolve the legal issues. You must then present these remaining facts intelligibly, accurately, and coherently. The basic principles for selecting and appropriately stating the facts of a case are best understood in the context of a specific problem.

Example: You represent Clara Finch in a land dispute. An interview with her and a subsequent investigation have revealed the following facts, stated in the order you learned them.

> In 1941, George Brauzakas purchased a forty-acre tract of land on the north side of County Highway Q, which runs east and west. Finch purchased five acres of this tract from Brauzakas in 1973 and built her home on this parcel. Finch's primary means of access to her home is by a dirt road running from the highway through William Amodio's (formerly Brauzakas's) property. Brauzakas sold the remainder of his land (thirty-five acres) to Amodio in 1975. Amodio has recently felled several large trees across the road through his property on its north side. There is no reference to Finch's use of the road in Amodio's deed to the property, and there is no recorded easement. Finch is an eighty-year-old widow living on a small pension. Finch has another access to her house by a dirt road leading from another highway, but that route takes her thirty miles and forty-five minutes out of her way. Amodio is a wealthy banker who bought the Brauzakas property on speculation that land prices would continue to increase. Amodio has stated several times that he blocked the road because he does not like Finch. Brauzakas and Finch had only an oral agreement that she could use his road as long as he owned the land.

There are two relevant appellate decisions in your state.

> **Carson v. Dow (1934)**
>
> The appellant, Carl Carson, brought this action for injunctive relief against Edward Dow, claiming that he had an express easement to run a natural gas pipeline across Dow's property, and that Dow refused him access. There is no recorded easement. The trial court held that there was no express easement because of the absence of any mention of the alleged easement in Dow's deed to the property or in any other written agreement. We agree. Absent some written contractual agreement, there can be no express easement.

Chapter 3
Law Office Memo

> **Watzke v. Lovett (1954)**
>
> Andrew Watzke purchased a tract of land from Peter Lovett. The tract in located on the shore of a lake and is surrounded on the remaining sides by property owned by Lovett. The only means of access to Watzke's property is by a road that crosses Lovett's property and connects to a public highway. Lovett has recently blocked the road, claiming that Watzke has no right to use it. Watzke conceded to the trial court, refused. We reverse.
>
> When a parcel of land is owned by one person, and that person transfers part of that parcel to another person, access to the transferred part cannot be denied if the only means of access is through the remaining part of the original parcel. A showing of strict necessity is required before an easement will be implied. The landlocked nature of Watzke's property satisfies that requirement in this case. Watzke has an implied easement to use the road over Lovett's property.

Certain facts have special significance in light of these two cases. The following is a procedure for selecting and stating them.

(1) Identify the legally significant facts.

The legally significant facts are those that will affect the legal outcome of your client's case. Some facts of a judicial opinion are more important than others. The most important facts are those the court used to determine whether to apply particular legal rules to the case it was deciding. Writing a legal memo reverses this perspective. Instead of looking backward to determine what facts a court thought were important, you must look forward to predict what facts in your client's case a court is likely to find significant. You can determine these facts only after you have identified the relevant rules and the corresponding issues.

Isolating the legally significant facts is a process of eliminating extraneous facts until only those necessary to resolve the legal issues remain. This process allows a clearer understanding an analysis of the problem, because it focuses the reader's and writer's attention exclusively on the facts of that matter. Identify all significant facts, regardless of whether they help or hurt your client's position.

When the legal rules are clear and unmistakable, you will need to identify relatively few significant facts. The ambiguity or vagueness of many legal rules, however, means that the legal significance of some facts will depend on how the rule is interpreted. These borderline facts should be included if the interpretation requiring them is plausible.

Emotional facts should be included if those facts have independent legal significance or are likely to influence the outcome by appealing to a judge's sympathy and sense of justice. When the law is straightforward and applies to your problem so clearly that there is little doubt concerning the outcome, emotional facts have little or no significance and should be omitted. When the law is not straightforward or the outcome is uncertain, however, emotional facts take on greater significance. Many exceptions to general rules have been made or expanded to reach a just result in light of the facts. Nonetheless, the value of emotional facts is speculative because a court may ignore them. Because a court cannot ignore legally significant facts, such facts give the best indication of the likely outcome.

The Carson and Watzke cases indicate that Finch could raise two possible legal objections. She could claim that she has an express easement or that she has an implied easement by necessity. The Carson court held that an express easement must be created either in a written agreement or in the deed to the property across which the easement runs. It is thus legally significant that there is no provision in Amodio's deed permitting Finch to use the road across Amodio's property and that there is no recorded easement. These facts will make it difficult for Finch to claim an express easement, but they must nonetheless be included in the Statement of Facts.

The claim that Finch has an implied easement by necessity involves a somewhat different set of legally significant facts. The court in Watzke held that when the only means of access to a person's property is through the property of the person who originally transferred the land, the person seeking access is entitled to an implied easement by necessity. In Finch's case, it is legally significant that there is a road across the Amodio property which Finch uses to get to her home, that there is another route to Finch's house, and that Brauzakas sold part of his property to Finch and the remainder to Amodio.

Although the significance of many facts will be immediately apparent, the significance of others will depend on how the legal rules are interpreted. For example, the Watzke court indicated that an easement will be implied only out of strict necessity. As a result, the existence of the second road may work to Finch's disadvantage. It may thus be significant that Finch is eighty years old and that the other road would take her thirty miles and forty-five minutes out of her way (facts which may have appeared at first to be emotional ones) because these facts tend to show that Finch's use of Amodio's road is more of necessity than convenience. These facts should be included in a Statement of Facts because they may have a bearing on the strict-necessity rule, even though there was another access in Watzke.

Finch's problem involves a number of emotionally significant facts you should exclude from analysis — particularly those that make it appear that the wealthy banker Amodio is spitefully imposing a hardship on the poor widow Finch. Although these facts might greatly influence how a judge would perceive the fairness of the situation, they have nothing to do with either of the legal rules concerning easements. Similarly, it is not significant that Amodio bought the property on speculation. Identify only the facts that are relevant to the possible application of a legal rule.

(2) Identify key background facts.

Legally significant facts tell part of the story, but these facts alone may not tell the whole story. Background facts are often needed to make the factual situation understandable and to put the legally significant facts in context. Include as many background facts as the reader needs to understand the problem, but no more.

In Finch's case, for example, it probably would help the reader to state that Brauzakas's tract was forty acres, that Finch's parcel is five acres, and that Amodio's is thirty-five acres. This information provides background for the implied easement question by clarifying Brauzakas's original ownership and subsequent division of the property. The dates on which Finch and Amodio bought their property from Brauzakas may be helpful, although the date on which Brauzakas purchased the land is not. In addition, it is useful to state that Brauzakas and Finch had an oral agreement, because this fact highlights the absence of a written agreement. The name of the highway, however, is probably not useful here. Nor is it helpful to state that Amodio blocked the access by felling several trees; the statement that he blocked the access will do.

(3) Organize the facts intelligibly.

The statement of legally significant and key background facts should tell your client's story completely and coherently. The most sensible and convenient method of organization is to relate the facts in chronological order. Chronological order is easy for the reader to understand because it is the usual way a story is told; it is convenient for the writer because the facts are stated as they occurred. Although you may organize facts in a number of ways, you should never organize them according to issues, even though you separately analyze the issues in the Discussion. Such segmentation invariably results in repetitious and disjointed factual statements.

In writing a Statement of Facts for this problem, you should begin with Finch's purchase of the property from Brauzakas and their oral agreement permitting her to use the dirt road across his tract. This chronological beginning of the problem sets the stage for the events that follow. You should then state that Brauzakas sold the rest of his land to Amodio. Amodio's deed for the property contains no recorded to Finch's use of the road, and there is no recorded easement. Recently, you would continue, Amodio has blocked the road to prevent Finch from using it. You should then add that Finch is eighty and that, while there is another access to her house, this alternative route takes her thirty miles and forty-five minutes out of her way. This last statement is difficult to place chronologically, but it fits here because it suggests the possible consequences of the blocked access. The reader would easily understand a statement drafted along these lines.

(4) Describe the facts accurately and objectively.

Describe legally significant facts precisely, for they are crucial to the outcome. It is improper and misleading, for example, to say simply that Brauzakas and Finch had an agreement concerning her use of the dirt road, because it matters whether that agreement was oral or written. It is also improper to say simply that Finch had another access to her property, because her age and the circuitous route are relevant to the legal rule concerning implied easements by necessity. These are legally significant facts, and you must

Chapter 3
Law Office Memo

describe them precisely. You may summarize background facts, but only if you do so accurately.

Be careful to describe the facts rather than evaluate, analyze, characterize, or argue with them. It is one thing to say that Amodio blocked the road, but it is quite another to say that Amodio wrongfully blocked the road. The latter is an evaluative statement that belongs only in the Discussion or Conclusion. Similarly, it is one thing to say that the alternate route takes her thirty miles and forty-five minutes out of her way, but another to conclude that the other route is impossibly difficult for a person of her age. State the facts objectively in the Statement of Facts; you can argue and analyze in the Discussion.

Consider these factual statements.

> ANSWER A: Clara Finch is an eighty-year-old widow living on a meager pension. She has a house on a small tract separated from the highway by property owned by William Amodio, a wealthy banker, who bought the land from the previous owner on speculation that prices would rise. The property, but Amodio has refused access out of dislike for Finch. Although there is another road that Finch could use, it takes her thirty miles and forty-five minutes out of her way.
>
> ANSWER B: Clara Finch's land is separated from the highway by William Amodio's land. Finch had a deal with the previous owner that she could use an old road through the tract for access to her five-acre lot. Amodio, whose property is thirty five acres in size, has blocked Finch's access to her property. There was no mention of Finch's easement in the agreement, and the easement is not recorded.
>
> There is another road Finch could use, but that route takes her a considerable distance out of her way, and she is eighty years old. Both Amodio and Finch bought their land from the same person. She bought five of his forty acres in 1973; Amodio bought the remaining thirty-five acres in 1975.
>
> ANSWER C: George Brauzakas, who owned a forty-acre tract, sold Clara Finch five acres of that tract in 1973. Finch then built her home on this land. They agreed orally that Finch could use an old road through his property for access to her home because her lot was separated from the highway by the remaining part of his tract. In 1975, Brauzakas sold this thirty-five acre tract to William Amodio. There is no recorded easement. Amodio has now blocked the dirt road across his property. Finch, who is eighty, has access to her house through a dirt road leading from another highway. That route takes her thirty miles and forty-five minutes out of her way.

Answer C is the best because it is a neutral and accurate description of the facts, stated in chronological order. Answer C includes the legally significant facts and just enough background facts for the reader to understand the problem.

Answer A is biased. The income or motives of the parties involved are not legally relevant; Answer A also omits such legally significant facts as the absence of a written agreement, a separate recorded easement, or a reference to an easement in Amodio's deed.

There are three problems with Answer B. First, it tries to describe separately the facts pertaining to two closely related issues. The result is repetitious and disjointed. Second, it uses vague terms such as "land" "deal" and "considerable distance" instead of more precise terms, thus raising unnecessary questions and perhaps changing the meaning of his statement. Third, it draws a legal conclusion by describing the road as an easement. Legal conclusions belong in the Discussion, not in the Statement of Facts.

4. Questions Presented

A basic principle of legal education and legal practice is that you receive answers only to questions you ask. The exactness of the question determines the precision and usefulness of the answer.

An office memorandum usually begins with a section stating the questions presented by the problem. This section alerts the reader to the specific issues addressed. It is, therefore, important to frame the question in this section as precisely as possible. A question that is too broad or too narrow misrepresents the scope or focus of your analysis and makes your discussion less effective.

Properly framing a legal question is a two-step process. First, you must identify precisely the legal rules that might apply to your problem. Second, you must identify the legally significant facts — the facts determine whether a particular rule applies to the situation.

The formula for framing a question is simple: does the relevant law apply to the significant facts? Both the law and the facts should be included in a succinct, one-sentence question. The question should be precise and complete. Generally, the legal rule should precede the facts.

When you have formulated a question by combining the relevant law with the significant facts, check to be sure that it conforms to the following principles:

(1) Be understandable.

A question should be as precise and complete as possible without being so complex that your reader cannot understand it. When a problem involves so many facts relevant to a single issue that including them in the question would make it too long and awkward, you should examine the significant facts and choose only the most relevant. You may be able to summarize or condense closely related facts, but you should do so only with great care. Whenever you generalize about the facts, you risk distorting them or making the issue seem broader than it really is. When in doubt, err on the side of being specific and awkward.

When a legal issue has several sub-issues, you should have a separate question for each. To make sure your reader understands that they are sub-issues, you may want to use a brief introductory question to identity the broad issue and set the sub-issues in context.

(2) Be objective.

Remember, an office memo should predict what a court is likely to do with a particular problem. Therefore, you must avoid advocating or anticipating a certain result. Include the significant facts favoring each side of the case. If you paraphrase facts to make the question more readable, do so objectively. You should also state the law objectively and not take a partisan approach. If the legal rule has several reasonable interpretations, state the rule so that you can discuss all these interpretations. When the interpretations differ greatly, you should present separate questions for each.

Example: Your client, Eric Vosberg, is a frail, chronically ill, thirteen-year-old boy. Deborah Starsky is a seventeen-year-old girl Vosberg and others know to be a neighborhood bully. She has been known to pick fights and has been found guilty of several misdemeanors in juvenile court. Two weeks ago, Starsky confronted Vosberg while he was on his way to a violin recital. She told Vosberg to put his nose against a nearby telephone pole. Vosberg complied. Starsky instructed Vosberg not to move until she gave him permission and then walked away. At no point did Starsky explicitly threaten Vosberg, touch him, or prevent him from continuing down the sidewalk. Vosberg remained at the pole for two hours and then ran home. He missed the recital and has suffered severe emotional problems as a result of the incident. Vosberg's parents want to know whether they can sue Starsky.

Your research has revealed only one relevant case.

Palmer v. Woodward (1960)

After making several purchases in Schwenson's Department Store, the appellant, Roger Palmer, left. He began to walk down the sidewalk when the appellee, Troy Woodward, a store detective, ran from the store and yelled, "Stop!" Palamer stopped.

Woodward approached Palmer, stood in his way, and put his hand on Palmer's chest. After telling Palmer he had to go back and see the store manager, Woodward gently grasped Palmer's elbow and led him back into the store. Palmer, sixty-eight, has failing health and a heart condition. He did not resist. As a result of the incident, Palmer suffered a mild heart attack and severe emotional distress.

Palmer filed suit for false imprisonment. The trial court dismissed Palmer's complaint, holding that restraint, a necessary element of false imprisonment, had not occurred. The trial court reasoned that Palmer voluntarily complied with Woodward's demands because he did not resist or make any attempt to free himself. We disagree.

The trial court correctly stated that false imprisonment requires the defendant to actually confine or restrain the plaintiff. The restraint must be obvious, and the plaintiff must be aware that he is being restrained. But the restraint does not have to be forceful; threats, express or implied, can be sufficient. In this case, the appellant is a frail, elderly man. The appellee is a six-foot, five-inch, 220-pound, semiprofessional football player who works part time as a store detective. Blocking another person's way is restraint when the aggressive person is obviously stronger, as he was here. In addition, the appellee touched the appellant by taking his arm and guiding him into the store. We hold that under the facts of this case, particularly the great disparity of physical strength, there was sufficient restraint. Reversed.

Consider the following attempts to state the question.

ANSWER A: Whether Vosberg can recover damages for false imprisonment.

ANSWER B: Whether Vosberg was sufficiently restrained to support a cause of action for false imprisonment.

ANSWER C: Whether the apparent strength of Vosberg and Starsky was so unequal that Vosberg can recover damages for emotional distress.

ANSWER D: Whether sufficient restraint to support an action for false imprisonment exists when a seventeen-year-old juvenile delinquent with a police record and a reputation of being a bully instructs a frail, chronically ill, thirteen-year-old boy who plays violin to remain in one place.

ANSWER E: Whether the fact that a seventeen-year-old female delinquent, who has been convicted several times and who has a reputation of being a bully and a fighter, gave instructions to a frail, thirteen-year-old boy, on his way to a violin recital, to put his nose against a phone pole and stay there until told otherwise, but never touched the boy or blocked his path and walked away immediately after the boy complied with the instructions, though the boy did not move from the pole for two hours, constitutes sufficient restraint to support an action for false imprisonment, when the boy missed the recital and suffered severe emotional problems as a result.

ANSWER F: Whether restraint sufficient to support an action for false imprisonment exists when a seventeen-year-old girl known as a juvenile delinquent and bully instructs a frail thirteen—year-old boy to remain in one place, and he does so for two hours after she has walked away, even though the girl neither touched him nor blocked his path.

The Palmer case indicates that your problem concerns what type of force, if any, is required to satisfy the restraint element of false imprisonment. Answer F is the best way of stating that question. Answer F correctly identifies the relevant law, includes the facts of the problem that a court is likely to find legally significant, and states the law before the facts. The question in Answer F is neither unduly narrow nor overly broad. It is readable and objectively stated. Answer F clearly identifies the precise legal question presented.

Answer A, by contrast, is useless. The question is too broad and makes no attempt to pinpoint the legal rule or the legally significant facts. The writer might just as well have stated the question: "Whether the law has been violated."

Answer B does pinpoint the legal question of restraint, but it fails to place that question in context because it omits the facts that will provide the basis for its resolution. A question framed this way is too unfocused to be of any value.

Unlike Answers A and B, which are too broad, Answer C is too narrow. By limiting the legal question to whether the strength of the parties is unequal, it fails to consider other factors that contribute to restraint. In addition, the mention of damages for emotional distress mistakes the real issue. Whether the plaintiff can recover damages for emotional distress is a different question from whether there has been restraint. In this respect, Answer C illustrates an important reason to ask the right question; if you ask the wrong question, you are likely to get the wrong answer. Even if your discussion covers the right issue, you have seriously misled the reader about the direction of the memo. Finally, Answer C, like Answers A and Answer B, omits the significant facts of the case.

Answer D is not objective. The question exaggerates the strength of the client's case because the facts included are relevant to only one side of the question. Answer D fails to note that Starsky did not touch Vosberg or block his path. Whenever you state a question, you must include those facts that hurt your case as well as those that help it. Answer D also includes some irrelevant facts, such as Vosberg's being a violinist.

Answer E is complete enough. It includes all the significant facts and properly states the issue of law. It is so complete, however, that it is awkward and unreadable. Answer E does not sort out the most relevant facts. Answer E also includes several facts that are not legally significant, such as concerning the violin recital and telephone pole. While you may want to include some background facts in the Statement of Facts, do not include them in the Questions Presented.

5. Sample Memo

TO: Gaby Duane
FROM: Clark Thomas
RE: Loman's Fashions — Breach of contract claim (advertising circular)
DATE: April 26, 2002
QUESTION PRESENTED[1]
Under New York law,[2] did[3] Loman's Fashions' description of a designer leather coat in an advertising circular constitute an offer[4] to sell the coat which

Chapter 3
Law Office Memo

became a binding contract when the text of the advertisement indicated that the coats were a "manufacturer's closeout" and that the early shopper would be rewarded, and when a shopper signified her intent to purchase the coat according to the advertised terms?[5]

SHORT ANSWER[6]

No.[7] Where, as here, the text of the advertisement merely stated that the sale was a "manufacturer's closeout" and that the "early" shopper would "catch the savings," the advertisement was not an offer to sell the coat which could be converted into a binding contract by conduct signifying an acceptance of the advertised terms.

FACTS[8]

Loman's Fashions, a retailer of women's and men's outerwear, distributed a circular in November advertising a manufacturer's closeout of designer women's leather coats for $59.99, coats that regularly sold for $300.00. The ad announced that the store would open at 7 a.m. on Friday, November 30, and stated that the "early bird catches the savings!" After about fifteen minutes, all the advertised coats had been sold. At 7:30 a.m., a shopper inquired about the coats and was told that there were none left, but she complained that Loman's was obligated to sell her a comparably valued designer leather coat at the advertised price. The store manager declined, and the shopper filed a complaint in Small Claims Court,[9] alleging that Loman's had breached a contract by failing to sell the advertised leather coats at the advertised price.[10]

Loman's president, Willi Loman, stated that the store occasionally gives rain checks when it is possible to replenish supplies of an item that Loman's can purchase at a discount. In this case, the manufacturer had discontinued the line of coats and Loman's was not prepared to sell other, designer leather coats at such a drastic markdown. Loman expressed concern[11] that, if the shopper's interpretation were to hold, Loman's would have to reconsider its marketing strategies; she had assumed that the advertised terms applied while supplies lasted. She asks whether Loman's would have any contractual obligation under these circumstances.[12]

DISCUSSION

[13] Loman's Fashions has been sued by a shopper for a breach of contract for

its failure to sell a designer leather coat that had been advertised for sale at a substantially marked-down price. Loman's contends that the advertisement was intended to apply while supplies of the item lasted, and that is it not obligated to sell the shopper a comparably valued coat at the advertised price. The issue in this case is whether a retailer's advertisement will be considered to be an offer that may be turned into a binding contract by a shopper who signifies an intention to purchase the items described in the advertisement. A court would likely conclude that the shopper did not state a cause of action for breach of contract because the advertisement did not constitute an offer which, upon acceptance, could be turned into a contract but rather and invitation to negotiate.

[14] In New York, the rule is well settled that an advertisement is merely an invitation to enter into negotiations, and is not an offer that may be turned into a contract by a person who communicates an intention to purchase the advertised item. *Geismar v. Abraham & Strauss*, 439 N.Y.S. 2d 1005 (Dist. Ct. Suffolk Co. 1981); *Lovett v. Frederick Loeser & Co.*, 207 N.Y.S. 753 (Manhattan Mun. Ct. 1924); *Schenectady Stove Co. v. Holbrook*, 101 N.Y. 45 (1885); *People v. Gimbel Bros., Inc.*, 115 N.Y.S. 2d 857 (Manhattan Ct. Spec. Sess. 1952). The only general test is the inquiry whether the facts show that some performance was promised in positive terms in return for something requested. *Lovett*, 207 N.Y.S. 2d at 755. However, a purchaser may not make a valid contract by mere acceptance of a "proposition." *Schenectady Stove Co.*, 101 N.Y. at 48. Nor does the purchaser have the right to select an item which the seller does not have in stock or is not willing to sell at a reduced price. *Lovett*, 207 N.Y.S. at 757.[15]

[16] An offer to contract must be complete and definite in its material terms; a general advertisement that merely lists items for sale is at best an invitation to negotiate unless it promises to sell an item in return for something requested. In *Schenectady Stove Co.*, for example, the plaintiff delivered to defendant a catalogue of prices containing a statement of terms of sale, but the catalogue did not state the amount of goods which plaintiff was willing to sell on those terms. Under these circumstances, the Court of Appeals held that no contract was ever made between the parties with respect to an order that defendant submitted

because the plaintiff had not made an offer that was complete and definite in all material terms. Hence, it was not possible for the defendant to make a valid contract by mere acceptance of a "proposition." 101 N.Y. at 48. Similarly, in *Lovett*, a department store advertised that it would sell, deliver, and install certain "well-known standard makes of radio receivers at 25 per cent. to 50 per cent. Reduction" from advertised list prices. The plaintiff had demanded a particular model of radio that was not listed in the ad, and the defendant had declined to sell it at the reduced price. 207 N.Y.S. at 754. The court held that an advertisement by a department store was not an offer but an invitation to all persons that the advertiser was ready to receive offers for the goods upon the stated terms, reasoning that such a general advertisement was distinguishable from an offer of a reward or other payment in return for some requested performance. *Id.* at 755-56. The court further held that, even assuming the plaintiff's "acceptance" turned the offer into a contract, the purchaser did not have the right to select the item which the defendant did not have in stock or was not willing to sell at a reduced price. *Id.* at 756-57.

[17] Loman's advertisement did not contain a promise to sell the leather coats in exchange for some requested act or promise. By its terms, the advertisement announced that it had a stock of coats to sell, and described the coats as a manufacturer's closeout selling at a substantially reduced price.[18] Nor did the ad give the public an option to choose any comparably priced leather coat if the advertised coats were no longer available. As the court noted in *Lovett*,[19] a prospective purchaser does not have the right to select items that the retailer does not have in stock or is not willing to sell at a reduced price. *Lovett*, 207 N.Y.S. at 757.

[20] The claimant here might argue that the advertisement did not contain limiting language, for example, that the coats were for sale while supplies lasted[21]. However, the ad indicated that the store, opening for business on the day of the sale at 7 a.m., was catering to early morning shoppers. By announcing that "the early bird catches the savings," the ad could fairly be read to mean that the supplies were not unlimited.[22]

CONCLUSION[23]

On these facts, the court will probably[24] find that the claimant has failed to state a cause of action for breach of contract because the ad did not constitute an offer but merely an invitation to negotiate.

Note

(1) The **question presented** states the question(s) the memo is to address: how does the relevant law apply to the key facts of the research problem? The question should be sufficiently narrow and should be objective.

(2) Generally, include the name of the jurisdiction involved, e.g. New York, the Second Circuit, etc.

(3) The Question Presented is usually one sentence. It often begins: "Whether..." or "Does..." Here, the writer has chosen "did." Although questions are usually framed so that they can be answered yes or no (or probably yes or probably no), sometimes they cannot (such as "Under New York law, has a retailer made a binding offer when...?").

(4) The author of this memo has been careful not to use language that assumes the answer to the legal question it raises. Here, since the question presented is designed to highlight whether the facts indicate that a formal contract offer has been made, you would not use the term "offer" in framing the question, i.e. you would not write "Did an advertising circular describing merchandise constitute an offer when it *offered* the merchandise for sale starting at a designated date and time?" because that formulation of the question assumes a legal conclusion — that the conduct at issue meets the requirements of an offer. Rather, reserve your legal conclusions (here, whether or not the advertisement constituted a formal offer) for the short answer section.

(5) Here, note how the writer has constructed the question in this memo to alert the reader to the following facts: description of merchandise in an advertising circular, statement in circular that item is a "manufacturer's closeout," statement in circular indicating that the early shopper will be rewarded.

Although the "question presented" section is short, it must (i) provide a concise reference to the legal claim and relevant doctrine and (ii) incorporate the most legally significant facts of your case. A complete and well-balanced question presented is incisive — it immediately gets to the heart of the legal question — and it orients the reader to the factual context.

You may not be sure which facts are most legally significant when you first start writing the memo. Your thinking may become clearer and better organized as the writing proceeds. You would ascertain which facts are legally significant by referring to the factual criteria (based on elements or factors) in the legal authority relevant to the question — e.g. statutes or case law. For this reason, many people do not write the final version of the question presented (or the short answer) until they have almost completed the "discussion" section of the memo.

(**6**) The **short answer** contains a clear answer to the question (i.e. a prediction) and an explanation of that answer. The balanced description of law and fact that you provide in the question presented should be mirrored in the short answer.

The short answer serves two functions: (i) it provides hurried readers with an accessible, bottom-line prediction as well as the core of the relevant law and facts; and (ii) it provides the more thorough readers with an outline or digest of your subsequent discussion section. The short answer should function as a roadmap to help readers feel oriented when they move on to the discussion.

(**7**) Begin the short answer with your conclusion: yes, no, probably yes, etc., if the question can be answered that way. Then give a brief (usually no more than four or five sentences long) self-contained explanation of the reasons for your conclusion, applying the rule to the facts of your case. As a general rule, include no citations.

(**8**) The **facts** section contains all the factual premises upon which your subsequent legal analysis is based. Certainly, all the facts cited in the application section (The "A" in IRAC or CRRACC) of your discussion should be presented as part of the story told in the facts section.

Bear in mind that the busy law-trained reader will value conciseness in this section, so try to present only those facts that are legally significant or that are necessary to make the problem clear. At the same time, bear in mind that the office memo should be a stand-alone document that can fully inform any colleague in your law office who may read it; therefore, the facts section should always contain a full and coherent recitation of the relevant facts, whether or not the principal reader of the memo already knows them (unless, of course, you were instructed to do otherwise).

(9) It is helpful to the reader to present the facts according to some organizational scheme. In this memo, the writer has addressed the heart of the incident — the advertisement, the sale of the coats, the arrival of the unhappy shopper — in chronological order in the first paragraph; a second paragraph collects relevant background information about the client.

In your own memo, you can recount the facts completely chronologically, you can put the most important incidents or facts first, or you can cluster the facts into discrete topics if the facts are complex and if this is the easiest way to understand them. Choose the organizational scheme that you think will make the facts most clear and memorable to the reader.

(10) In your fact section, be sure to specify what legal claims are being considered or are being brought, and be sure to describe any legal proceedings that have already taken place.

(11) Identify your client and briefly describe your client's goal or problem.

(12) Since memo writing is predictive writing, you should try to maintain an objective and impartial tone as you recount the facts. This is not to say that you should omit facts that have an emotional impact. Rather, the facts section of an office memo should not be written in a tone that conveys a preference for a particular theory of the case, that implicitly advocates for one side in the dispute, or that telegraphs any of the legal conclusions to be drawn in the discussion section. Since you are not advocating for any side, you ought not color or characterize the facts as you would if you were writing a brief. Also, do not comment upon the facts in the facts section or discuss how the law will apply to them.

(13) The **umbrella section** of the discussion introduces or prefaces your first section of in-depth legal analysis; for example, it restates the key facts and issue presented, and introduces the overarching legal rule. Note how the writer alerts the reader to the key point of the doctrine, that general advertisements are treated in law as invitations to negotiate, not offers.

(14) The **rule statement** synthesizes key elements of the cases relevant to the issue in your case into a general statement of the rule. To produce an

accurate and well-crafted rule statement, you must have a good understanding of the existing legal authority on which your rule statement is based.

(**15**) Note how the writer pulls together key cases that comprise the rule, then identifies the standard of inquiry by which courts apply the rule.

(**16**) If the rule statement serves as the thesis sentence for a longer discussion about a legal rule that has developed over time in a series of cases, the **rule proof** serves as your explanation and elaboration of that thesis sentence.

Note as you read this section how the writer fleshes out the facts, holding, and reasoning of the Schenectady Stove Co. and Lovett cases, focusing on facts that are similar to the Loman case.

(**17**) A good **application** section weaves the cases into your facts. Language from the cases should be prominent and woven into your discussion of these facts. In the rule proof you discuss cases to support the rule statement. In the application section, you might draw analogies or contrasts between the cases discussed in the rule proof and your facts as a way to reach your conclusion.

(**18**) Note how the writer focuses on the specifics of the language of the advertisement.

(**19**) Note how the writer draws a direct comparison to similar facts in the Lovett case.

(**20**) The use of a **counterargument** is a good way to convey that the existing legal authority is not clear, unequivocal, or unified when applied to facts like yours. It may be the case that you cannot predict with certainty the outcome of your case, given your facts.

(**21**) Note here how the writer points to the absence of limiting language in the advertisement to support an argument that a shopper would be led to believe that appearing at the appointed time was sufficient to qualify for the reduced-price item.

(**22**) In a longer, more complex discussion, include here a short statement of your position on the question or issue explored in a given IRAC (or CRRACC) unit — your **conclusion** for that unit.

(**23**) The overall conclusion contains a summary of the main points of your analysis. In your application section you may have struggled with areas of uncertainty in the legal doctrine and/or competing policy rationales. You may have also grappled with a seemingly contradictory assortment of facts: some seem to fit into the requirements of the rule; others suggest that the rule is not satisfied. You may have weighed arguments against counterarguments. After you have done all this, you must take a position and make a statement about how the court will apply the law. Given the more fully fleshed out short answer, the writer here has opted for a brief restatement of the ultimate conclusion.

(24) As a legal writer, it helps to have an assortment of qualifiers to acknowledge how certain or uncertain you are of the actual judicial outcome. Your conclusion can convey that you are completely confident the court will rule as you predict or that, given the state of the legal authority, the outcome is really a toss-up and could go either way. Or you can convey any level of confidence in between. Keep in mind that the reader will be judging your credibility as a legal thinker based on (among other things) the congruity of your tone with the data at hand.

Exercises

1. Suppose you were Marie Lin, a lawyer assistant, and Randall Byars, who was in the trouble with Stephen Graham, was your client, please write an office memo to your senior lawyer, David Black.

Randall Byars recently signed a contract to purchase a house in the community to which he has been relocated. He has since discovered that at certain times of the year atmospheric conditions are such that the fumes from a nearby chemical plant become trapped at ground level. The fumes smell noxious and cause watery, burning eyes. Although this problem was not apparent when Byars was shown the house, the seller, Stephen Graham, was aware of the problem. This was the primary reason Graham sold the house, but he never mentioned the problem to Byars. Byars is your client and wants to know whether he can get out of this contract. The highest court in your state has decided these two cases.

Stewart v. Avery (1984)

The appellee, Jessica Avery, sued to rescind a contract for the purchase of a house. The appellee contends that the appellant deceived her by not disclosing that the house contained high levels of radon — odorless and colorless radioactive particles that can cause cancer. Normally, the rule of *caveat emptor* applies to the purchase of real estate, requiring the buyer to thoroughly inspect the property before agreement to purchase it. Here, however, such an inspection would not have revealed the high levels of radon. Such a defect is a critical factor in the transaction, affecting the value of the property and its potential resale value. Thus, rescission is appropriate to relieve the appllee from the burden of this agreement, obtained through the appellant's silence on a matter he surely knew was material to the transaction. The decision of the trial court to rescind the contract is, therefore, affirmed.

Waters v. Morton (1991)

The appellee was granted rescission of a contract for the purchase of a house. The appellee did not discover until after the purchase that the septic tank and drain lines were inadequate. This deficiency resulted in the overflow of raw sewage into the front yard after every heavy rain. This condition was apparent only then.

Passive concealment of defective realty constitutes an exception to the rule of *caveat emptor*. This exception places a duty on the seller to disclose facts not apparent to the buyer that would probably affect his decision to buy.

Here, even the most diligent of examinations would not have disclosed this defect, because the problem was apparent only after a heavy rain. The appellant knew of the deficiencies in the sewage system, yet he allowed the appellee to purchase the property without disclosing these facts. Such conduct constitutes fraud and warrants rescission of the contract. Affirmed.

2. Suppose you are David Hesler, a law clerk with ABC Law Firm in Minnesota. Ben Lee, a 60-year-old Chinese visitor to America, came to your office to seek legal advice. Ben visited MN Amusement Park on Dec. 16, 2008. He was asked to sign a release form at the entrance which released the MN Amusement Park from liability for any injuries sustained by the participant. Ben does not know much English; he looked around and found nobody available to help. Then he signed the form without reading it and

entered the park eagerly. Unfortunately, Ben got injured on a Park ride. He came in to ask whether he can sue the MN Amusement Park for its negligence. Please use these facts and the information below to write a 600- to 800-word office memo to a senior lawyer in your firm.

You did some research and found some relevant cases:

(1) *Garrison v. Combined Fitness Ctr.*, 559 N.E.2d 187, 190 (MN. App. Ct. 1990)

The courts upheld exculpatory clauses in release forms if they are clearly written in language that can be easily understood.

(2) *Owen v. Vic Tanny's Enterprises*, 199 N.E.2d 280, (MN. App. Ct. 1964)

The courts held that the exculpatory language in a release form must clearly express the intention of the parties to insulate the defendant from liability for injuries sustained by the plaintiff.

(3) *Rudolph v. Sante Fe Park Enter., Inc.*, 461 N.E.2d 622, 624 (MN. App. Ct. 1984)

The court held that a person cannot avoid a contract simply by saying that he did not read it before he signed it.

Chapter 4
Writing Briefs

The lawyer as advocate is the counterpart of the lawyer as counselor. To the client, the lawyer is a counselor; to the outside world, the lawyer is an advocate. As an advocate, the lawyer exercises persuasion in a variety of ways to achieve results favorable to the client. Many times a lawyer will help a client avoid a lawsuit by convincing a potential adversary that the client's position is solid. At other times, a lawyer may convince a government agency to adapt a more favorable attitude toward the client's position. While effective advocacy can help keep a dispute out of court, it can also increase the likelihood of success if litigation is necessary.

The brief is the formal document a lawyer uses both to convince a court that the client's position is found and to persuade a court to adopt that position. Briefs are similar to office memos in many respects, and many of the principles that apply to briefs. Both must honestly state the law, the facts of the case, and the reasons for their conclusions clearly and concisely. The advice in a memo, of course, is worthless if it cannot be defended in litigation.

Briefs differ from memos, however, in two important respects. The first difference is the tone of the document: briefs argue; memos discuss. The writer of a memo is developing a legal strategy with other attorneys; the writer of a brief is submitting a legal argument to opposing counsel and a judge or panel of judges, all of whom will scrutinize it. Open and honest assessment of the client's position, required for memos, is absolutely wrong for briefs. The brief writer must make the client's position seem as strong as possible, emphasizing favorable arguments and minimizing the force of opposing argument. It is not enough that the client's position appear logical or even desirable; it must seem compelling.

The second difference is the thinking process used in drafting the documents. The brief writer knows the basic conclusions in advance and searches for argument and materials supporting those conclusions and showing that his client's position is stronger and should prevail. The memorandum writer, by contrast, is concerned with objectively determining whose position is most sound and usually will not come to a conclusion until relatively late in the process of research and analysis.

There are two kinds of briefs. A brief to a trial court (sometimes called a memorandum of law or memorandum of points and authorities) is the document presented to a trial court in support of, or in opposition to, various motions, or to convince the court to decide the merits in a particular way. A brief to an appellate court is the document presented to a reviewing court challenging or defending a trial court's decision in a case.

Following is a generally accepted format for both the brief to an appellate court and the brief to a trial court:

Brief to an Appellate Court	Brief to a Trial Court
Title Page	Caption
Index	
Authorities Cited	
Opinion(s) Below	
Jurisdiction	
Constitutional Provisions, Statutes, Regulations, and Rules Involved	
Standard of Review (required by some courts)	
Questions Presented	Questions Presented (optional)
Statement of Facts	Statement of Facts
Summary of Argument	
Argument	Argument
Conclusion	Conclusion
Appendix(es)	

Chapter 4
Writing Briefs

The name of each section (except the Title Page and Caption) should be underlined or capitalized and placed immediately above that section.

When drafting a brief you should be aware of three things. First, trial and appellate courts usually have specific rules concerning the format and content of briefs. These rules ensure some uniformity and make it easier to compare arguments made in opposing briefs. Specific court rules control when they vary from the general rules given here. Second, the importance of many of the elements of an appellate brief may seem obscure at first, and many of the court rules will concern seemingly minor items such as length, page, size, and citation form. Although some of these elements and rules may seem tedious and overly technical, you should take them seriously. Many courts reject incorrectly presented briefs. Third, briefs are rarely drafted in the order these element appear. You will usually write the Argument, Summary of Argument, Statement of Facts, and Questions Presented before you write the other elements.

Section 1   Briefs to a Trial Court

Lawyers submit briefs to a trial court to persuade the court to decide some aspect of litigation in their client's favor. They write briefs in a variety of contexts and at many stages of litigation. These briefs all have one thing in common; however, their audience is the trial judge.

1. Elements of a Brief

The following is a description of each element of a brief. The Discussion also explains when an element in a trial court brief differs from its counterpart in an appellate court brief. Examine Appendixes (Brief Samples) in conjunction with this chapter.

(1) Title Page or Caption

The Title Page of a trial court brief identifies the court, the docket number, the name of the case, the side represented, and the names and addresses of counsel. The Title Page distinguishes the brief from many others received by the court and ensures that the brief will be placed in the proper file.

The first page of the brief to a trial court has a Caption, which looks like this:

UNITED STATES DISTRICT COURT
FOR THE DISTRICT OF SUPERIOR

WESTBROOK NEIGHBORHOOD ASSOCIATION,
Plaintiff,
Vs.
ELLISON RE,YCLING. INC.,
Defendant.

Civ. Docket No. CZ-8071-93
Hon. F. A. Hollender

A TRIAL COURT BRIEF
IN SUPPORT OF DEFENDANT'S
MOTION TO DISMISS

The Caption substitutes for the Title Page; it identifies the court, the name of the case, the docket number, the motion or other matter under consideration, the judge, and the side represented.

(2) Questions Presented

This section states the legal issues involved in a brief and tells the court the matters you intend to address. The Questions Presented in a brief is similar to those in a memorandum. Both must include the legal rule and a summary of significant facts, and both must be precise and understandable.

Unlike the Questions Presented in an office memorandum, though, the questions in a brief should be slanted toward your client's position and should reflect your interpretation of the law. If you are using that interpretation to emphasize certain facts in your argument, your questions should contain these facts. In addition, the questions should be stated so that they prompt an affirmative answer. Your brief should project a positive tone; it should argue for a particular conclusion rather than simply against the contrary conclusion. If you are appealing an unfavorable trial court decision, for example, your questions might begin: "Whether the trial court erred..." Your opponent, appealing the same decision, might begin: "Whether the trial court properly held..." Both questions suggest an affirmative answer.

There are two styles of presenting the questions in a brief, and these styles differ principally in their argumentative tone and completeness. The better style, which you should use, is to state the question so completely and so persuasively that it answers itself.

> Whether the trial court deprived the defendant of his right to due process of law under the Fourteenth Amendment by admitting into evidence a confession that was extracted from the defendant after twenty-two consecutive hours of interrogation by rotating teams of defectives.

This way of presenting the question combined the relevant legal rule and the significant facts so that the only reasonable answer seems to be "yes." This style is very effective, although you should not risk your credibility by overstating or distorting your position. The other style states questions in their barest form.

> Whether admission into evidence of the defendant's confession violated his right to due process under the Fourteenth Amendment.

This question does not provide significant facts, nor does it make the answer obvious, although it does frame the issue in a way that would be acceptable to both sides.

Many briefs to a trial court are so short or straightforward that the Questions Presented section is unnecessary. The section is necessary, however, in long or complex trial court briefs, which often contain multiple issues.

(3) Statement of Facts

The Statement of Facts in a brief, also known as Statement of the Case or simply Statement, is a descriptive account of the facts from your client's point of view. Although this statement cannot omit any damaging facts, you should write it to promote the court's understanding of and sympathy for your client's situation. Many lawyers and judges believe that the Statement of Facts, is the most important section of any brief.

(4) Argument

The Argument is the foundation on which the rest of the brief is constructed. Like the Discussion in an office memorandum, it is the heart of the document. Although the Statement of facts and Summary of Argument are important, and sometimes decisive, your client generally wins or loses on the quality and substance of what you say in the Argument. An effective Argument in a brief is developed using the basic concepts of legal writing. The Argument should be clear and compelling; it should reflect a sound understanding and thoughtful analysis of the relevant law. Although the Argument is similar to the Discussion, it is different from the Discussion in two important ways.

First, this section of the brief should be an argument rather than an objective discussion of the law. You should state, in forceful and affirmative language, your strongest argument and issues first and present your client's position on each issue or sub-issue before you refute position of your opponent. These and other principles of advocacy presented in the Argument section will help you present your case more convincingly.

Second, the Argument should contain point headings. Point headings are conspicuous thesis statement that prefaces each logical segment of your Argument. Because they are capitalized, underlined, or formatted in a prominent way, point headings make it easier for the reader to understand the structure and content of your Argument. Point headings are always included in appellate briefs, but their use in trial court briefs is optional.

(5) Conclusion

This section describes what you want the court to do. It precisely state what relief you are requesting from the court — particularly if the relief you seek is more complicated than affirming or reversing the lower court's judgment. The request for relief is usually one sentence in length. In trial briefs with complex arguments, you may include brief summary of the argument supporting your conclusion. Immediately following, you should include the address, phone number, and signature of at least one of the attorneys who presented the brief. You should also include the date. The Conclusion section in trial brief should look like this:

For the foregoing reasons, plaintiffs respectfully request that the defendant's motion for summary judgment be denied.

Respectfully submitted,

_____

Charles McGrady
Attorney Appellants
Smith, Dunmore &Coffin
420 Brookshire Commons
Greensboro, N.C. 27402
(010) 423-0706

March 1, 2014

2. Tactical Considerations

The following tactical considerations apply specifically to briefs written to a trial court. Although the examples in this chapter involve civil cases, the principles described here also apply to criminal cases. Briefs to a trial court can be classified into the following four categories.

(1) Briefs submitted in support of or in opposition to motions that are dispositive of some or all of the issues in the case without a trial. These briefs are generally filed either before or after discovery. Civil cases begin when the plaintiff files a complaint alleging that the defendant has done or do something illegal and requesting relief. If the defendant believes that the complaint is not based on a valid legal theory, that the court lacks personal jurisdiction, or that there is some other fundamental defect on the face of the complaint, it will probably file a motion to dismiss based on Rule 12(b) of the Federal Rules of Civil Procedure or the parallel state rule. The defendant will attach a "memorandum of law in support of motion to dismiss," which is a brief explaining why the motion should be granted. A brief to a trial court, particular one that supports or opposes a motion, is often called a "memorandum of law" or "memorandum of points and authorities." The plaintiff will file a brief opposing the motion. The trial court will then decide whether to grant the motion.

If the case is not dismissed, it proceeds to discovery. During this period, the Federal Rules of Civil Procedure and their counterpart state rules allow each side to learn more about the facts surrounding the case. After discovery is complete, either side may file a motion for summary judgment (or partial summary judgment) under Rule 56 of the Federal Rules or the parallel state rule. A party filling a summary judgment motion claims that the material facts are not in dispute and that she is entitled to judgment as a matter of law. Again, each party will file a brief with the trial court supporting its position, and the judge will decide whether to grant the motion.

(2) Briefs submitted in connection with discovery disputes. The basis methods of discovery are written questions to opposing parties or potential witnesses(interrogatories), written requests to the other side to admit certain facts(requests for admission), written requests to the production of documents, and oral questions to potential witnesses(depositions). The trial courts expect that discovery will ordinarily be conducted in a fair and responsible manner. Occasionally, however, a party will claim that the other side is asking for privileged information, is making an overly burdensome request for the production of documents, is not responding to proper discovery requests, or in some other way is violating the rules governing discovery. When that happens, a party will often file a motion for some type of relief with the trial court and a brief in support of its motion, and the other party will file an opposing brief.

(3) Briefs submitted in connection with evidentiary or procedural disputes. Before or during the trial, disputes often arise about whether a particular piece of evidence should be admitted, or how the case should proceed. When that happens, a party is likely to file a motion with the trial court to exclude the evidence in question or for other appropriate relief. The other side will then file a reply brief, and the judge will decide how to proceed.

(4) Briefs submitted on the substantive issues in the case before and after trial. The trial is the main event in litigation. The plaintiff must present evidence to establish all of the facts necessary to prove its claims. The defendant must present evidence to rebut the plaintiff's proof or establish the facts necessary to support any affirmative defenses. The evidence presented generally consists of witnesses' testimony and documents. Some trials are finished in a few hours. Others continue for months. After evidence has been received, the

Chapter 4
Writing Briefs

judge or jury (depending on the case) renders a decision.

Briefs may be submitted at the commencement and at the conclusion of trials to provide the court with each party's view of the facts and how the issues should be resolved. A pre-trial brief defines the issues for the judge and demonstrates how the law applies to facts a party hopes to establish. In non-jury case, a post-trial brief ties all of the evidence together (with citations to the record) and urges the court to reach certain conclusions based on the application of the law to that evidence. In cases decided by juries, a post-trial brief may present legal arguments supporting or opposing a motion for judgment not withstanding the verdict or a motion for new trial.

Each Type of brief has different requirements. Pre-trial and post-trial briefs in non-jury case are generally the longest because they contain a full rendition of the relevant facts and complete discussion of the issues. Brief written on discovery, procedural, or evidentiary issues, on the other hand, are usually short and generally include only an abbreviated discussion of the facts and law. Briefs on dispositive motions fall in the middle. They tend to be longer and more detailed than briefs on procedural, or evidentiary issues, but shorter than pre-trial or post-trial briefs. The legal analysis, however, is frequently as detailed as a pre-trial or post-trial brief, primarily because of the importance of these motions. Of course, the existence of a clear legal bar to the claim or defense should be conveyed to the court in one or two pages.

The following problem will help illustrate the basic tactical considerations that apply to briefs filed with trial courts:

Peter Miller was a passenger in a small private plane that crashed in a swamp in the state of West Florida. The plane was owned by the pilot, Dennis Chisolm, who was Miller's friend. The crash was caused by a defective fuel pump which, because of Chisom's neglect in maintaining the plane, was not corrected. Chisolm, who is 67 years old and retired, escaped with minor injuries. Miller suffered serious injuries, including permanent spinal damage that has left him confined to a wheelchair. Since the crash Chisolm has become extremely depressed from guilt for having injured his friend. Psychiatric counseling has not helped.

Your firm represents Chisolm. Shortly after the crash Miller settled with

Chisolm for $1.5 million, the limit of Chisolm's insurance policy plus one-half of Chisolm's life savings. He decided to settle based on your firm's advice that the settlement would end the matter as far as he was concerned and that he would have no further liability arising from the accident. Chisolm is living off the balance of his saving of $500,000. He has no other source of income.

Miller has recently commenced suit against Arson Industries, the manufacturer of the engine and fuel pump, seeking $10 million in damages. Arson has filed a third-party complaint against Chisolm, seeking contribution for any liability Arson may have to Miller. Miller has offered to accept the same settlement from Arson of $1.5 million, but Arson has refused to discuss settlement at this figure. You have been requested to prepare a brief in support of a motion for summary judgment against Arson's third-party complaint on the grounds of the "settlement-bar" rule.

Your research has revealed these West Florida cases.

Sarasota Pools v. Buccaneer Resorts (W. Fla. 1989)

Paula Jensen, a guest at the defendant's resort, was injured when the pool's diving board cracked, causing Jensen to strike the side of the swimming pool. The diving board had been improperly installed by the pool contractor, Sarasota Pools, and then improperly maintained by the resort. Jensen settled with Buccaneer for $75,000 and filed suit against Sarasota. She obtained a judgment of $50,000. Sarasota has brought this suit against the resort for contribution. The trial judge dismissed the complaint. The district court of appeals affirmed. We affirm.

Much disagreement exists in the various states and among the lower courts in this state concerning the rights of contribution between joint tortfeasors when the plaintiff has settled with one or more of them. Two leading views have emerged. Under the first, all tortfeasors may recover against one another for each one's percentage of faults regardless of the settlement, but the setting tortfeasor receive credit against their liability for settlement fund paid to the plaintiff. Under the second, settling tortfeasors cannot recover from non-settling tortfeasors for contribution; neither can non-settling tortfeasors sue settling tortfeasors. The second view is called the "settlement-bar" rule. A settling tortfeasors has literally "bought his peace" by settling and is entitled to freedom from any further litigation arising out of the incident. The plaintiff's claim against the non-setting tortfeasors is reduced to reflect the settlement proceeds received.

After much consideration we are persuaded that the settlement-bar rule is the better alternative. We find this rule to be much easier to enforce and fairer because it provides more predictability so parties can know the consequences of their conduct in advance. We also find that the settlement-bar rule has the salutary effect of encouraging settlement and avoiding litigation, which is much needed relief, given the congestion in our courts. Accordingly, we adopt the settlement-bar rule for all contribution actions in this state.

Raseen v. Harrison Construction Co. (W. Fla. Dist. Ct. 1993)

Ahmad Raseen's house in Sliver Lake, West Florida collapsed during Hurricane Andrew. He sued hurricane Construction Co., the contractors building the house, claiming that they were negligent in construction, and Design for Living, the architects, claiming negligent design. Hurricane and Designs cross-claimed against each other. After commencement of the trial, Raseen settled with Designs for $30,000. Designs then moved to dismiss Hurricane's cross-claim against it. The trial court granted the motion on the basis of the court's decision in *Sarasota Pools v. Buccaneer Resorts*. The jury subsequently returned a $150,000 verdict against Harrison. Harrison appealed, claiming that the trial court erred in dismissing Design, We agree.

Designs' settlement in this case appears grossly disproportionate to the liabilities involved. The record suggests that Designs is primarily liable for the collapse of the plaintiff's house. The court should hear the evidence, determine the percentage of liability each should bear on Raseen's damages, and enter judgment accordingly. The settlement-bar rule thus far has been applied in this state only to personal injury cases, which present special difficulties in proving damages and assessing fault. We use no reason to extend it to a case such as that before us now involving only proper damage. In addition, it is difficult to understand how any public policy of reducing litigation would be served because the trial had commenced when the settlement with Designs occurred. Reversed.

Sunshine Health Care, Inc. v. Rollins (W. Fla. Dist. Ct. App. 1991)

Dr. Alfred Rollins is licensed to practice medicine in this state. Sunshine is a health maintenance organization that employed the doctor. The genesis of this case was Rollins's treatment of Ina Rivkind at the Sunshine Clinic for a dog bite. There is little question that Dr. Rollins was negligent in treating the wound, which caused the bite to become infected. Ms. Rivkind subsequently was required to have a serious operation to cure the infection, which has left her with permanent disfiguring marks on her arm. Ms. Rivkind threatened to sue Dr. Rollins for malpractice and the clinic for negligence in hiring the doctor because there is serious question about the doctor's credentials. In separate negotiations before any suit was filed, Ms. Rivkind agreed to a $90,000 settlement with the clinic and a $5,000 settlement with the doctor. The clinic brought this action against the doctor for contribution arising out of the settlement. The trial court dismissed. We affirm.

There is a strong policy in this state of upholding settlements and holding parties to the terms of their bargain. Sarasota pools v. Buccaneer Resorts. This policy is especially strong where, as here, both wrong doers have settled with the plaintiff. It makes no difference that each party had not known how much the other was settling for. They both received the benefit of their respective bargains — the end of litigation. The settlement-bar rule precludes either of them from now reopening the dispute in an attempt to redistribute the liability.

You have also located a pertinent law review article, portions of which appear below.

Elizabeth B. Burns, the Settlement-Bar Rule: Tough Choices, Tough Answers, 89 Tallahassee L. Rev. 135(1993)

Perhaps one of the greatest areas of philosophical disagreement in modern law concerns the problem of contribution among joint tortfeasors when the plaintiff has settled with one or more of them. The question most often arises in cases of personal injury, but not exclusively so. Many instances of property damage cases involve personal injury or are cases in which an injury just as easily could have occurred. Although some cases have drawn a distinction between personal injury and property damage, applying certain rules of contribution in the former and not in the latter, there is no rational basis for doing so. The problem is highlighted in a case involving both personal injury and property damage. Is there any logic to applying two different rules to such a case? The answer is no.

...

Each of four different views on the contribution question has merit. Each also requires courts to make tough choices among competing considerations. In

Chapter 4
Writing Briefs

Sarasota Pools V. Buccaneer Resorts, the West Florida Supreme Court selected the settlement-bar rule as the law in West Florida. Under this rule a settling tortfeasor literally buys his peace with the world. He cannot be sued by anyone who may also be liable to the plaintiff but neither can he sue anyone. The incident and the litigation are over as far as a settling tortfeasor is concerned.

The settlement-bar rule has much to commend it and serves many valuable policy goals. First, it is easy to enforce. The only legitimate question is whether there has been a bona fide settlement. If the settlement is collusive or a sham, the court can disregard it and rule on the contribution claim as if no settlement occurred. Second, the settlement-bar rule is fairer to the settling tortfeasor in that it gives him the benefit of his bargain. Any settling tortfeasor certainly believes that it gives him the benefit of his bargain. Any settling tortfeasor certainly believes that once he settles with the plaintiff, his obligations with respect to the incident are at an end. The settlement-bar rule enforces that expectation. Third, the settlement bar rule provides predictability and certainty in this troublesome area of the law. A defendant knows that he can either litigate or settle. If he chooses the latter he can do so with confidence that he will not later be drawn into any subsequent litigation arising out of the incident. Finally, and perhaps most importantly, the settlement-bar rule encourages settlements, thus reducing litigation. This is perhaps the greatest policy consideration supporting the rule. The cost of litigation today is enormous and is a social cost that we all share. Significant resources are conserved every time a dispute is settled short of litigation. Because encouraging settlements is the primary policy underpinning the rule, there would seem to be no justification for applying the rule when that policy is not served.

. . .

The settlement-bar rule does not come without cost. The major cost is potential unfairness to other non-settling defendants. The plaintiff is permitted to proceed against them for the full amount of the plaintiff's claim, less than what the plaintiff received from the setting tortfeasor who is barred from contribution, therefore, may be held to a greater share of liability than he should legitimately have to bear. For example, if the plaintiff's damages are $100,000 and the plaintiff settles with Defendant A for $10,000, Defendant

B would be fully liable for the balance of $90,000, even if Defendant B's share of responsibility for the plaintiff's damages may only be 20%.

The short answer to this dilemma, however, is that the non-settling tortfeasor could have settled but chose not to do so and instead risk litigating the claim. Presumably, the non-settling tortfeasor did this knowing he had no contribution rights. One would imagine that the lack of contribution rights would be a significant incentive for a non-settling tortfeasor to settle.

3. Narratives in Law: The Statement of Facts

The Statement of Facts in a brief to a court performs specific work: we can think of it as a strategic staging or presenting of facts in a way that addresses the legal issues in a case, without overtly arguing them. Typically, a judge will read the Statement of Facts in a brief before reading the Argument; a well-crafted Statement of Facts that engages in covert persuasion can influence the way in which the arguments will be evaluated. At its best, a Statement of Facts will have the attributes of a narrative, including a plot line based on a certain temporality, a series of events, a cast of characters, and a point of view. If it is skillfully crafted, it will elicit interest and build dramatic tension. Unlike other narratives, though, a Statement of Facts in a brief is subject to parameters that are based on the elements of the law that applies. The facts you choose to include in the Statement of Facts should bear a relationship to the factual criteria in the case law or statute that governs the legal issue. For example, in a case involving the special relationship doctrine in torts, in which New York case law has identified four elements for meeting its requirements (knowledge, assumption of duty, direct contact, reliance), plaintiffs and defendants should include facts in the Statement that tend to support or disprove these elements.

Thus, in the Statement of Facts there is interplay between law and fact. The Statement of Facts should be written with a consciousness of what will be argued in the Argument; there should be a correspondence of facts in both, though the language, level of detail, and tone will differ. With these parameters in mind, consider the possible approaches to developing a narrative that you've encountered in other contexts. Narratives can be character-driven, event-driven, place-centered. Narratives can unfold in chronological order of events, through flashbacks, or through some other point in time that is neither

Chapter 4
Writing Briefs

at the beginning nor the end of the sequence of events constituting "what happened." Narratives can be told from the perspective of a particular person, including the narrator or some other person, or a narrative can shift its perspective in the course of the telling.

In a Statement of Facts in a brief, the need to present a compelling, coherent plot or story line that addresses the legally significant facts will limit some of the options otherwise available to storytellers. The narrative should "flow" (e.g. it would be risky here to experiment with post-modern approaches that fracture time frames or juxtapose perspectives — it won't accredit your client's case if you confuse or disorient the reader!). The reader should be able to get a clear sense of "what happened," though the choice of where to begin the narrative (i.e. what, in the telling of it, constitutes the beginning) can be critical to creating a compelling effect. As always, you would need to think strategically when choosing where to "begin." It's also crucial to narrate in a way that embeds the point of view of your client (and that avoids highlighting the perspective or the experience of the opposing party). Typically, presenting a narrative from your client's perspective involves making your client or its representative the subject or agent in the story line — the focus of attention and action.

The Statement of Facts is not the only written factual narrative that advocates produce in a litigated case. The Complaint is also a source of facts, and in some instances, such as in a motion to dismiss, it is the only source available to the parties, because its allegations are taken as true. The Complaint serves legal and rhetorical functions that are distinct from the way in which a Statement of Facts works. The legal function of the Complaint is primary: it alleges facts necessary to state all elements of a legal claim. Thus, it is written from the perspective and within the knowledge base of the pleader. Secondarily, the Complaint may have a persuasive or narrative function — when it is framed with more detail. As writing, it is its own legal genre. Its form has legal significance: the factual substance must be set out in separately numbered paragraphs; each paragraph should deal with one idea that can be admitted or denied in an answering pleading; the language should be clear and precise. The Complaint may not present a narrative that is artful in the telling, but at the very least it purports to narrate a legal story — its facts fit within all the requirements prescribed for a cause of action. If the Complaint is fairly specific, it may also get across a factual narrative — what happened and to whom — and usually this presentation of facts will occur in a chronological order.

Yet, given these considerations of function and form, the Complaint is rarely a good model of a narrative for the Statement of Facts. Even when working within the more specialized modes and genres of legal writing, it's important for advocates to cultivate a sensibility about storytelling and language that is literary. The goal, then, for plaintiffs, is to create an engaging narrative in the Statement of Facts, without simply replicating the elements and the organization of the Complaint. The challenge for both plaintiffs and defendants is to identify a credible plot line, which can derive from a variety of sources: from the facts of the case; from the legal doctrine itself — from ideas that emerge from the cases or statutory criteria; from legislative policy; or from the accumulated bank of human experience, and the frameworks or values prevalent in a culture. That task is complicated for defendants when the Complaint is the only source of facts because, as noted, it is written from the plaintiff's perspective. Defendants may draw upon fair inferences from the facts that are alleged, however, and may point out negative facts — facts that are not alleged in the Complaint — that arguably are necessary to meet the requirements of the cause of action. Both parties should consider the choices that are possible concerning character, perspective, sequencing of information, selection of facts, and level of factual specificity. In short, to maximize the persuasive impact of the Statement of Facts, advocates should keep in mind the attributes and uses of narratives.

4. Checklist for Drafting a Trial Brief

(Modeled after a brief writing checklist prepared by Professor Janet Calvo, CUNY School of Law)

I. Introduction (or Preliminary Statement)

Does the Introduction articulate the party's claim and introduce the theory of the case by referring to the case facts?

Are the parties identified?

Is the procedural history included?

II. Statement of Facts

Does the Statement set forth the facts in a narrative that will be easy to follow for a reader who is unfamiliar with the case?

Does it include all legally significant facts?

Does it include relevant background facts?

Does it include facts that have an emotional resonance or sympathetic value for the party on whose behalf you write?

Are the facts stated accurately?

Does the Statement include the facts that you use in the Argument?

Has the Statement been edited to remove legal conclusions and editorializing?

Do favorable facts appear in positions of emphasis?

Does the Statement include significant unfavorable facts without overemphasizing them?

Does the Statement present and develop the theory of the case?

III. Question Presented (or, alternatively, Summary of Argument)

Does the Question combine the legal claim and controlling legal standard with the legally significant facts that raise the legal issue?

Is the Question framed so as to suggest an affirmative answer?

Does the Summary (if applicable) present a short statement of the legal and factual theory of the case?

IV. Point Headings

Do the point headings and subheadings provide the reader with an outline of the argument?

Are the headings framed as legal assertions that are favorable to the party you represent, and are they supported with legally relevant facts?

Do the headings answer the question(s) presented?

V. Argument

A. Overall

Is the Argument organized into points and subpoints?

Do the points and subpoints follow the CRRACC paradigm (Conclusion/Rule Synthesis/Rule Proof/ Application of Rule to Facts/Counterargument/

Conclusion Restated)?

Does the Argument address the procedural context and the arguments based upon it?

B. Content of Rule

Is the synthesized rule (legal standard) set forth clearly and completely?

Does the synthesized rule discuss the "common threads" (as that term is used in Laurel Oates et al., The Legal Writing Handbook (3d ed., Aspen), at pp. 78-82) or patterns among cases?

Is the synthesized rule framed favorably for the party you represent, supporting the conclusion that you want the court to reach?

C. Rule Proof

Does the Rule Proof carry forward and develop each of the ideas stated in the Rule Synthesis in a section of one or more paragraphs that begins with a thesis (idea) sentence?

Do the cases discussed in the Rule Proof illustrate and support the idea expressed in each thesis sentence?

Does the Rule Proof address the holdings, legally significant facts, and reasoning of the cases discussed?

Are the facts of the cases included in the Rule Proof related to/illustrative of the legal point that you have asserted?

Are the parts of cases that counter your argument distinguished or explained?

Does the Argument raise and address relevant policy arguments?

D. Application of Rule to Fact

Does the Application relate all the components of the rule/legal standard to the facts of the case that you are arguing?

Does the Argument demonstrate how underlying policy objectives in the law are met if the court accepts the application of law to fact?

Does the Application of rule to fact illustrate the theory of the case?

E. Counterargument

Does the Counterargument address and dispose of the arguments raised by the opponent, without overemphasizing them?

F. Organization

Does each paragraph within a point or subpoint advance the argument being made?

Are there clear transitions between paragraphs?

If the thesis or topic sentences of each paragraph within a point or subpoint were arranged in order, would a sound structure or outline of the point emerge?

Do the sentences within a paragraph relate to one another coherently, such that each successive sentence builds on the idea that is being addressed in preceding sentences?

G. Form

Have you checked all sentences for correct grammar, spelling, and citation form?

VI. Conclusion

Section 2 Briefs to an Appellate Court

Appellate and trial court briefs differ in several ways. Appellate briefs focus more on broad policy because appellate courts are more concerned with establishing and applying rules that will work in many situations. Trial court briefs tend to focus more on the facts of an individual case because trial courts are closer to the parties and more concerned with deciding cases according to established precedent than with establishing new law. Appellate briefs are usually accompanied by an edited transcript of the record from the lower court.

1. Elements of a Brief

The following discussion focuses primarily on appellate briefs because they have more elements than trial court briefs. The Discussion also explains when an element in a trial court brief differs from its counterpart in an appellate court brief. Examine Appendixes (Brief Samples) in conjunction with this chapter.

(1) Title Page

The Title Page of an appellate brief identifies the court, the docket number, the name of the case, the side represented, and the names and addresses of counsel. The Title Page of briefs filed in the highest state appellate court or the Supreme Court of the United States also identifies the term of the court and the court from which the appeal is taken. The Title Page distinguishes the brief from many others received by the court and ensures that the brief will be placed in the proper file. Appendixes show a standard Title Page for appellate briefs, though there can be minor stylistic variations.

(2) Index

The Index is a table of contents for the appellate brief and is sometimes labeled as such. It lists each element of the brief and the page on which that element begins. In addition, the point headings used in the argument should be stated in full in the order they appear, with page numbers corresponding to their locations. The point headings, described in detail later, are specialized thesis sentences that introduce parts of your argument. This outline of the point headings gives the reader a concise and easily understandable summary of your argument. The briefs in Appendixes show a basic format for the Index.

(3) Authorities Cited

This section, also called Table of Authorities or Citations, lists all of the legal and other materials used to support the Argument in an appellate brief and shows every page on which those materials are cited. This list of authorities permits a judge or opposing counsel to determine quickly where you examined specific cases, statutes, or other materials. It also provides a quick reference for complete citations to any materials used in the brief.

The Authorities Cited section is usually divided into several basic categories, including cases, constitutional provisions, statues, and miscellaneous materials. Each of other categories can be subdivided. Subdividing is for the reader's benefit. It will often be helpful to have a separate section for cases decided by the court to which the brief is addressed. For example, you might list cases under the headings "Michigan Cases" and "Other Cases," or you might list them under "United States Supreme Court Decisions" "Sixth Circuit Court of Appeals Decisions" and "Other Federal Decisions." You might also create categories to emphasize specific statutes, administrative rules, secondary authorities, or the legislative history of a particular act. Avoid cluttering the brief, however, with numerous subcategories that have only a few citations.

Cases, secondary authorities, and materials should be listed in alphabetical order in each category. Statutory sections, constitutional provisions, and other materials that cannot be listed alphabetically should be listed in numerical order. The brief in Appendixes show how to list Authorities Cited.

Chapter 4
Writing Briefs

(4) Opinions Below

This section of an appellate brief indicates where the decisions of the lower courts or government agencies that have decided this case can be located, in case the reviewing court wants to read them. Provide a citation for them. Provide a citation for these previous decisions if they have been reported; if they have not yet been reported, say so and their location in the record. For example:

> The opinion of the Court of Appeals for the District Circuit is unreported and is reprinted at pages 1a-2a of the appendixes to the petition for certiorari (Pet. App.). The opinion invalidated a rulemaking order of the Federal Communications Commission. The Commission's rulemaking order is reported at 7F. C. C. R. 8072 (1992) and is reprinted at Pet. App. 3a—36a.

(5) Jurisdiction

This section of an appellate brief, also called a Jurisdictional Statement or Statement of Jurisdiction, provides a short statement of the jurisdictional basis for the appeal. Because jurisdiction itself is often an issue in trial courts and is also asserted in the complaint, this section is unnecessary for briefs to trial court. Some state appellate courts require a Jurisdictional Statement only in limited circumstances. The Jurisdiction section should briefly inform the court of the factual circumstances, court rules, or statutory provisions on which appellate jurisdiction is based. Thus:

> The judgment of the Unites States Court of Appeals for the Seventh Circuit affirming the decision of the United States District Court was entered on September 7, 1990. The petition for a writ of certiorari was filed on November 27, 1990, and this Court is invoked under 28 U.S.C. §1254(1).

(6) Constitutional Provisions, Statutes, Regulations and Rules Involved

This section tells the court what codified provisions are relevant to the determination of the case and where in your brief the judge can scrutinize the exact language of these provisions. The name of this section varies according to the materials included. When you have one or two provisions that are relatively short, you should state the exact language in full. When you have many provisions or the provisions are lengthy, you should provide the name and citation in this section and indicate that the provisions are stated in full in one or more appendixes at the end of your brief.

Thus:

> Section 29 of the Mobile Home Commission Act, Mich. Comp. Laws Ann. §125.2329(West Supp.1993), provides as follows:
> A utility company notifies the department ten days before shutoff of service for nonpayment, including sewer, water, gas, or electric service, when the service is being supplied to the licensed owner or operator of a mobile home park or seasonal mobile home park for the use and benefit the park's tenants.

Or:

> The texts of the following statutes relevant to the determination of the present case are set forth in the Appendixes: Section 3? (2) (6) and 10(b) of the Federal Insecticide, Fungicide, and Rodenticide Act, 7 U.S.C. §§136a(c) (2) (6), 136h (b) (Supp, III 1991); Tucker Act, 28 U.S.C. §1491(1988&Supp.IV 1992)

(7) Standard of Review

This section contains a concise statement of the appropriate standard of review to be exercised by the appellate court, with citation to authority supporting the applicability of that standard. The location of the standard of review within the brief may be specified by court riles. The appellate court's standard of review will vary, depending on the legal issues involved and the procedural posture of the determination being appealed. The various standards of review are generally not contained in the court rules, but are developed in case law. They are discussed in greater detail in Chapter 6(Briefs to an Appellate Court). A typical standard of review section reads as follows:

> The issue before this Court is whether the trial court erred in dismissing the complaint for lack of personal jurisdiction. The court's review of the grant of a motion to dismiss is De Novo. *Larkin v. Smith Realty Co.*

If a dispute exists over the applicable standard, your discussion will be more detailed. You will have to demonstrate why your position on the appropriate standard is correct and why your opponent's is wrong.

(8) Questions Presented

This section states the legal issues involved in a brief and tells the court the matters you intend to address. The Questions Presented in a brief is similar to those in a memorandum. Both must include the legal rule and a summary of significant facts, and both must be precise and understandable.

Unlike the Questions Presented in an office memorandum, though, the questions in a brief should be slanted toward your client's position and should reflect your interpretation of the law. If you are using that interpretation to emphasize certain facts in your argument, your questions should contain these facts. In addition, the questions should be stated so that they prompt an affirmative answer. Your brief should project a positive tone; it should argue for a particular conclusion rather than simply against the contrary conclusion. If you are appealing an unfavorable trial court decision, for example, your questions might begin: "Whether the trial court erred..." Your opponent, appealing the same decision, might begin: "Whether the trial court properly held..." Both questions suggest an affirmative answer.

There are two styles of presenting the questions in a brief, and these styles differ principally in their argumentative tone and completeness. The better style, which you should use, is to state the question so completely and so persuasively that it answers itself.

> Whether the trial court deprived the defendant of his right to due process of law under the Fourteenth Amendment by admitting into evidence a confession that was extracted from the defendant after twenty-two consecutive hours of interrogation by rotating teams of defectives.

This way of presenting the question combined the relevant legal rule and the significant facts so that the only reasonable answer seems to be "yes." This style is very effective, although you should not risk your credibility by overstating or distorting your position. The other style states questions in their barest form:

> Whether admission into evidence of the defendant's confession violated his right to due process under the Fourteenth Amendment.

This question neither provides significant facts, nor does it make the answer obvious, although it does frame the issue in a way that would be acceptable to both sides.

Many briefs to a trial court are so short or straightforward that the Questions Presented section is unnecessary. The section is necessary, however, in long or complex trial court briefs, which often contain multiple issues.

(9) Statement of Facts

The Statement of Facts in a brief, also known as Statement of the Case or simply Statement, is a descriptive account of the facts from your client's point of view. Although this statement cannot omit any damaging facts, you should write it to promote the court's understanding of and sympathy for your client's situation. Many lawyers and judges believe that the Statement of Facts, is the most important section of any brief.

(10) Summary of Argument

This section is a concise statement of your major conclusions and most important reasons supporting them. It conveys to a judge the essence of your argument and is particularly useful when a judge has not had time to read the entire brief before oral argument. For this reason, make sure that your summary is specific to the case under review and not merely a list of general legal principles. The Summary of Argument should be self-contained; the reader should not have to look elsewhere to understand the argument. Like the Conclusion in an office memorandum, the Summary of Argument should contain no citations to cases, or regulations unless the authority is well known or absolutely essential to the reader's understanding. Each major conclusion should be in a single paragraph. The briefs in Appendixes show examples of the Summary of Argument.

(11) Argument

The Argument is the foundation on which the rest of the brief is constructed. Like the Discussion in an office memorandum, it is the heart of the document. Although the Statement of facts and Summary of Argument are important, and sometimes decisive, your client generally wins or loses on the quality and substance of what you say in the Argument. An effective Argument in a brief is developed using the basic concepts of legal writing. The Argument should be clear and compelling; it should reflect a sound understanding and thoughtful analysis of the relevant law. Although the Argument is similar to the Discussion, it is different from the Discussion in two important ways.

First, this section of the brief should be an argument rather than an objective discussion of the law. You should state, in forceful and affirmative language, your strongest argument and issues first and present your client's position on each issue or sub-issue before you refute position of your opponent. These and other principles of advocacy presented in the Argument section will help you present your case more convincingly.

Second, the Argument should contain point headings. Point headings are conspicuous thesis statement that prefaces each logical segment of your Argument. Because they are capitalized, underlined, or formatted in a prominent way, point headings make it easier for the reader to understand the structure and content of your Argument. Point headings are always included in appellate briefs, but their use in trial court briefs is optional.

(12) Conclusion

This section describes what you want the court to do. It precisely state what relief you are requesting from the court — particularly if the relief you seek is more complicated than affirming or reversing the lower court's judgment. The request for relief is usually one sentence in length. In trial briefs with complex arguments, you may include brief summary of the argument supporting your conclusion. Immediately following, you should include the address, phone number, and signature of at least one of the attorneys who presented the brief. You should also include the date. The Conclusion section in an appellate brief should look like this:

For all the foregoing reasons, the judgment of the Ingham County Circuit Court should be reversed and the case remanded for a new trial.

Respectfully submitted,

_____

Charles McGrady
Attorney Appellants
Smith, Dunmore &Coffin
420 Brookshire Commons
Greensboro, N.C. 27402
(010) 423-0706

March 1, 2014

(13) Appendixes

This section contains the quoted statutes from the section of your brief called Constitutional Provisions, Statutes, Regulations, and Rules Involved. There can be a separate Appendix for each major category of statutes in the brief. There should also be an Appendix for any diagrams or charts you include. If you use more than one Appendix, give each a short descriptive title. Each of the sample briefs in Appendixes contains its own Appendix showing the relevant Statutes.

2. The Argument

Advocacy is the craft of persuasion. It is the means by which an attorney persuades a court to adopt one's client's position as its own. An effective advocate will show a court that deciding for one side would be logical and desirable, and that deciding for the other side would not. Courts in an adversary system depend on advocates to illuminate the strengths and weaknesses of competing positions. An advocate thus assists the court in deciding a case. Many times, the arguments, cases, and even the language of the winning brief will appear in the court's opinion. For better or worse, the skill and resources of counsel are often as important to a decision as the relevant law.

Coherence and credibility are essential to effective advocacy. The advocate's research must be complete, the analysis sound, and the conclusions sensible. Clear organization, thoughtful analysis, and a logical progression are essential. A writer who is not understandable is not effective.

Honest about the law and the facts is also essential to effective advocacy. A brief should rely on shading, emphasis, and overall strength of argument for its persuasive value, rather than on omission or distortion of the relevant law or misstatement of facts. The subtlety of this distinction in certain cases makes it no less important.

The Model Rules of Professional Conduct, which have been adopted in most jurisdictions, prohibit an attorney from knowingly making "a false statement of material fact or law to a tribunal." They also prohibit an attorney from knowingly failing "to disclose to the tribunal legal authority in the controlling jurisdiction known to the lawyer to be directly adverse to the position of the client and not disclosed by opposing counsel."

The Model Rules of Professional Conduct and the Federal Rules of Civil Procedure also establish a minimum standard for the kind of argument an attorney can make. The Model Rules state that a lawyer may not "bring or defend a proceeding or assert or controvert an issue therein, unless there is a basis for doing so that is not frivolous, which includes a good faith argument for an extension, modification or reversal of existing law." This ethical rule is reinforced by Rules 11 of the Federal Rules of Civil Procedure and parallel rules that exist in many states. Rule 11 is intended to ensure that briefs, motions, and other papers filed in count have a reasonable factual and legal basis. Under Rule 11, a lawyer implicitly certifies that a paper has a reasonable basis by filing or otherwise presenting it to a court. Rule 11(b) provides:

> By presenting to the court (whether by signing, filing, submitting, or later advocating) a pleading, written motion, or other paper, an attorney or unrepresented party is certifying that to be the best of the person's knowledge, information, and belief, formed after an inquiry reasonable under the circumstances,
>
> i. it is not being presented for any improper purpose, such as to harass or to cause unnecessary delay or needless increase in the cost of litigation;
>
> ii. the claims, defenses, and other legal contentions therein are warranted by existing law or by a no frivolous argument for the extension, modification, or reversal of existing law or the establishment of the new law;

iii. the allegations and other factual contentions have evidentiary support or, if specifically so identified, are likely to have evidentiary support after a reasonable opportunity for further investigation or discovery; and

iv. the denials of factual contentions are warranted on the evidence or, if specifically so identified, are reasonably based on a lack of information or belief.

Rule 11 allows a court to impose sanctions against lawyers who violate the rule. Formal sanctions include reasonable expenses incurred by the opposing party because of the filing of the paper and reasonable attorney fees. Informal sanctions include embarrassment as well as loss of your profession by clients and potential clients.

The importance of honesty to your professional future cannot be overstated. Federal Judge Lynn N. Hughes puts it plainly:

Honesty in fact and law determines not only the outcome of the cases but also your future as a lawyer. If you appear before me well prepared and if you present your case with integrity and class, I will forget you by dinner. But if you misrepresent your facts or law or if you try cute evasions, I will remember you after you have turned gray. Do not sell off your integrity for any client. No matter how smart you may be, if I cannot approach your presentation with trust, you are but half heard at best.

The Following principles will help you present the Argument forcefully, persuasively, and honestly.

(1) Present your strongest issues, sub-issues, and argument first.

When your client's case involves several independent issues, present the strongest issue first, followed by the next strongest issue, and the next, and conclude with the weakest. Similarly, when several arguments support your client's position on an issue or sub-issue, present them in descending order of strength. The "strongest" issues, sub-issues, or arguments are those most likely to persuade a judge to rule in favor of your client.

If you apply this principle, your brief will be more persuasive for several reasons. First, to capture the court's full attention, you must demonstrate that your client's legal position is impressive. The beginning of the Argument sets

Chapter 4
Writing Briefs

the tone for what follows. Because the strongest issues or arguments are necessarily the most compelling ones, beginning with them enhances your credibility. Second, the less persuasive issues and argument are more compelling when you use them to buttress stronger issues and arguments than when you present them strictly on their own merits. Conversely, stronger issues and arguments seem less compelling when you present them after weaker issues and arguments. Third, crowded dockets-even at the appellate level — often mean that a brief will not necessarily be read in its entirety by all the judges or clerks. If you present the strongest issues and arguments first, they are much more likely to be read.

A corollary to this guideline is this: Omit weak argument and issues. In prewriting and drafting briefs, think of as many arguments and issues as possible. Some of these arguments will be weak because there is scant authority to support them or because the rule in question has never been applied to the facts before the court. Sometimes, of course, you will have to include such argument in your brief because you have nothing stronger. When you do have stronger arguments, however, you should omit the weak ones because weak argument undermines your credibility and divert attention from more persuasive arguments.

If you have arguments of near strength, consider which arguments will have the strongest appeal to the court to which you are submitting your brief. If you are writing to an appellate court, look for examples in which the court has treated a similar issue or a case with similar policy considerations. If you are writing to a trial court, consider the court's function. It is bound by decisions of the appellate courts within its jurisdiction. As previously noted, a trial court is more likely to base a decision on settled law than on unsettled law. Thus, in most cases it would be the better strategy to base your first argument on settled law within the jurisdiction.

Consider the following situation:

> On November 5, Palula Jennings was elected to her first term as Justice of the Peace for Monroe County, a position that enabled her to perform civil weddings and hear small claims cases. Immediately after her election, she reversed her previous support

for a highly controversial court reform proposal — one that was an issue in many of election races, including hers. After she took office on January 2, a group of citizens circulated petitions for her recall. The petitions, filed with the appropriate county official on March 15, included a statement that the basis for the recall was her "opposition to the court reorganization plan."

Section 5 of the State Elections Act provides:

The petition or petitions, which shall clearly state the reason or reasons for the recall, shall not be filed against an officer until the officer has actually performed the duties of that office to which he or she has been elected for a period of six months during the current term of that officer.

After filling a suit to prevent Jennings's recall, her attorney filed a motion for summary judgment. Relying on section 5, he prepared two outlines of a brief in support of that motion:

ANSWER A: The petitions are invalid under the Elections Act because they do not meet the section 5 requirement of a clear statement of the reasons for recall. The statement on the petitions that Jennings opposes the court reorganization plan does not clearly inform voters whether it is her position, her change of position, or both, that motivates the recall.

The petitions are also invalid because, contrary to section 5, they were submitted before Jennings had been in office for six months, because the petitions were submitted on March 15, less than two-and-one-half months after Jennings took office on January 2, the six-month requirement was not fulfilled.

ANSWER B: The petitions are invalid under the Elections Act because, contrary to section 5, they were submitted before Jennings had been in office for six months. Because the petitions were submitted on March 15, less than two-and-a-half months after Jennings took office on January 2, the six-month requirement was not fulfilled.

The petitions are also invalid because they do not meet the section 5 requirement of a clear statement of the reasons for recall. The statement on the petitions that Jennings opposes the court reorganization plan does not clearly inform voters whether it is her position, her change of position, or both, that motivates the recall.

Answer B is better because the six-month argument is stronger than the clear-statement argument. The six-month argument addresses an unmistakable error; section 5 is explicit and leaves little doubt about what is required. The clear statement argument addresses a more debatable issue. In the absence of any relevant case law, "opposition to the court reorganization plan" may not be reasonably understood as a clear statement. Beginning with that argument, as Answer A does, is a less forceful way of presenting the case.

(2) When issues are equal in strength, present the most significant issues first.

The most significant issues are not necessarily the strongest ones. The most significant issues are those that, if resolve favorably, would help you client most. In a criminal case involving two equally strong issues, for example, you should first discuss the issue that would exonerate the defendant, and then discuss the issue that would merely win the defendant a new trial.

This principle is subordinate to the first principle because a strong but less significant argument is more persuasive than a weak but more significant argument. Likelihood of success should be your main consideration. Assume, for example, that a convicted pickpocket could raise two issues on appeal. He could argue with strong precedent that the judge erred in permitting him to be convicted solely on the basis of hearsay, and he could argue with tenuous support that the statute under which he was convicted was unconstitutionally vague. The hearsay issue should be presented first, even though it is less significant than the constitutional question, simply because it is more likely to succeed. If, however, the vagueness issue were at least as strong as the hearsay issue, it should be presented first. Winning on the vagueness issue would result in his release rather than just a new trial.

Presenting the most significant issues first is important for the same basic reasons as presenting the strongest issues first. If you present a serious issue first, the court is more likely to take the entire brief seriously than if you begin the brief with an issue concerning a technical violation of an obscure law. In addition, less significant issues seem more compelling when you use them to buttress important issues than when you use them to introduce an argument.

Consider again the Jennings example.

The petition drive against Paula Jennings garnered 7,850 signatures. In the last election, 32,000 people in Monroe County voted for a candidate for governor. The State Elections Act further provides:

Sec. 2 Every elective officer in the state expect a judicial officer is subject to recall by the voters of the electoral district in which the officer is elected.

Sec. 6 The petitions shall be signed by a number of qualified and registered voters equal to not less than 25% of the number of votes cast for candidates for the office of governor at the last preceding general election in the electoral district of the officer sought to be recalled. The person or organization sponsoring such recall shall have ten days to file additional signatures after any determination that petitions submitted contain an insufficient number of qualified and registered voters.

Jennings's attorney has prepared two outlines of a brief to the trial court concerning these sections:

ANSWER A: The petitions are invalid because they challenge an officer specifically exempted from recall by the Election Act. Election 2 expressly expects "a judicial officer" from the Act, a term that necessarily includes a justice of the peace performing such judicial activities as deciding small claims cases.

Even if there were no such exemption, the petitions would still be invalid because, contrary to section 6, they do not contain signatures equal to 25% of the votes for governor in Jennings's electoral district in the last election. Because the petitions have only 7,850 signatures and 32,000 people in the district voted for a candidate for governor in the last election, they are 150 signatures short of the section 6 requirement.

ANSWER B: The petitions are invalid because, contrary to section 6 of the Election Act, they do not contain signatures equal to 25% of the votes for governor in Jennings's district in the last election. Because the petitions have only 7,850 signatures and 32,000 people in the district voted for a candidate for governor in the district in the last election, they are 150 signatures short of the section 6 requirement.

Even if there are enough signatures, the petitions would still be invalid because they challenge an office specifically exempted from recall by the Elections Act. Section 2 expressly expects "a judicial officer" from the Act, a term that necessarily includes a justice of the peace performing such judicial activities as deciding small claims cases.

Chapter 4
Writing Briefs

Answer A is better because it places the issue of the substantive validity of the petitions before the issue of sufficient signature, even though both issues are very strong. A favorable decision on the exempt-officer issue would foreclose the recall effort altogether, but the sufficient signature issue may only delay the recall because section 6 allows ten days for the filling of additional signatures. Answer A emphasizes the more significant issue, and gives the less significant issue more strength by discussing it after and therefore in light of, the more significant issue. Answer B, by contrast, emphasizes the less significant issue and obscures the more significant issue.

Answer A also shows a more logical progression of thought than does Answer B. Answer A states, in effect, that the Election Act does not apply, and even if it does apply, the requirements of the Act were not met. Each issue is independent of the other. Answer B, on the other hand, illogically states that the requirements of the Elections Act were not met, and even if they were, the Act does not apply. Answer B assumes that Elections Act applies to this situation when discussing the first issue but not when discussing the second. Answer A is better because it arranges the issues both logically and in order of significance.

How should the argument and issues for sections 2, 5, and 6 of the Election Act be combined? Explain.

(3) Present your client's position on each issue or sub-issue before answering counterarguments.

This principle is a slight modification of the rule requiring you to state the reasons for a conclusion before responding to reasons against it. In a memo your conclusion may support your client or it may support your opponent. But in a brief, your Conclusion must not only convince the court to decide for your client, it must also convince the court to decide against your opponent. Your client's position should define the order and the tone of argument on any given issue or sub-issue. You can make that position much clearer by stating and justifying it before answering counterarguments. If you attack your opponent's argument before advancing your own, you face two potential problems. One, you risk not stating your position intelligibly, or worse yet, not having your main argument read at all. Two, you sound defensive and imply that your opponent's point of view is more interesting or important to the court.

If there are several argument opposing your client's position on an issue or sub-issue, present the strongest ones immediately after you have explained your client's position. Your opponent's counterarguments are likely to be the most interesting to the court, and you gain credibility by promptly confronting them.

Example: Lan LeVasseur was convicted of second degree murder on the basis of a voiceprint identification, because the victim had been operating a tape recorder just before the crime occurred. LeVasseur has appealed on the ground that voiceprint identification is inherently unreliable. Although courts in his state have not decided this issue, courts in two neighboring states with identical rules of evidence have decided the following cases:

> **State v. Decker (1963)**
> Alan Decker was convicted of Arson on the basis of a voiceprint identification from the recording of a wiretapped telephone conversation. The sole issue on appeal is the propriety of the trial judge's ruling that permitted the voiceprint to be admitted unless its scientific basis and reliability are generally recognized by competent authorities. Voiceprint analysis, however, is not so recognized; there is little literature on the subject and great disagreement among experts as to its accuracy. For that reason, we reverse and remand for a new trial.
>
> **State v. Manning (1973)**
> Margerita Manning was convicted of second-degree murder in connection with the bombing of an office building that led to the death of a secretary employed there. Some twelve minutes before the explosion, local police received a phone call warning that the building should be evacuated. That call was taped and was used in a subsequent voiceprint identification that formed the evidentiary basis for Manning's conviction.
>
> The record before this court indicates that voiceprint analysis is a widely accepted and scientifically accurate method of identification that has the support of many experts. Because its scientific basis and reliability are generally recognized, the trial judge committed no error in admitting the voiceprint identification into evidence.

The prosecutor's brief on appeal might be organized in either of the following ways:

ANSWER A: The voiceprint analysis was properly admitted into evidence. In this state, scientific tests are admissible when their reliability and scientific basis are generally recognized by competent authorities. *People v. Greene*. Although this state's courts have not addressed the admissibility of voiceprints under this rule, other state's courts have. In *State v. Decker*, the court held that a voiceprints analysis was improperly admitted because of the lack of scientific literature and disagreement among experts as to its accuracy was at an early stage of development. In the 1973 case of *State v. Manning*, however, the court held that a voiceprint was properly admitted into evidence, because by that time the reliability and scientific basis for voiceprint analysis were widely recognized by experts. Manning reflects significant developments in the field over ten years and underscores the correctness of the trial judge's ruling in this case.

ANSWER B: The voiceprint analysis was properly admitted into evidence. In this state, scientific tests are admissible when their reliability and scientific basis are generally recognized by competent authorities. *People v. Greene*. Although this state's courts have not addressed the admissibility of voiceprints under this rule, other state's courts have. In 1973 case, *State v. Manning*, the court held that the reliability and scientific basis for voiceprint analysis are recognized by experts and, hence, that voiceprint can be admitted into evidence. Manning reflects significant developments in this field and underscores the correctness of the trial judge's ruling in this case. Although a 1963 case, *State v. Decker*, held to the contrary, it was decided before voiceprint analysis had become a widely accepted and scientifically reliable identification technique.

Answer B is preferable because it describes the favorable case before it responds to the unfavorable case, rather than other way around. Answer B states that voiceprint analysis is widely accepted and was thus proper in this case, and then distinguishes Decker as out of date. This response to Decker is consistent with the prior analysis of Manning, and is persuasive in that context. Answer A is less clear because the older case is distinguished before the affirmative argument is even stated. Even when Manning is discussed, the analysis is not as sharply focused as it is in Answer B. In addition, Answer A is defensive, and gives greater weight to the counterargument.

(4) Use forceful and affirmative language.

Word choice is as important as structure in an argument. Words can make an argument seem confident or defensive, bold or halting, credible or dubious. They can also make a position seem conservative or radical. Words cannot be submitted for a good argument, but they can greatly enhance it. The lawyer whose arguments are stated with authority and confidence is the most convincing to a court. The following guidelines are illustrative.

A. Present argument from your client's point of view. The tone of your argument should be positive rather than negative or defensive. Thus, you should frame both your arguments and your rebuttal of counterarguments in terms of why your client should win rather than why the opponent should lose. By presenting arguments from your client's point of view, you show control over the issues and write a more persuasive brief.

Example: The plaintiffs brought an action under the federal Noise Control Act 1972, alleging section 1337 of the Judicial Code as the sole basis of jurisdiction. The defendant has filed a motion to dismiss on the ground that the plaintiffs did not allege an amount in controversy of $50,000 or more. The plaintiffs' argument to the federal district court might be stated in either of the following ways:

ANSWER A: The defendant incorrectly contends that the plaintiffs' failure to allege $50,000 as an amount in controversy deprives the court of jurisdiction. Section 1337 of the Judicial Code provides original jurisdiction to the federal courts of "any civil action or proceeding arising under any Act of Congress regulating commerce," but it does not require an allegation of amount in controversy. Because the federal Noise Control Act, under which the plaintiffs brought this action, is a congressional regulation of commerce, the defendant's contention is untrue. Section 1332 requires an allegation of an amount in controversy for federal jurisdiction, but the plaintiffs do not rely on section 1332.

ANSWER B: This Court has jurisdiction to hear this case. Section 1337 of the Judicial Code provides original jurisdiction to the federal courts of "any civil action or proceeding arising under any Act of Congress regulating commerce," but it does not require an allegation of an amount in controversy. The plaintiffs have alleged jurisdiction

Chapter 4
Writing Briefs

> under the federal Noise Control Act, a congressional regulation of commerce. The defendant's claim that an amount in controversy was not alleged is thus irrelevant. Because the plaintiffs do not rely on section 1332, which requires an allegation of amount in controversy for federal jurisdiction, this Court has jurisdiction.

Both answers cover the same ground, but they convey different messages. Answer B says the plaintiffs have jurisdiction; Answer A says the defendant's claim is unsure, but it never clearly says the federal district court has jurisdiction. Answer B is better because it is more positive and lucid. Answer B turns the defendant's denial of jurisdiction into an affirmative argument that the court has jurisdiction. It demonstrates control over the direction and the tone of the argument. Answer A, which is dominated by the defendant's viewpoint, does not.

B. Present the law from your client's point of view. Balanced descriptions of the law belong in office memos but not in legal briefs. The law should be characterized to favor, and be consistent with, the client's position. The legal rules and principles, of course, determine what arguments can be made. But they should also be an integral part of the law to the facts. The description of the law would otherwise disrupt the flow and direction of the Argument.

Example: Consider this illustration.

Mary Elston brought an action against Juan Guerrero, the driver of a car that struck her van from the rear, causing Elston a serious back injury. At trial, Guerrero's attorney attempted to introduce evidence to show that Elston's van had seat belts and that most, if not all, of Elston's injuries could have been avoided had she been wearing a seat belt. The trial judge refused to admit that evidence. The state's appellate courts have not addressed this question. The case was tried under the state's comparative negligence rule, and Guerrero's attorney was attempting to mitigate damages. The jury returned a verdict for Elston and awarded $225,000 in damages. On appeal, Guerrero's attorney might characterize the relevant law from other states in two ways:

ANSWER A: When seat belts are available to the plaintiffs in an auto negligence action and the plaintiff's failure to use them caused or contributed to their injuries, the defendant in some states is entitled to have damage award reduced accordingly. E. g., *Bentaler v. Braun*. This rule is based on the reasonable view that the use of seat belts reduces serious injuries and fatalities from automobile accidents and that those riding in bars should know of this additional safety factor. *Braun*. Cases to the contrary are based on the questionable premises that the duty to fasten seat belts arises only if the plaintiff anticipates the accident, that not all vehicles have seat belts, and that not all people use them. E. g., *Kopischke v. First Continental Corp*. When seat belts are available, though, it is manifestly unfair to penalize a defendant for the plaintiff's failure to exercise a simple precaution that is surely in the plaintiff's best interest.

ANSWER B: The courts of other states are divided on whether a defendant in an auto negligence action is entitled to have the damage award reduced when seat belts available to the plaintiffs and the plaintiff's failure to use them caused contributed to her injuries. Most courts, however, deny mitigation. A minority of the courts have held that the use of seat belts reduces serious injuries from auto accidents, and that those riding in cars should know of this additional safety factor. E. g., *Bentzler v. Braun*. The majority of cases are premised on the view that the duty to fasten seat belts arises only if the plaintiffs anticipates the accident, that not all vehicles have seat belts, and that not all people use them. E. g., *Kopischke v. First Continental Corp*. The issue is which party should bear the cost of the plaintiff's failure to use seat belts. Braun probably represents the better reasoned view because the use of seat belts reduces injuries.

Answer A is better because it is confident, forceful and presents the law in the light most favorable to Guerrero. Answer B, by contrast, is passive and balanced in tone. The writer does not sound convinced and thus is not convincing. Answer A show the courts how to decide in Guerrero's favor; it states the position favoring mitigation, presents that position as if it were clearly better, and encourage the courts to select Braun as preferable policy. Unlike Answer B, it deemphasizes the division of the courts and the minority position of the Braun case by merely implying these facts. Answer A, in short, describes the law in a way that advances the Argument.

C. Make your client's position seems objective. Because courts generally do not like to innovate, your client's position should appear to reflect the existing law even when a decision in your client's favor would break new legal ground, you must make it seem that a favorable decision is required by law, justice, and common sense. Whenever possible, avoid wordy references to your client's position, suggestions that your client's position is merely an interpretation of the law, and explicit indications that it diverges from the law. Conversely, you should characterize the opposition's case as distant from the existing law or as were interpretation. You should, however, avoid a sarcastic or insulting tone.

Consider the following:

A complaint filed with the State Bar Association charged Leon Gibbon, an attorney, with depositing in his personal checking account the funds of several estates for which he was doing probate work and converting $147,000 of these funds to his personal use. A hearing panel of the State Bar Association agreed with the complaint after an evidentiary hearing and voted to suspend Gibbon from the practice of law for five years. Gibbon appealed to the Stated Bar Grievance Board, which affirmed the panel's findings and increased the suspension to lifetime disbarment. Gibbon appealed the Board's disbarment decision to the state's highest appellate court. The State Bar Association's attorney might characterize its position on appeal in either of these ways.

ANSWER A: The State Bar Association interprets the State Bar Grievance Rules to provide the Grievance Broad with discretionary authority to increase a five-year suspension to disbarment. The State Bar Association agrees with the Grievance Broad's conclusion, after reviewing the detailed records, that "the uncontradicted evidence of serious violations of the State Rules of Professional Conduct warrants disbarment." The Board's failure to make a detailed statement of the reasons for disbarment is therefore irrelevant, not withstanding the obvious importance of this matter to Gibbon.

ANSWER B: The State Bar Grievance Broad has discretionary authority to increase a five-year suspension to disbarment. After reviewing the detailed record, the Board concluded that "the uncontradicted evidence of serious violations of the state Rules of Professional Conduct warrants disbarment." In light of that conclusion, a more detailed statement of reasons would serve no useful purpose.

Answer A emphasizes the State Bar Association's position, but Answer B emphasizes the correctness of the Grievance Broad's decision. Answer B is better because it sounds more objective than Answer A. Answer A is also verbose and less forceful because it begins with "The State Bar Association interprets..." Finally, it suggests more weakness in the State Bar Association's position than necessary ("Board's failure" "obvious importance of this matter to gibbon" and "interprets the...Rules"). The difference between the two answers is one of emphasis; the skillful use of emphasis makes a more persuasive argument.

(5) Fully argue your client's position.

Because the brief is a statement of reasons for adopting a certain position, these reasons should be stated as completely as possible. The principle requiring an explicit statement of all the analytical steps needed to reach a conclusion takes on a new dimension in advocacy. Here are two guidelines.

A. Make effective use of the facts. As Statement of Facts for a Brief shows in more detail, the fact is the essential of legal reasoning, but the facts may also be used to gain empathy for the client. By marshaling and emphasizing the appropriate facts, you can often overcome a weak legal position and make a court see the desired outcome as compelling. Similarly, you can minimize the strength of your opponent's position by de-emphasizing damaging facts — explaining them, summarizing them, or describing them blandly. Always use the facts to your client's advantage — in briefs to both trial and appellate courts.

Edgar Brown was convinced of first degree murder. Defense counsel has two drafts of the brief on appeal:

ANSWER A: The trial judge erred by not charging the jury with the lesser included offense of voluntary manslaughter. A defendant is entitled to a jury charge for manslaughter whenever there are enough facts to convince a reasonable person that the homicide was committed under the influence of an irresistible passion caused by an insult or provocation sufficient to excite a reasonable person. *People v. Valentine.* The defendant in that case was convinced of first degree murder for killing a man who repeatedly insulted the defendant during a quarrel by calling him a window peeper and a liar, among other things. The court held that these facts would justify a verdict of voluntary manslaughter and that the trial court erred by giving jury instructions that precluded convinced for that crime.

Brown's case is similar to Valentine because the record shows that Brown committed the homicide after being taunted about a sensitive personal matter. Brown described the decedent as "my best friend from army days," even though the decedent had broken Brown's nose in a fight the previous year. Brown was depressed and unemployed and the killing occurred during a weekly poker game after the decedent called him a "welfare bum" and a "loser." Any reasonable person in Brown's position would have been similar provoked.

ANSWER B: The trial judge erred by not charging the jury with the lesser included offense of voluntary manslaughter. A defendant is entitled to a jury charge for manslaughter whenever there are enough facts to convince a reasonable person that the homicide was committed under the influence of an irresistible passion caused by an insult or provocation sufficient to excite a reasonable person. *People v. Valentine*. The defendant in that case was convinced of first degree murder for killing a man who repeatedly insulted the defendant during a quarrel by calling him a window peeper and a liar, among other things. The court held that these facts would justify a verdict of voluntary manslaughter and that the trial court erred by giving jury instructions that precluded convinced for that crime.

Brown's case is similar to Valentine because the record shows that Brown committed the homicide after being taunted about a sensitive personal matter. Brown was extremely depressed after his layoff from an auto plant, where he had worked for seventeen years. He had been unable to find other work because of the local high unemployment rate. Both he and his wife testified that he had trouble concentrating after ha was laid off, that he frequently forgot things, and that their marriage was strained. The homicide was committed during a weekly poker game with friends. Like the decedent in Valentine who repeatedly insulted the defendant, the decedent in this case, Brown's "best friend from army days," begin to taunt Brown about being a "loser," a "welfare bum," and a "social parasite." Although Brown and the decedent had engaged in a brief fistfight a year earlier, several persons, including the decedent's wife, testified they had long since made up. After the decedent ignored repeated warnings to quit, Brown suddenly lunged at him with a paring knife used to make sandwiches. Brown later could remember nothing of the homicide expect experiencing blind rage. A reasonable person on Brown's position would have been similarly provoked.

Answer B is better because its invalid detail forces the court to see the issue from Brown's viewpoint. The additional facts not only pace the incident within the manslaughter rule but they also paint a sympathetic portrait of a harassed man pushed to the breaking point. The facts are set out in chronological order, showing Brown's growing frustration and unhappiness. Answer A's analysis of the facts, by contrast, is poorly organized, omits important facts, and does not describe precisely what happened. Answer A mentions the fistfight in a damaging way, while Answer B carefully excuses and blends this point into the argument. Answer A is unpersuasive because it does not provide insight or foster empathy for Brown's situation. To be an effective advocate, you must learn to recognize the most valuable facts and weave them strategically into your legal argument.

B. Make effective use of legal policies. In writing briefs, relationship between rules and policies is important. Policies define the reason for the legal rules in question. The result you advocate must be significant from a policy standpoint; technical of the law, therefore, are usually not enough. Policy arguments are also important when the legal rules or the facts do not provide you with a strong position, particularly at the appellate level. As discussed in Chapter 4 and 5 (Briefs to a Trial Court and Briefs to an Appellate Court), policy argument are generally more important in appellate briefs than in briefs to trial courts.

Example: Section 8 of the Township Rural Zoning Act requires a public referendum on the "adopting of a zoning ordinance" when 8% of the registed voters in the township sign petitions requesting a referendum. Seymour Township adopted its zoning ordinance in 1962. Several weeks ago, the Township Broad rezoned an eighty-acre tract from agriculture to residential. Township residents gathered sufficient signatures to request a referendum, but a trial court ruled that section 8 applied to the initial decision to zone, not to subsequent zoning amendments. The citizens' brief to the court of appeals could be summarized in the following ways:

> ANSWER A: Section 8 of the Township Rural Zoning Act requires the requested referendum. Section 8 applies to the "adoption of a zoning ordinance," a term that includes not only the initial decision to the zone but also subsequent amendments. Because such amendments obviously become part of the ordinance, they should be treated in the same manner.
>
> ANSWER B: Section 8 of the Township Rural Zoning Act requires the requested referendum. Section 8 applies to the "adoption of a zoning ordinance," a term that includes not only the initial decision to the zone but also subsequent amendments. Because such amendments obviously become part of the ordinance, they should be treated in the same manner.
>
> This conclusion is important to the underlying purpose of section 8 — ensuring that the ordinance is acceptable to majority of those living in the township. Because zoning amendments might make the ordinance unacceptable to those citizens, the referendum requirement should apply equally to zoning amendments and the original ordinance. Zoning amendments, moreover, significantly affect the quality of life of township residents by prescribing the existence, location, and density of new developments. The public ought to be able to vote on these important decisions. Finally, because the right to vote is a fundamental one, any perceived ambiguities about the scope of legislative grant ought to be resolved in favor of that fundamental right.

Answer B's completeness makes it far more compelling than Answer A. Answer A is merely an argument about the meaning of the language in the section 8, an argument that sounds uninspired and lame because it does not make effective use of the underlying policies. Answer B reaches the same conclusion, but it relies far more on the underlying policy of majority approval for zoning decisions than in the meaning of the words. It states that the legislative intent requires that section 8 be applied to zoning amendments, regardless of the ambiguous language of the law.

3. Tactical Consideration for Writing Appellate Briefs

Once the trial court enters a judgment, whether it is a judgment of dismissal, summary judgment, or judgment on the merits after a trial, the case is finished unless the losing party appeals. To appeal a case, the losing party (the appellant) must allege that the trial court committed a specific reversible error. For example, the appellant may assert that the trial court erred by failing to admit certain evidence, by misinterpreting or failing to follow a rule of procedure, by not applying the proper legal rule, by incorrectly interpreting the rule, or by failing to follow a rule of procedure, by failing to properly instruct the jury. If there is conflicting evidence at trial, the appellant my also challenge the trial court's findings of fact — the determination of which version of the facts is correct. Appeals challenging factual findings, however, are rarely successful.

Generally, a party may appeal only from a final judgment. The final judgment rule is designed to prevent piecemeal appeals until a matter has finally been resolved by the trial court. Sometimes, however, and under very limited circumstances, appeals are permitted from orders entered by the trial court prior to the entry of final judgment. These are known as interlocutory appeals. In federal courts some interlocutory appeals are brought as of right, but most are heard only if the trial court, in its discretion, certifies the order for interlocutory appeal and the appellate court, in its discretion, decides to hear the appeal. Rules governing interlocutory appeals in state courts vary significantly. State rules of appellate procedure should always be consulted.

Losing litigants have a right of appeal from final judgments to an intermediate appellate court in the federal system and in most state instances and some states to appeal to the highest state court or, in the federal system, to the United States Supreme Court. In the overwhelming majority of appeals, however, the highest court has discretion whether to hear the case. If the court declines to hear the case, the decision of the intermediate appellate court is final.

A losing litigant appeals by filling a notice of appeal in the appellate courts having jurisdiction over the matter. Each party then submits briefs to the appellate court explaining why the trial court did or did not commit reversible error. Appellate briefs are subject to extensive rules concerning content, length, and style. Each appellate court requires litigants to follow its rules. Appellate briefs also lead to be longer and more formal than briefs to trial courts. The roles for style and advocate however remain the same. Several tactical considerations should be kept in mind when preparing appellate briefs.

Chapter 4
Writing Briefs

(1) Focus on the claimed errors of the lower court.

An unsuccessful litigant cannot appeal simply because he does not like the trial court's decision. Nor can he prevail on appeal simply by demonstrating that the trial court has made a mistake. An appellant must convince the appellate court that the trial court erred and that the error adversely affected the outcome. The appellee, on the other hand, must attempt to persuade the appellate court that the trial court ruled correctly on all points claimed to be error and that, even if any rulings were harmless because they did not affect the outcome of the trial.

Because an appellate court is interested only in correcting mistake made by the trial court you should frame your argument in terms of the error you claim the trial court made or on the error your opponent alleges. The appellate court from the outset must fully appreciate the nature of the error and the procedural context in which it occurred.

Consider this principle in the context of the *Miller v. Arson Industries* case. You were unsuccessful in obtaining summary judgment in Chisolm's favor. The trial judge denied Chisolm's motion with the following opinion and order:

Third party defendant Chisolm has filed a motion for summary judgment with this Court requesting an order of dismissal based on the settlement-bar rule. Chisolm relying on the decisions in *Sarasota Pools v. Buccaneer Resorts* and *Sunshine Health Care, Inc, v. Rollins*, contends that he is entitled to be dismissed because he settled with Miller, the plaintiff in this case.

The Court disagree Sarasota is a very different case and not controlling. In Sarasota, the plaintiff settled with one tortfeasor, Buccaneer Resorts, and then litigated against the other, Sarasota Polls, obtaining a judgment. Sarasota afterward brought suit against Buccaneer for contribution. The court concluded that the settlement-bar rule should apply and affirmed the lower court's dismissal of the suit.

The decision in *Raseen v. Hurrison construction Co.*, relied on by Arson Industries, is more instructive. The court there refused to dismiss for two reasons. The first was that the trial had already commenced when the settlement with one tortfeasor occurred and that tortfeasor sought dismissal. Although the court attempted to distinguish Sarasota for the second reason — that Raseen did not involve personal injury — the read distinction is in the timing.

That brings us to Chisolm's case. Suit is now opening between Miller and Arson. The case appears unlikely to be settled Granting Chisolm's motion will not conserve judicial resources or encourage settlements. This court is not convinced that the rule even persuaded Chisolm to settle. The present case therefore is not the same as the wholly independent second trial sought by the non-settling tortfeasor in Sarasota. It is more like the situation in Raseen. It is therefore ordered that third-party defendant Chisolm's motion for summary judgment is hereby denied.

The trial judge subsequently certified his order for an immediate interlocutory appeal, and the court of appeals accepted the appeal. You are handing the appeal.

Consider the following:

ANSWER A: The trial court should have dismissed Arson's third-party complaint. In *Sarasota Pools v. Buccaneer Resorts*, the West Florida Supreme Court held that a settling tortfeasor is not liable to a non-setting tortfeasor in contribution. The Sarasota case is controlling here.

ANSWER B: The trial court erred in denying Chisolm's motion for summary judgment. The West Florida Supreme Court held in *Sarasota Pools v. Buccaneer Resorts* that a setting tortfeasor is not liable in contribution to a non-settling tortfeasor. The Sarasota case is controlling, and the court's failure to follow the clear mandate of the Supreme Court is reversible error.

Answer B is better. Answer B clearly focuses the appellate court on the mistake made by the trial court that Chisolm claims is reversible error. Answer B also correctly describes the procedural setting of the trial court's decision and thus provides a framework for the remainder of the argument.

Answer A has a thesis sentence and properly states the law, but it does not do so in terms of the alleged trial court error. Answer A is too abstract and thus lacks the persuasiveness of Answer B.

(2) Base your argument on the appropriate standard of review.

Appellate courts exercise different standards of review, depending on the nature of the case and the case's procedural posture when the trial court's decision was issued. The standard of review determines the latitude afforded to the appellate court to substitute its judgment for that of the trial court. Generally, appellate courts exercise plenary review, which is a *de novo* review, of all legal conclusions. This means they are free to substitute their judgment for that of the trial court on legal conclusions without giving any deference to the trial court's decision or reasoning. Appellate courts, however, are usually limited to a clearly erroneous of similarly restricted standard for review of the trial court's finding of fact. This restricted standard of review is a reflection of great deference given to trial judges, who observe the witness first hand, in determining credibility when conflicting versions of the same event are introduced into evidence. In jury trials, it is also a reflection of the jury's role as the finder of fact.

Appellate courts generally exercise *de novo* review of summary judgments and dismissals granted on the pleading. The standard of review for such decisions varies from state to state, however, and you should always check the law in your jurisdiction to determine the appropriate standard of review.

Always frame your argument to an appellate court in terms of the appellate standard of review. You should state the standard of review at the beginning of the brief and, if it furthers your argument, periodically remind the court of the appropriate standard. The rules of many appellate courts require a statement of the applicable standard of review to be included in the opening sections of the brief. Even when such a statement is not required, always draft your main arguments with the applicable standard of review in mind.

Consider the following examples:

> ANSWER A: The court erred in denying Chisolm's motion for summary judgment. The scope of review of a grant or denial of summary judgment is de novo. This court therefore is not bound by the trial court's conclusions.
>
> [Sections of argument omitted]
>
> The trial court incorrectly concluded that applying the settlement-bar rule in this

case would not conserve judicial resources or encourage settlement. To the contrary, Chisolm's dismissal from the case would constitute a significant savings of judicial energy. If Chisolm's action is not dismissed, the court must consider issues of Chisolm's negligence in order to apportion the liability between Chisolm and Arson. The issue of Chisolm's negligence will inevitably extend the trial and consume greater resources than if it were not in question. Moreover, enforcement of the settlement-bar rule may encourage Arson to settle, because Arson will know that if it loses, it must bear full responsibility for the plaintiff's damages without resource against Chisolm. In any event, the policy is to encourage settlements in the first instance. Chisolm was encouraged to settle in the first instance on the better that he would have no further liability. This Court is free to and should reject the trial court's erroneous conclusions to the contrary.

ANSWER B: The court erred in denying Chisolm's motion for summary judgment.

[Sections of argument omitted]

The trial court was wrong in concluding that no judicial savings would accrue by applying the settlement-bar rule. Judicial economy would be served by trying only the issue of whether Arson was negligent and the percentage of fault each should bear for Miller's damages. The court was also wrong in concluding that application of the settlement-bar rule would not encourage settlements. The court's focus is too narrow. Enforcement of the policy encourages settlements generally even if it does not encourage Arson to settle in the present case. Chisolm certainly was encouraged to settle based on the belief that he would have no further liability.

Answer A is better. Answer A states the standard of review at the outset and again during the argument when the trial court's finding are discussed. Answer A thus reminds the appellate court that it is considering a denial of a motion for summary judgment and that it may therefore freely substitute its judgment for that of the trial court.

Answer B, on the other hand, does not remind the court that its scope of review is *de novo*. Even though appellate judges are presumed to know the scope of review, the failure to expressly remind the court of its scope of review risks the appellate court's inadvertently or subconsciously giving undue weight to the trial court's conclusions.

Chapter 4
Writing Briefs

(3) Emphasize that a decision in your client's favor would further the policies underlying the law.

An argument that incorporates policy is stronger than one based solely on the law. Appellate briefs should contain a more extensive discussion of policy than trial court briefs. Appellate courts are responsible for providing guidance to the trial courts and for determining the direction of the law within their jurisdictions. Appellate judges, therefore, are very interested in understanding the policies supporting the applicable legal rules and determining whether those policies would be served by applying the rules to the case before them. This is especially true of the highest appellate court in a jurisdiction. A good appellate brief should clearly articulate the policies underlying the key legal rules and demonstrate how a decision in your client's favor would or would not further those policies.

Considering the following:

ANSWER A: The trial court erred in denying Chisolm's motion for summary judgment. In *Sarasota Pools v. Buccaneer Resorts*, the West Florida Supreme Court adopted the settlement-bar rule, which precludes any action for contribution by or against a setting tortfeasor. Sarasota is controlling. In that case, the injured party settled with the resort. She afterward filed suit against the non-settling pool contractor and obtained a judgment. The pool contractor then commenced an action for contribution against the resort. The court held that the settlement-bar rule precluded such a suit. The court reasoned that the policy of encouraging settlements and providing parties who settle with the benefit of their bargain would be further limited by such a ruling. Other decisions are in accord, e.g. *Sunshine Health Care, Inc. v. Rollins*.

The facts of the present case are virtually identical. Chisolm settled with the plaintiff shortly after the incident. The plaintiff then sued Arson, and Arson brought this claim against Chisolm. The settlement-bar rule should preclude Arson's suit just as it did the claim in Sarasota Pools. The policy articulated in Sarasota Pools of encouraging settlements would be served by such a ruling.

ANSWER B: The trial court erred in denying Chisolm's motion for summary judgment. In *Sarasota Pools v. Buccaneer Resorts*, the West Florida Supreme Court adopted the settlement-bar rule, which precludes any action for contribution by or against a setting tortfeasor. Sarasota is controlling. In that case, the injured party settled with the resorts and filed suit against the non-settling pool contractor, obtaining a judgment. The pool contractor then commenced an action for contribution against the resort. The court held that the settlement-bar rule precluded such a suit. Other decisions are in accord, e.g. *Sunshine Health Care, Inc. v. Rollins*.

The court in Sarasota articulated several policies fostered by the settlement-bar rule. The court stated that the rule was much easier to enforce and much fairer than the alternatives. The court further observed that the rule provided more predictability, allowing the parties to know the consequences of their conduct in advance. The court also said that the settlement-bar rule had the salutary effect of encouraging settlements and providing much-needed relief for the congestion in our court system. Legal commentators have agreed. In her article, *the Settlement Bar Rule: Tough Choices, Tough Answers*, 89 Tallahassee L. Rev. 135 (1993), Elizabeth B. Burns pointed to the rule's tendency to encourages settlements as its single most beneficial policy.

The facts of the present case are virtually identical to those in Sarasota. Chisolm settled with the plaintiff shortly after the incident. The plaintiff then sued Arson, and Arson brought this claim against Chisolm. The settlement-bar rule should preclude Arson's suit just as it did the claim against Sarasota Pools.

The policies underlying the settlement-bar rule would be well served by its application to this case. Chisolm would not have settled but for the belief that doing so would end his liability. The trial court's conclusion that the rule did not encourage Chisolm's settlement is simply wrong. This Court exercises plenary review in this manner and should disregard the trial court's erroneous determination. Moreover, to look at the current situation and determine whether the policy of encouraging settlement would be served is myopic. The proper question is whether the settlement-bar rule encourages settlements generally, not whether the rule should be disregarded after one tortfeasor settles if the remaining tortfeasors refuse to settle. The policy of conserving judicial resources would also be served by applying the settlement-bar rule to this case. The difficult issue of apportionment of fault between Arson and Chisolm would be removed from the case, leaving for trial only the issue of Arson's negligence.

Answer B is better. It effectively explains the key policies underlying the rule and demonstrates that the Supreme Court and a legal commentator have recognized the rule. Answer B then demonstrates how application of the rule to Chisolm's case would further the policies underlying the rule. It fleshes out the bare legal rules, making the argument much more compelling and significant to an appellate judge.

Answer A should look familiar to you. It is similar to the better answer under the third principle in Chapter 4 (Briefs to a Trial Court). The answer is good for a trial brief but deficient for an appellate brief because it includes no extended discussion of policy. While Answer A correctly states the rules of law and mentions the supporting policy, it does not explain the underlying policy considerations and demonstrate how they would be served by applying the settlement-bar rule.

(4) Explain how decision in your client's favor would foster harmony or consistency in the law.

Appellate courts are concerned with the orderly development of the law. They want to ensure not only that the policies supporting the rules are being served but also that their decision will not create disharmony in the law or set bad precedent. You must therefore strive to convince the appellate court that a decision in your client's favor is consistent with previous decisions and that it would foster, rather than discourage, a rational development of the law.

Considering the following:

ANSWER A: The West Floroda Supreme Court's decision in *Sarasota Pools v. Buccaneer Resorts* is controlling.

[Argument on law and policy]

The trial court's decision therefore should be reversed. Its decision is contrary to Sarasota and Rollins. For the reasons given, Raseen was incorrectly decided and should be disregarded.

ANSWER B: The West Floroda Supreme Court's decision in *Sarasota Pools v. Buccaneer Resorts* is controlling.

[Argument on law and policy]

A decision reversing the trial court would therefore be in complete accord with Sarasota and Rollins. To the extent that Raseen was correctly decided, it is not to the contrary. The trial in Raseen had already commenced when the settlement was reached. The public policies of encouraging settlements and conserving judicial resources would not have been furthered by application of the settlement-bar in that case.

Answer B is preferable because it clearly articulates how a decision in Chisolm's favor would be consistent with the uniformity or harmony in this area of the law. Even the troublesome Raseen decision is harmonized. Answer A is little more than a summary. It fails to demonstrate how a decision in Chisolm's favor would contribute to the orderly development of the law. It does not attempt to harmonize the Raseen decision, leaving the court with two divergent lines of authority from which to choose. Answer A therefore is less persuasive than Answer B.

4. Checklist for Drafting an Appellate Brief

(The following guidelines explain why the YMCA Model Supreme Court brief is written in the style shown in the sample.)

Briefs will be submitted in the following format.

(1) Typewritten or word processed on white 8-1/2 x 11 inch paper.

(2) 1.5 or double spacing between lines is generally used, as demonstrated in the sample.

(3) Typeface must be a legible font such as Courier or Times, generally 10 to 12 point size on a word processor, or pica type (10 characters per inch) on a typewriter. Excessively small or large fonts are difficult to read.

(4) One inch (1″) margins should be used.

(5) Uncopyable or illegible briefs will be returned for correction.

(6) Briefs shall not exceed ten (10) pages, excluding the title page and table of contents, but including all other elements. (note: It is doubtful that a quality brief can be developed in fewer than 6 pages.)

(7) All pages except the title page and contents shall be numbered, the page after the Table of Contents being page 1.

(8) To facilitate copying, original briefs must not be bound by more than one staple in the upper left hand corner.

(9) Signatures of both team members must appear at the end of the document in the location indicated in the sample.

Content

Briefs must contain the following elements in the order listed.

(1) Title Page: The title page shall be in the form shown in the sample brief that follows this section. It contains:

Chapter 4
Writing Briefs

- The words IN THE YMCA MODEL SUPREME COURT OF THE STATE OF NEW MEXICO.
- The Case number (or numbers). Case number(s) will be noted in the case packet.
- The name of the appellant and the respondent as stated in the case.
- Identification of the brief as being that of the Appellant or the Respondent.
- Court from which the case originated.
- Notation that an Oral Argument is requested.
- Name and address (either home or school is acceptable) of Attorneys appearing before the court. (In this case, list the members of the team. In a real brief, the opposing council is known in advance and their names are also included, something not possible in the Model Supreme Court.)

(2) Table of Contents: The table of contents in the Model Supreme Court is a separate, single page that lists each element of the brief (excluding itself and the title page) and the page on which each element begins. Because the Argument is the most complex part of the brief, the headings and subheadings used within the argument section should also be listed in the contents with the corresponding page number. Usually this is done in outline form as shown in the Sample Brief.

(3) Table of Authorities: The table of authorities in the Model Supreme Court is a list, no more than one page long, of all materials used to support the argument. It includes every page in the brief where the particular excerpt is found. It is similar to the bibliography of a term paper, except that the citation format is different, and cases are usually grouped by type: state statute, case law, Constitutional provisions and other materials.

This list not only verifies the sources used by the attorney, but is useful for the Court and for other attorneys to quickly determine what cases, statutes or other materials are being cited, and to easily locate these references in the original research materials used in preparing the case. Correct citation format shall be used as described later in this manual.

Note: participants are not to cite any additional material in their cases other than what is included in the case packet. This is not to say that students aren't allowed to pursue additional resources such as dictionaries of legal terms, guidebooks on brief writing, or manuals on the preparation of oral arguments. But they cannot cite or refer to any source as authority for their briefs or oral arguments other than the resources provided. Factual statements or arguments of law must be able to be backed up by the resources in the case packet.

(4) Statement of the Issues: This is a very short introductory statement of the legal issues or points of law involved in the case. It tells the Justices precisely what legal issues the attorney team wants the Court to decide. These statements should be phrased to help one argue FOR a particular conclusion rather than simply against the other side. In the Model Supreme Court cases, there will be two primary legal issues (generally, each member of the team will take one issue to research and prepare an argument).

These issues are stated in question form and should be phrased in such a way that a "yes" answer will support one's position. These statements are very short, generally no more that one sentence per issue, and are generally placed just before the Statement of the Facts.

For Example,

The appellant may phrase an issue this way:

"Did the trial court err in holding that...?"

The respondent may phrase the issue in the same case this way:

"Did the trial court correctly conclude that...?"

(5) Statement of the Facts: The Statement of the Facts is a retelling of the facts from the client's point of view. However, the facts provided in Model Supreme Court Cases are not to be added to nor disputed. For a Model Supreme Court brief, this section should be about one page long, and not more then two pages.

Attorneys explain the situation in a way that helps their client. This is a very important part of the brief that sets the stage for the argument, and should be presented both to help the court understand the case and show the client in the best possible light. But, remember not to assume facts not given, and do not distort, change, or add to the facts!

For example, here is how parties in a real Supreme Court appeal used the Statement of Facts in different ways to support their positions.

Chapter 4
Writing Briefs

The Appellant/Defendant's brief began this way: "[John Doe] was a mentally ill nineteen year old when he participated in a robbery with a juvenile female..."

The Respondent/Plaintiff's brief began: "Since [John Doe] pleaded guilty..."

(6) Argument: This is the core of the brief. Students may find the argument to be somewhat like writing a persuasive essay with lots of research references. It presents support for the issues presented earlier. Solid research is used to back every part of the argument. Arguments must be well-organized and convincing; attorneys will win or lose their case based on the quality and substance of what is said.

Each point the team wants the court to consider in deciding the case must be described, and the reasons explained with appropriate references to research materials used, and text citations inserted as frequently as needed. Citation format examples appear later in this manual.

In the Model Supreme Court, arguments for each of the two issues should be at least one, but no more than three pages each. The total argument section should not exceed six (6) pages. Attorney teams are advised to have each member take one issue to research and prepare that portion of the argument for the brief. Remember: the total brief, except for title page and table of contents, must stay under the ten page limit.

As an example of how an argument could be written, imagine the following scenario where a team wanted to argue the point that Judicial Immunity protected a County Sheriff from liability in a particular case. That portion of the argument might be written like this:

The doctrine of judicial immunity is firmly entrenched in American law as held by the US Supreme Court when it stated "a like immunity extends to other officers of government whose duties are related to the judicial process." Barr v. Mateo, 360 US 564, 569, 79 S. Ct. 1335, 3 L. Ed. 2d 1434, 1440 (1959). Accordingly, the doctrine of judicial immunity shields Sheriff Innocent from any liability arising from his release of the defendant, because he was acting upon the order of Judge Knowsit.

As shown above, the team first explains the rule of law, then shows how it applies to the particular case. If needed, a short direct quote is included to help the Court recall the precedent or law in question.

The team then makes additional arguments to demonstrate that Sheriff Innocent was not liable. They continue to cite relevant cases, statutes and constitutional provisions that further bolster their overall argument. (Reminder: participants are not to cite any additional material in their cases beyond what is included in the case packet.)

Structurally, each part of the argument is first directed at supporting the various issues of one's own case, then also opposing the contentions anticipated to be brought up by the opposing party.

Stylistically, the argument is written in forceful, active, positive language. (A team wants the court to rule FOR their client, not simply against the opposing counsel.) The argument also forms the core of one's oral presentation and will be used by the Justices to make their decision.

The writing of the argument, as shown in the sample brief, uses headings and subheadings to begin each section of the narrative and help clearly organize the argument. The same structure of headings and subheadings should be summarized in the table of contents. The idea is to do everything in terms of both form and substance to help the Court understand the reasonableness and logic of the argument, and thus decide in one's favor.

The following outline style is one commonly used when writing arguments in New Mexico:

I. ISSUE (bold and all caps)

A. <u>Main Point</u> (Bold, Underlined, First Letter Caps)

1. **Supporting Points** (Bold, First Letter Caps)

Note: This is also handy way to prepare one's notes for the oral argument. It is more effective to have an outline to refer to than the written text. One reason to outline an oral argument is because Justices are free to interrupt an oral argument and ask questions at any time. Questioning can take an oral argument off track very quickly. Therefore, an outline is better than a prepared speech because it allows the Attorney a more effective way to remember what points have been covered and makes it less likely that someone will lose his or her place.

Chapter 4
Writing Briefs

(7) Conclusion: This is where the Attorney team summarizes their argument and specifically states the result desired. The conclusion in a Model Supreme Court brief can be as short as one sentence, and should not exceed a single short paragraph. The signatures of the Attorney team follow the conclusion, as shown in the sample.

Section 3 Effective Advocacy in Brief Writing

More than anythinge else, good brief writing requires good writing. A well-written brief has much in common with a well-common oped piece in a newspaper or a well-written magazine article. All hold the reader's attention, have a point of view, and clearly state a position. Lawyers who want to write good briefs will benefit from reading widely in literature, including periodicals, containing good writing. Look at the following example from E. B. White's book about a little girl named Fern and her pet pig Wilbur.

> Carrying a bottle of milk, Fern sat down under the apple tree inside the yard. Wilbur ran to her and she held the bottle for him while he sucked. When he had finished the last drop, he grunted and walked sleepily into the box. Fern peered through the door. Wilbur was poking the straw with his snout. In a short time, he had dug a tunnel into the straw. He crawled into the tunnel and disappeared from sight, completely covered with straw. Fern was enchanted. It relieved her mind to know that her baby would sleep covered up, and would stay warm.

For several reasons, the writing in this paragraph is clear and holds the reader's interest. The words are evocative. Fern "peered"; Wilbur "poked" and "crawled"; Wilbur finished not "his milk" but "the last drop." These sentences vary in length. White isn't afraid of writing a three-word sentences. Clauses are located at the beginning and ends of sentences. They don't pop up unexpectedly in the middle of a different thought.

White also knows what he is trying to say. He knows what ideas he wants to present and in what order they should be presented.

A legal writing benefit not only from good writing style, but also from the certainty and clarity in White's writing. A lawyer can only write a clear, well-organized brief if he knows what he wants to say and in what order to present his points. Brief writing is easier and the final product sharper when a lawyer has outlined it before beginning to write.

1. Shun Legal Jargon

One especially good example of this problem is the use of "appellant" and "appellee." Good briefs generally do not use those terms except on the title page. State and federal appellate rules urge counsel not to use those terms, but instead to use the actual names of the parties or other equally unique identifiers. Indeed, although perhaps not strictly "jargon," you should cast a suspicious eye on any words or phrases in the brief that do not serve a clear purpose.

In avoiding jargon, you are not prohibited from using legal terms of art. In a negligence case, you must discuss "standard of care." In criminal cases, you must examine the various degrees of intent. When you use those terms of art you must be careful to explain what you mean, and when you can get away with using plain English non-legalese, do so.

2. Parts of the Briefs and How They Advocate

The purpose of a brief is to advocate. Every section, paragraph, sentence, and word of a brief should advocate in its own fashion. When you write a brief, make every part of the brief assist in making your client's point. More importantly, when you revise a brief, look at every section, paragraph, sentence and word to make sure that it serves as its advocacy function.

When you write the brief, try to put yourself in the judge's place. Write with his point of view in mind. He doesn't know all the facts of the case and must be educated from the group up. He may know nothing of the substantive law relating to the case, so you must give him a full picture of that area of law in terms that he can understand. Try to put yourself in the judge's shoes at each phase of brief writing — outlining, drafting and editing to ensure that you are doing the best job of making your client's case to the forum that will be deciding it.

Appellate briefs have standard organizational structures mandated by rules; trial and motion briefs are somewhat more flexible. The following taxonomy relates directly to appellate briefs but may be adapted to other formats.

(1) Statement of the Issues

The statement of issues is probably the most important part of the brief because it frames the case for the court. I advocate using the "deep issue" as conceived by the legal writing teacher Bryan Garner. This format uses one or two sentences followed by a question, and it is limited to 75 words or less. The sentences provide the necessary facts and, when appropriate, state the applicable legal standard. For example:

> The city determined that a police officer should receive a "Class 3" disability pension. The officer appealed, and the Public Employees Retirement Board upgraded the pension to "Class 2." The upgrade has no financial effect on the City; the PERF statute is not a party in the administrative proceeding. Does the City have standing to bring a judicial review petition?
>
> Plaintiffs allege that seatbelt enforcement law does not require reasonable suspicion for a police officer to stop a motorist suspected of violating the seatbelt law, and that standard appears nowhere in the law's text. The general legal principle is that constitutional protections against unreasonable searches are implicit in criminal statutes. Does the seatbelt enforcement law violate the Indian Constitution because it does not explicitly incorporate the reasonable suspicion requirement?
>
> Langen admitted violating the law governing real estate brokers by misappropriating money from his escrow account. The Real Estate Commission imposing sanction had not acted within the 60-day time period set by statute. Did Langen Waive his claim that the Commission failed to timely act by failing to present this claim to the Commission?

This format conveys the necessary factual and legal context in straight forward sentences. The format many lawyers have been taught, confining the issue statement to a single sentence, often requires circumlocutions and wordiness that robs the issue statement of effectiveness. Other nostrums about issue statements, such as that they must start with the word "whether", are equally hoary and should not restrict the writer.

The statement of issues must be objective enough to inform the court of the topic it will be considering, but sufficiently laden with information from your case to suggest the answer. A court is not helped by the following questions: Whether there is sufficient evidence to support a conviction?

An astute law clerk might discern that this case is criminal, but learns nothing about the charge or the evidence, which are key matters in determining the answer to the question. This question neither suggests the proper answer (a persuasive question) nor draws the reader's interest (an analytical question). An effective statement of issues will begin to tip the court's thinking in favor of your client early in the appellate process.

Well-drafted statements of issues advance the advocacy of the briefs and are crafted artfully to communicate each side's "slant" on the case at the very beginning of the brief, before there has been time for explicit advocacy or explanation. They give the court a feel for your position, and may even begin to convince the court that you are right, before a judge gets beyond the first page or two of your brief.

(2) Statement of the Case

This part of the brief may seem an unlikely place for advocacy, but do not overlook it. One way in which it can advocate is to omit information that is unnecessary to the court's consideration of the case (or, in its extreme form as permitted by Indiana Appellate Rule 8.3, it can be omitted altogether in the appellee's brief if there is no reason to deviate from appellant's statement). A statement of the case that contains extraneous information is boring and potentially misleading. Only the matters essential to a particular appeal should be contained in the statement of the case.

The statement of the case also provides your first opportunity to briefly summarize the issues you want the court to decide. In Indiana Appellate Rules and Federal Rules of Appellate Procedure both invite this kind of summary, asking that the statement of "the nature of the case" provides a vehicle for briefly explaining the factual circumstances and principal issues raised by the case, giving the court the flavor of the case well before the argument section of the brief. Here is an example.

> In this case, plaintiffs have challenged Indiana's procedure for intercepting tax refunds to satisfy debts resulting from overpayments of Food Stamps. The State Defendants have conceded that the notices they sent to Food Stamp recipients in connection with this process were deficient, as the District Court found. The State Defendant contests, however, the District Court's finding that the procedure for

> interception statute, Indiana Code 6.8.1.9.5, is facially unconstitutional. Finally, they appeal the District Court's order that repay tax refunds intercepted in the past because the order violates the Eleventh Amendment.

Our office often succumbs to the temptation to accept the other side's statement of the proceedings as permitted by Rule 8.3. The danger in accepting the statement without checking it is that jurisdictional defect will be overlooked. Only by carefully going through the record to ensure that jurisdictional prerequisites are satisfied can the appellee's attorney be sure it's not a problem in the case that will permit dismissal without briefing.

(3) Statement of Facts

As Judge Friedman of Federal Circuit has written, "The facts are the most important part in a brief. If the court can be persuaded to take a particular view of the facts, the legal conclusions may follow almost automatically." Many advocates believe that the court should know how it wants to decide any case by the time it has concluded reading the statement of facts, so that argument section of the brief only has to provide the court the legal tools of needs to justify that result.

The statement of facts cannot contain any misstatement because such error, especially in the statement of facts, compromises the advocate's credibility. A lawyer who makes an inaccurate statement in the factual section of the brief risks his credibility in the court's eyes as to all other aspects of his advocacy. Make the statement of facts objective, and omit argumentative words or phrases. Follow each sentence with a citation to the record. In writing the facts, remember the substantive standards that apply. In appeals after trials in Indian, for example, the appellate court is to look at the facts most favorable to the judgment. You can present other facts in the record to the appellate court as well, but you must be careful not to present other facts in the record to the appellate court as well or to present only the version of the facts that was rejected by the fact-finder.

But even in this format there is great room for advocacy in the language describing and placement of salient facts. For example, it is usually more effective if you put your best facts in short sentences and bury the less favorable facts in longer sentences. Bad facts often can be deemphasized by use of passive voice, which you should otherwise avoid. Word choice is the key in the statement of facts. Make sure you are careful to use language that is not misleading but that characterizes the facts favorable to your client. (For example, a defendant is more likely to say that the witness testified that he "used a weapon." While the prosecution in the same case will say the witness described how the defendant "repeatedly slashed the victim's throat and chest, nearly decapitating the victim.") You should not use the statement of facts to regurgitate long passages from the record, but the statement of facts often can be spiced up by adding some colorful quotations.

Here is a recounting of a crime that would make a good statement of facts. It is not taken from a legal brief but from a work of journalism:

> As [Officer] O'Donnell remembers the events of February 11, he and [Officer] Bill Sheehan turned onto Canton Street, a wooded but heavily traveled road that feeds onto Route 128, at about seven-thirty and saw a Pontiac Grand Prix parked a few feet from the curb, with its emergency lights flashing. The driver, as seen in silhouette through the fogged window, seemed slumped in his seat. Parking the cruiser and walking back toward the Grand Prix, Sheehan and O'Donnell were met by a man dressed in fatigues, who had come out of passenger side to say that his friend was ill but no help was needed. The two policemen, suspecting a drunk driver, continued to the Grand Prix and looked in. "Hey, what's all the blood?" O'Donnell said. Someone said "Hey," there was a blinding flash as O'Donnell turned, and he felt himself falling. There were more shots, and then O'Donnell, felling a foot next to him, grabbed at it and began struggling with the man in fatigues, only to have him break loose and run. O'Donnell drew his own gun and fired, bring the man down in the middle of Canton Street. As it turned out, O'Donnell had two minor wounds and serious powder burns of the face. Bill Sheehan lay dying on the street, a bullet from a snub-nosed 38 in his head. The man slumped in the driver's seal had a similar slug in the head, and died not longer after reaching the hospital. He was identified as Captain John Oi. The man in fatigues was Armand Therrien. His wounds were not critical, and the following morning, in Massachusetts General Hospital, a Westwood police officer was able to inform him that he was being charged with the murder of John Oi.

This narrative contains simple language, without jargon or cliché. The sentences tend to be short, but vary somewhat in length. The tone of entire paragraph is calm and straightforward, but by the end the reader is entirely convinced that Therrien is culpable for two deaths.

Great statement of facts shares two attributes illustrated by the excerpt. First, the neutral tone and unbiased viewpoint convey an impression that the story is completely factual and accurate. Second, the careful selection of facts and words to describe those facts turns this neutral presentation into a convincing argument for the lawyer's position.

(4) Summary of Argument

This section is particularly important in some courts where staff attorneys or clerks use the summary to evaluate cases, where judges read only the summary prior to oral argument, or where judges hearing many arguments in a single settling quickly need to refresh their recollections immediately prior to argument. In all cases, you should write a thorough, clear summary, without citations, that provides a clear and accurate outline of the argument.

The summary of argument is part of the argument. Do not just regurgitate your argument headings. Pick the salient features of your argument and artfully boil them down to a concise, accurate and persuasive summary. You should write the summary of argument at last, after you are certain of the way in which your argument will take shape.

(5) Argument

The argument is the portion of the brief where you blend the facts and the law in a manner designed to convince the court to arrive at the result you advocate. Logical and compelling organization is the key to this portion of the brief. You should thoroughly outline the argument before beginning to write, considering all the alternative arguments and determining how best to arrange them.

At the outlining stage, one of the most important tasks is to decide which legal theories you will use and which you will discard. As Judge Alarcon of the Ninth Circuit has written, use a scalpel and not a shotgun in shaping your appeal. There is no "magic" number of points that should be argued in a brief, but the task of weeding out of weak arguments and concentrating on good arguments is vital. When you include weak arguments, they undercut the good arguments in your brief. In the brief, you should focus on your best arguments, usually placing your best arguments first in the brief (although, by convention, jurisdictional arguments usually go first, even before your best substantive arguments).

Mark Herrmann and Katherine Jenks have explained that the difference between a "writing" brief and is that the "winning" brief writer is willing to select and concentrate on the arguments that have the best chance of winning. The "great" brief, the long, ponderous, academic treatise that looks good on the shelf and may impress the client, is less likely to win because the court is likely to wade through its many complex arguments and difficult prose. Herrmann and Jenks acknowledge that although you can't win with an argument you don't make, you increase your overall odds of winning by streamlining your brief and jettisoning marginal points.

Punctuate your argument with argument headings that are pithy and actually argumentative. Headings should not be mere labels (e.g. "default" "plain meaning of statute"), but should be sentences that relate directly to your case (e.g. "The Appellant Procedurally Defaulted This Issue Because He Failed to Raise It in the Appeal of His Conviction").

Here are a few rules for writing the argument.

I. Argument should be affirmative.

State your point, not your opponent's. Argue for the result you want, not against the result your opponent wants. Too many briefs start out like this:

> Appellant argues that the clear statutory language supports his construction.

Don't use your valuable space (especially when it's the first sentence of a section of the argument) to restate your opponent's position.

Here are some alternatives:

> The statutory language does not support Appellant's position.
> The statutory language gives the Appellant no support.
> The statutory language supports Appellee's position because the disputed phrase, "doing business in," is independent only if interpreted in the manner appellee urges.

Each of these alternatives is better than the sentence that restates your opponent's position. The last alternative is he best because it is a clear, affirmative statement of your position that is supported by enough detail to put some flesh on the bones of the general preposition it states. It is also an effective, albeit indirect, rebuttal of the other side's argument.

II. Write with topic sentences.

Tightly organize each portion of the argument, and begin each paragraph with a topic sentence that relates directly to the portion of the thrust of the argument as a whole. When you edit a draft brief, go through the argument paragraph by paragraph, asking the question "Does the topic sentence of this paragraph make a strong advocacy statement for my client that relates directly to the portion of the argument in which it is contained?" Too often, the point of the paragraph, which should be contained in the topic sentence, is buried at the end of the paragraph. Here is an example of this inverted structure:

Defendant's refused instruction #6 reads:

> Merely presenting where firearms are located or association with persons who possess firearms is not along sufficient to support a finding of constructive possession.
>
> Defendant argues that the trial court erroneously refused this instruction. However, the record demonstrates that the substance of the proffered jury instruction was covered by another instruction which was given to the jury.

This paragraph begins with a fact, not an argument. It then restates the opponent's argument before making its point. Here is an alternation of the paragraph that improves it:

> The trial court correctly declined to give defendant's proffered instruction because the substance of the instruction was covered by another instruction that was given to the jury. The declined instruction states that "Mere presence where firearms are located or associated with persons who possess firearms is not alone sufficient to support a finding of constructive possession." The trial court's instruction numbered 8, however, provided exactly the same information as was contained in the declined instruction.

This formulation is better advocacy. It makes the point of the paragraph in the first sentence, and then supports the point in the balance of the paragraph. It argues affirmatively, explaining why the trail courts decision should be affirmed, not why the appellant's argument is incorrect. It does not restate the appellant's argument.

III. Use authority in text: avoid boilerplate.

It is important to support our arguments with authority, but it is just as important to integrate that authority into the text of your argument. It is less effective to banish authority to its own paragraphs, which are full of nothing but general statements of law supported by citations. The most effective way to argue is to begin with a topic sentence that deals explicitly with your case, then to support that sentence with detail from your case and with quotations or citations. Here is an example:

> The law does not permit James to repudiate the 1992 Agreed Entry that ratified the 1991 modification of his child support obligation. A party may not claim benefits under a transaction or instrument and, at the same time, repudiate its obligations. *Caito v. Indianspolis Produce Terminal Inc* (1974), 162 Ind. App. 590, 596, 320 N. E. 3d 276, 283. In this case, James claimed a benefit under the 1992 Agreed Entry by obtaining a resolution of the proceedings against him (albeit one he now finds unsatisfactory) and by postponing his trial to jail. He cannot now seek to repudiate the agreement which brought him those benefits. When a party enters into a settlement, he is stopped from asserting that he is not bound by it. *Krick v. Farmers & Merchants Bank of Boswell* (1972), 151 Ind. App. 7. 279N. E. 2d 254, 160.

This paragraph integrates the facts of the case with the authority being cited. It does not relegate all of the authority to a boilerplate ghetto which may be useful to a clerk who is citing a draft opinion, but which is of little persuasive value to a judge who wants to read an analysis that applies the law to the facts of this case, not a treatise restating abstract legal propositions.

Another hazard of boilerplate is telling the judge what he already knows. Especially in the criminal context, it is likely that the judge who will be reading your brief has applied the standard of sufficiency of the evidence at least as many times as you have. As Judge Garth of the Third Circuit has written:

Chapter 4
Writing Briefs

> Most Judges are familiar with the relevant cases and law, but have to be educated as to how those cases and law are to be applied to the facts the appeal before them. When I sit on a case presenting a Brady issue (the government must disclose to defense counsel any exculpatory material known to the government), I do not need an extensive discussion of the law or the Brady principle, nor do I need 63 citations of the cases applying Brady, all of which say the same thing. What I do want to know is how the facts of this case fall, if they do, within the Brady doctrine, and whether the facts of this case satisfy each of the Brady requirements.

So why provide the judge with two paragraphs of boilerplate, without a single reference to the facts of your case? Far better provide half a dozen sentences explaining the facts of your case, a single sentence stating the standard with one or two recent citations, and end it.

IV. Make policy argument.

Policy is important in some cases. In the simplest cases, where the law is settled and can be applied rather mechanically to the facts, policy arguments are of little use (for example, appellate courts no longer need to be told why they should defer to trial courts on issues of credibility). But in cases raising novel issues, especially relating to constitutional or statutory interpretation, it is vital to provide the court with policy rationales supporting your position. The court needs to be told indeed, convinced why it should rule in your favor. When a court potentially can support either result with the law, it will want to do what it considers right or fair, and you should tell the court why your result is the right or fair one. Here is an example of a policy argument:

> Indiana's system requiring prior approval; for construction of nursing home beds eligible for medical does not deprive Medicaid recipients of a free choice among providers. In light of the facts that Indiana already has the highest per capita numbers of nursing home beds in the United States, R. 333, no system that limits the construction and conversion of beds based on demonstrated need can be said to limit access. According to the information Appellants provided to the trial court, more than a quarter of Indiana's nursing home beds are empty. R. 333. Medical recipients, as well as non-Medicaid patients, have access to many nursing homes but neither group has access to every bed at every facility.

This paragraph doesn't rely on citations and precedent to convince the appellate court. Rather, it gives the court good, practical reasons for deciding in favor of result it advocates. In the particular case from which this paragraph is drawn, both sides had good legal arguments. The practical consequences, as illuminated in the briefs, probably weighed heavily in the court's final decision.

The paragraph section of the brief is where you must blend facts, law and policy in a coherent persuasive manner. A clear outline and logical flow are vital. The argument should be affirmative. Each paragraph should be related to the main flow of the argument through a topic sentence. Briefs that meet these criteria will be a cut above those that appellate courts usually see.

V. Conclusion.

The conclusion must state exactly the relief you want for your client, or alternative forms of relief if they are acceptable. The conclusion should state the relief you want and nothing more. Some others believe that the conclusion should summarize the argument, but there is another location (i. e. the summary of argument) more appropriate for such things.

3. Other Matters

(1) Pejoratives

Do not directly criticize opposing parties or counsel in your briefs. Use of such ad hominem attacks almost is always counterproductive. Andrew Frey and Roy Englert, experienced appellate counsel formerly with the Solicitor General's office, have provided this example about appropriate tone and its effects based on an Indiana case.

> Tone matters too. In a recent, highly publicized criminal case, appellate counsel did a masterful job of identifying the issues and mustering legal and factual support for his client's position. He did so, however, in a self-righteous tone, overstating accusations of prosecutorial misconduct, belittling the trial judge, and portraying his client as the victim of a person who, the jury had found, was herself the victim of the client's serious criminal conduct.
>
> The lawyer, who is prominently affiliated with an elite East Coast institution, should have been careful to adopt a respectful tone toward the Midwestern state judges he was addressing. We read the briefs before the case was argued. We concluded that if

Chapter 4
Writing Briefs

the judges thought the issues otherwise close, human nature probably would make them want to rule against the defendant because of his lawyer's imperious tone. We are not mind readers, but we do know that the defendant lost appeal by a 2-1 vote.

(2) Length

Briefs are called briefs for a reason. How long should a brief be? As short as possible to perform the work is necessary. There are no hard-and-fast rules of length, but court appreciates short briefs when it is possible to make all the points you need to make and support them adequately in a short brief. Judge Evens of the Seventh Circuit, when he was a district judge, wrote the following about a brief he felt was too long: 1) The story of the creation of the world is told in the book of Genesis in 400 words; 2) the world's greatest moral code, the Ten Commandments, contains only 279 words; 3) Lincoln's immortal Gettysburg Address is but 266 words in length; 4) the Declaration of Independence required only 1,321 words to establish for the world a new concept of freedom. Together, the four contain a mere 2,266 words. On this routine motion to amend a civil complaint, plaintiff's approximately 41,596 words spread over an agonizing 124 pages. In this case, the term reply "brief" is obviously a misnomer. Rather than impressive, the "brief" is oppressive.

When a court imposes a page limit on briefs, never try to evade that page limit by skimping on margins or switching type faces in a manner prohibited by rule. The Seventh Circuit is especially persnickety on questions of type size and margin dimensions, and it has sanctioned lawyers who have sought to chest on length in these manners. Judge Kozinski of the Ninth Circuit has made clear how judges are affected by lawyers who cheat on page limits:

It tells the judges that the lawyer is the type of sleazeball who is willing to cheat on a small procedural rule and therefore probably will lie about the record or forget to cite controlling authority.

That characterization is to be avoided at all costs. If you also absolutely have to write a brief that is longer than the prescribed limit, ask permission in advance.

Be ruthless in limiting footnotes. Resist the impulse to show the court how much you know on a marginally-related topic by including a short treatise in a footnote. As Judge Alarcon of the Ninth Circuit has written, "Footnotes force the reader to break his concentration on your discussion of an issue to chase after an often extraneous diversion." Justice Breyer made history in his first term as a Supreme Court justice by including no footnotes whatsoever in any of his opinions, and American law has not been noticeably diminished by his action. Justice Breyer has said "either a point is sufficiently significant to make, in which case it should be made in the text, or it is not, in which case, and don't make it."

(3) Addenda

Proving addenda containing salient materials can significantly improve a brief. This proposition is especially true for federal courts, where the rules require that the lower court's decision, other relevant documents from the lower court and copies of relevant statutes and regulations be included in an addendum or appendix to the brief, which may be bound with the brief if it is short enough. A good appendix, containing copies of relevant statutory sections or lover court documents such as finding and conclusions or jury instructions, assists judges in understanding your argument. Judges have very heavy workloads and will smile when they find that they don't have to get up from their desks in the office or couches at home to find the materials they need. They'll be even more grateful if they're reading in the back seat of a car being driven to a distant hearing where they simply can't get access to the relevant law book or record volume to check out an assertion in a brief.

(4) Citations, Questions and Abbreviations

Avoid long quotations. Find only the best language and use it. The most artful advocates can find short quotations that support their points and that fits seamlessly into text of a paragraph that is otherwise in the advocate's voice.

I. Avoid string cites. Use the most recent case and the older case that established the preposition. Always use pinpoint cites to the exact proposition for which you are citing a case. Whenever you use a signal before a case, add a parenthesis after the citation explaining the relevance of the case's holding to the point you are making.

II. Avoid acronyms. Instead of using "OMPP" for "Office of Medicaid

Chapter 4
Writing Briefs

Policy and Planning," use "Medicaid." Instead of using "DMH" for "the Division of Mental Health," use "the Division." These words are easier for uninitiated judges to remember. If you avoid acronyms altogether, the Judges won't be having to page back and forth in the brief to find your initial references so that they can decipher them.

(5) Writing Style

Here are ten specific suggestions about writing style.

I. Use active voice.

II. Try not to use forms of the verb "to be." Substitute active verbs instead.

III. Minimize the use of adverbs and adjectives. Use more precise nouns and verbs instead. This principle is especially true of the words "clearly" "plainly" and the like that are often found in brief. When judges read these words, their guard immediately goes up because the statements they support generally are anything but "clear" or "plain."

IV. Prune unnecessary words and sentences.

V. Make sure your pronoun antecedents are clear.

VI. Keep the subject and verb near one anthor.

VII. Try to use a standard subject-verb-object order in most sentences.

VIII. Shift clauses to the end of sentences. They're especially bad if they're stuck in the middle of sentence.

IX. Use simple, familiar, concrete words.

X. Don't overuse commas. Commas should be used to separate items in a series, to separate independent clauses joined by a coordinating conjunction, to separate introductory clauses or phrases, and to separate nonrestrictive parenthetical elements or appositives from the rest of a sentence. Commas may occasionally be useful on order situations, where thay can avoid confusion.

Good brief writing, like much of good lawyering, does not come easily. It takes hard work, creative thinking, self-criticism and plain old practice. The guidelines in this chapter will make brief writing easier and improve the final product.

Section 4   Ten Misconceptions that Result in Bad Briefs[①]

There is an art to writing effective briefs, and each brief is different. But many ineffective briefs contain the same mistakes, regardless of the brief's subject matter or the brief's intended judicial audience. One recent survey revealed that more than 93% of the responding practicing attorneys and judges (both state and federal) believed that the briefs and memoranda they saw were "marred by basic writing problems," including a lack of focus (76.1%), failure to develop an overall theme or theory of the case (71.4%), and failure to be persuasive (66.4%). Another recent survey of 355 federal judges found that "judges are critical of lawyers' inability to use relevant, controlling authority to their advantage."

The demands of a high volume law practice contribute to these drafting errors. A heavy caseload allows little time for the brief writer to achieve the critical distance from the document necessary to edit and revise effectively.

In addition, many attorneys have misconceptions about the role of a judge that lead to basic drafting errors. Because judges want the result of a case to turn on the merits, rather than on which party hired the better lawyer, they sometimes reach out in cases where the briefs are poorly organized and opaque to independently divine the applicable law and record facts. However, it is not the judge's job to sift through the advocate's possible arguments to determine which argument is strongest or to figure out how the law applies to the facts of the case. Judges will not always have the time, the inclination, or the patience to figure out what a disorganized brief's arguments are or should have been.

In spite of the demands of a high volume law practice, lawyers can avoid committing many common brief-writing errors by making a significant attitudinal shift during the writing process. Lawyers should try to put themselves in the place of their intended readers — the busy judge and the often inexperienced law clerk. The ten most common ways to write a bad brief that

---

① Sarah E. Ricks, Clinical Associate Professor & Co-Director, Pro Bono Research Project, Rutgers School of Law-Camden. J.D. Yale Law School.

Jane L. Istvan, Senior Attorney, Appeals, City of Philadelphia Law Department, J.D. Yale Law School.

the authors have identified are all rooted in a failure to recognize that, like lawyers, judges also have a high volume practice. And, unlike many lawyers who specialize in one area, often judges are generalists who regularly confront widely differing legal subjects. Judges need lawyers to explain to them clearly and concisely what the applicable law is and how it applies specifically to the facts of a particular case. When a judge who has spent all day trying a contract case sits down to consider the merits of a free speech case at 4:30 p.m. that afternoon, he needs help in recalling the relevant legal doctrines in free speech cases and applying them to the facts of the pending case. The following explanation of recurring brief writing misconceptions and errors can assist lawyers in assessing the effectiveness of a brief from the perspective of the intended reader. This article can help lawyers avoid ten of the most common ways to write a bad brief.

I. MISCONCEPTION NO. 1: DON'T WASTE TIME ORGANIZING OR OUTLINING YOUR ARGUMENTS. THE JUDGE CAN FIGURE OUT YOUR BEST ARGUMENTS.

This is a key part of doing a busy judge's work for her. To be effective, the brief must meet the needs of the reader — the court. "[J]udges value well organized, tightly constructed briefs second only to good legal analysis. For efficiency reasons, they seem to prefer traditional methods of organization, such as the use of a summary or roadmap of the arguments to follow and the placement of an advocate's strongest arguments first." A busy judge is more likely to be persuaded by a brief that organizes and prioritizes the arguments. Below are some tips for organizing briefs and making them easier to read.

A. Tip: If You Can, Give Your Brief an Organizing Theme

An organizing theme should be a message that shines through detailed facts and case law for a busy judge. This theme should be logical and easy to grasp. It should make emotional sense and should permeate every part of the brief. Some call this a *theory of the case*. In a recent survey of legal professionals including judges, the majority of respondents ranked the most important element of legal style as "an integrated statement of the theory (or theories) that favors the client's position."

Example: Let's say you're briefing a hostile work environment case where an employee complained of sexual harassment and the employer disciplined the perpetrator. Your theme could be:

Title VII holds employers responsible for their own discriminatory conduct. It does not hold employers responsible for every incident of harassment committed on their premises.

Every part of the brief should support that theme: the facts section, the headings, the introductory paragraph summarizing the argument, the explanation of the governing law, the key facts selected to support the legal argument, and, in an appellate brief, the question presented.

B. Tip: Use CRAC as a Default Analytical Structure for Each Legal Conclusion

Generally, to prove each legal conclusion your brief advocates, the brief should follow the following format, which some call CRAC (Conclusion — Rule — Application — Conclusion).

(1) First, Summarize how the law applies to your facts — a legal conclusion you want the court to reach.

Example: There was no hostile work environment in this case because the undisputed facts demonstrate that the City took adequate remedial measures when the Plaintiff complained about sexual harassment.

(2) Next, explain the legal propositions upon which you rely.

Prove that the law is what you say it is. Explain the binding case law that sets forth the test for establishing a hostile work environment and explain how the courts define adequate remedial measures.

(3) Then, explain how those legal propositions apply to your facts.

Describe the record facts that establish that the City took adequate remedial measures. Repeat the language of the legal test when applying it to your facts. Explain how legal principles from applicable statutes, case law, or both, and factual similarities to applicable case law compel the conclusion that the City took adequate remedial measures as a matter of law. Distinguish your client's facts from the key facts of cases that did find a hostile work environment.

(4) Finally, reiterate the legal conclusion you advocate.

For each legal conclusion your brief seeks, do this before moving to the next argument.

Example: Since the City took adequate remedial steps in response to the

Chapter 4
Writing Briefs

Plaintiff's complaints, there was no hostile work environment.

C. Tip: Make the Logical Relationships Between Ideas Easy for the Reader to Grasp

(1) Use Headings

Using headings helps the court (and you) figure out where your argument is going. "Briefs with frequent headings often are more logical because of the discipline needed to organize the arguments into sections that are distinctively labeled." Effective headings are not general statements; rather they articulate your client's specific legal argument.

Example: "Smith's Due Process Rights Were Violated When She Was Fired as a Teacher Without Notice or a Hearing."

Not: "Smith's Due Process Rights Were violated."

(2) Use a Table of Contents

To help the court easily grasp the brief's logical structure, put the headings into a table of contents. One Texas judge explained how a table of contents helps the court by increasing judicial efficiency: "a detailed table of contents... [including] [s]ubheadings [is] critical to the speed with which a judge ... can write an opinion because they enable the opinion writer to quickly reference the argument being addressed." Most appellate court rules require a table of contents. Even if not required by court rules, a table of contents is a good idea for briefs that exceed ten pages.

(3) Use (But Do Not Overuse) Bullets and Numbered Lists

In the body of the brief, use numbered lists, if applicable. If the legal test or legal argument can be logically presented in an enumerated list, help the court by listing it. Wayne Schiess succinctly illustrates how to use these aids to assist the reader:

Enumeration, like this: The important factors are (1) the audience, (2) the document length, and (3) the document's purpose;

- Tabulation, like the bulleted items you are reading now;
- Enumeration and tabulation together, like this — The important factors are:

    i. the audience,
    ii. the document length, and

iii. the document's purpose,

iv. use transitions

Try to make the logical relationships between ideas even easier to grasp by using transitions, such as "in addition" "by contrast" or "in the alternative." If you are arguing in the alternative, use transitions in the headings to make it easy for the court to grasp that you recognize that two arguments are not consistent with each other. For example, if the brief argues the court lacks jurisdiction and then argues the merits, use a transition to signify that the arguments are in the alternative, such as "Even if this Court Has Jurisdiction..."or "Regardless..."

D. Tip: Summarize Before Launching into Detail

Summarize the crux of the argument in an introductory, roadmap, or executive summary paragraph. In a recent national survey of federal judges, "[s]eventy-six percent of the judges said it is essential or very important to include an introductory paragraph that explicitly outlines the arguments to follow." While required for appellate briefs, this is also helpful in trial court briefs as a courtesy to the reader — the court.

E. Tip: Address Threshold Issues First

Unless you have a strategic reason to do otherwise, address threshold issues (like jurisdictional or statute of limitations arguments) before the merits. After all, if the threshold argument persuades the court, it may not need to reach the merits.

F. Tip: Open with Your Strongest Argument

"Always lead from a position of maximum strength. This strategy requires you to produce an intelligent answer to the following question: What argument, objectively considered, based on precedent and the court's previously-stated policy concerns, is most calculated to persuade the court to your benefit?" In a recent survey of legal professionals, about 30% of judges and attorneys "wanted the first issue presented to be the one most likely to get needed relief, and also to be the most significant issue presented by the case."

II. MISCONCEPTION NO. 2: DON'T BOTHER TO FIND CITES FOR THE FACTUAL AND LEGAL ASSERTIONS YOU MAKE IN YOUR BRIEF.

Assume you are the moving party. The easiest thing for a judge to do is to deny your dispositive motion and move on to trial. If she is going to deny a

Chapter 4
Writing Briefs

party its right to a jury trial, she wants to be confident that she is doing the right thing, and she is going to want to be able to explain and justify that decision. Therefore, you need to do the judge's work for her and make it easy for her to find the points in case law and in the factual record that prove your argument.

A. Pincite to the Exact Pages of a Case or the Precise Sections of a Statute or Regulation

Before filing, check to ensure the pincites are accurate. As a Georgia federal judge warned, "Misleading or incorrect citations, however unintentional, detract from the persuasiveness of the brief." Checking the accuracy of your pincites is also good self-discipline. It helps ensure that your recollection of the governing law is accurate, not wishful thinking.

B. Don't Make Unsupported Factual Assertions

Make sure the record you are creating for the trial court includes the facts you want to assert in the brief. Whether in a trial brief or on appeal, cite to your record and provide helpful quotes to let the judge know that you are not distorting the record. Precise record citations make it easy for the judge or law clerk to locate the specific fact that supports your argument. This is also good self-discipline. Like accurate pincites to the relevant law, precise record citations help ensure that your recollection of the factual record is accurate, not wishful thinking.

III. MISCONCEPTION NO. 3: IF YOU DO PROVIDE CASE CITATIONS, DON'T BOTHER TO EXPLAIN TO THE COURT WHY THEY ARE RELEVANT. QUOTE FROM CASES A LOT. AND THROW IN SOME BIG BLOCK QUOTES FOR GOOD MEASURE.

Doing the court's work for it includes citing case law effectively and demonstrating to the court how that case law supports the position that you want the cow to adopt. "The secret ambition of every brief should be to spare the judge the necessity of engaging in any work, mental or physical."

A. Tip: As a General Rule, Avoid String Cites

Skeptical readers, like courts, do not trust attorneys enough to rely upon string cites. Nor are string cites an effective way to teach the court the governing law. Instead, prove to the court that each case you cite is on point. As one state supreme court justice cautioned, it is "essential" to tell the court why a case is cited: "[T]he purpose of a citation should be explained. A case may be important for its facts, its holding, its reasoning, its approval of other authority, or an observation that is dictum." Explain the purpose of the citation either in the text or, for a less important case, in a parenthetical. Parentheticals are also useful when citing several cases to illustrate the same principle.

B. Tip: Discuss Your Best Cases in Detail

Use parentheticals for the rest of the cases. In explaining your best cases, be sure to include the key facts and reasoning that the brief later will argue make the pending case analogous to, distinguishable from, or controlled by the precedent case. For the brief's application of the law to persuade the court, the explanation of the law needs to lay the groundwork for the brief's later analogies and distinction.

C. Tip: If the Court Will Need to Parse the Language of the Legal Test, Then Quote It

Quoting the legal test is both helpful to the court and good self-discipline to ensure that your memory of the legal test is not more favorable to your client than its reality. Summarizing the language of a legal test may gloss over nuance.

D. Tip: Except for Quoting the Legal Test, Rarely Quote from Cases

Your summaries of the legal authority are more succinct. Save quotes for the rare occasions "when the opinion's language is just so juicy and on point that you could not say it better or more concisely yourself." In articular, use block quotes sparingly. Many readers confess to skipping them. Save block quotes for when: (1) the quote is completely on point; (2) the quote sets forth a legal test; or (3) you can plug in the names of your litigants to demonstrate the quote's application to your case.

E. Tip: When Quoting More than Just a Few Words, Introduce Your Quote and Draw Your Reader's Attention to Key Passages in the Quotation

Introduce your quote by explaining why it is in your brief. The introduction both "induces the reader to read the quotation — which might otherwise be skipped — by providing a key to its meaning." If the brief writer has accurately represented the legal significance of the quoted language, it helps to earn the court's trust.

If the quote is long, underline, *italicize*, or **bold** key short passages to pique interest. Use these techniques sparingly, as special type is no substitute for

Chapter 4
Writing Briefs

forceful logic and overuse can annoy the reader.

IV. MISCONCEPTION NO. 4: DON'T BOTHER SPELLING OUT EXACTLY HOW THE LAW APPLIES TO YOUR CLIENT'S FACTS. THAT'S THE JUDGE'S JOB.

An effective brief meets the needs of the reader — the court. In a recent survey of members of the legal profession, over 60% of federal judges and about 40% of both state judges and practicing attorneys identified the most important clement of legal analysis as "effectively weaving the entire body of authority into an argument to give the reader a clear understanding of the applicable body of law." The court does not share your familiarity with your client's facts and needs your help to understand which facts are legally significant and why. Explicitly apply the law to your client's facts. Explain how the facts of a particular case make it distinguishable, analogous, or controlling. Below are some tips to help you apply the law to the pending case more explicitly.

A. Tip: Repeat the Language of the Legal Test When Applying the Law to Your Client's Facts

Example: The employer provided employee Smith with a meaningful opportunity to respond to the allegations against him because the employer met with Smith to permit him to refute the charges before the employer decided to suspend him.

B. Make Analogies Between Your Client's Facts and the Facts of Decided Cases Explicit and Easy for the Court to Grasp

Example: Like the unattached garage in *Picaroni*, which was separated from the house by a walkway, in this case the trailer was separate from Ms. Peluso's main house.

C. Make Distinctions Between Your Client's Facts and the Facts of Decided Cases Explicit and Easy for the Court to Grasp

Example: Unlike the attached garage and enclosed patio in *Cook*, which qualified as integral parts of the main house because they were akin to additional rooms, here Ms. Murray's trailer does not share any door with the main residence.

D. Make It Easy for the Court to See that the Result Your Brief Advocates Is Consistent with the Policies Underlying the Results in Binding Precedent

Example: The public policy served by considering the attached garage and patio in *Cook* to be part of the "inhabited dwelling house"— imposing a more serious sanction for the crime of burglarizing a place likely to be populated — would not be similarly served by expanding the definition to include the trailer here.

V. MISCONCEPTION NO. 5: DON'T WORRY ABOUT WHETHER YOUR RECITATION OF THE FACTSIS COMPELLING. BRIEFS ARE ALL ABOUT LAW, NOT FACTS.

Where you are writing a trial-level or an appellate brief, do not make the facts a sterile recitation of the record. Rather, use the facts section to advance your argument. Pull facts together into a compelling story that helps sell your case without overt argument and without slanting the facts unfairly. Open with a summary of the facts and the core of the brief's legal theme or theory. Emphasize favorable facts by using concrete, easily visualized words and by supplying more detail. "To read a story from the client's perspective, the reader must be able to… sense somehow what the people in the story must have heard, seen, tasted, smelled, felt and believed." Neutralize an unfavorable fact by juxtaposing it "with other facts that explain, counterbalance, or justify it." Use topical (not argumentative) headings to break up a long story into digestible chunks and to focus the narrative. Word choice matters. "[W]hat we call something goes a long way toward what or how a reader will think of that thing. For example, do we call the dog that bit the plaintiff a 'pet,' a 'guard dog,' a 'Doberman,' or, simply by its name, 'Chocolate'?"

Try to create empathy for your client by working in relevant information from the record about the client's honorable traits, such as a criminal defendant's struggle to overcome a violent childhood or a corporation's longtime financial support of adult literacy programs. Professors Brian Foley and Ruth Anne Robbins recommend that lawyers borrow fiction-writing concepts, such as classic conflicts (e.g. *Man Against Institution*, *Man Against Leader*, or *Man Against Powerful Entity*) to frame the facts and infuse the client's legal position with emotional force.

To illustrate some of these techniques, below is an excerpt from the Statement of Facts of a civil rights brief. The brief argued that the court should not hold the government actors liable for a crime because a private person, not the government, raped and murdered the victim. The theme of the brief was that the crime victim had no constitutional right to be rescued from the violence inflicted by the criminal, a private actor, because no state actor had personally put the victim in danger or prevented the victim from being rescued by private parties.

The brief's author organized the Statement of Facts below to further that theme. Notice how the Statement of Facts opens by summarizing the most compelling fact at the heart of the brief's theory — that the rapist/murderer had no connection to the government. Note that a fact favorable to the brief's theory — that even before police had arrived, the neighbor who could have broken into the apartment to rescue the victim had decided not to break in — is emphasized in several ways. It is stated. It is underlined. It is described in detail. Its presence in the record — three times — is itself stated.

Note how the author emphasizes another fact favorable to the brief's theory. When police were deciding whether to forcibly enter the victim's apartment, they asked the witness who had called 911 whether the noise he had heard had in fact come from the apartment — and the witness equivocated. That fact is stated. It is described in detail. It is illustrated with a quote from the record and underlined to draw the court's attention to key language.

Note how the Statement of Facts below attempts to neutralize an unfavorable fact — that another neighbor did not think the witness who called 911 had equivocated on the source of the noise. It is de-emphasized — while at the same time not deceptively omitted or described — by juxtaposing it with the admission of equivocation by the neighbor who called 911. It is de-emphasized by placement at the middle of a paragraph, sandwiched between two favorable facts.

Note how the Statement of Facts attempts to create empathy for its potentially unsympathetic clients — the two police officers who did not rescue the victim. They are not labeled simply "police," but instead are named: Officer Scherff and Officer Woods. Since rescue of the murder victim would have required the police to break into a private home, the Statement of Facts creates empathy for the officers by articulating their acute awareness of the constraints on their government power to enter private homes forcibly. The

Statement of Facts suggests Officer Woods was brave and was willing to break into private homes when necessary to save lives by mentioning that he had done so before. The Statement of Facts creates empathy for the police by detailing the solid investigatory steps the officers *did* take in easily visualized language.

Finally, note that the Statement of Facts emphasizes not only the record evidence that favors the brief's theory, but concludes by emphasizing the absence of evidence that would support the opposing side.

STATEMENT OF FACTS

In the early morning hours of May 7, 1998, a private individual with no connection to municipal government raped and murdered Shannon Schieber in her Center City Philadelphia apartment.

On May 7, 1998, between approximately 12:00 a.m. and 1:15 a.m., Ms. Schieber's next door neighbors, Leah Basickes and Parrnatrna Greeley, heard a noise. 110a; 64a. Greeley thought the sound came from the direction of Shannon Schieber's apartment, but Basickes disagreed and made it "very clear" that the noise came from outside. 11 la; 61a—65a.

The couple took no action, and sometime after Basickes went to bed, Greeley heard "a strangle" or "strangulation sound." 69a. Greeley exited his apartment, crossed the hall, and banged on Schieber's apartment door, yelling into the apartment, but he heard no further noises. 65a—66a. He then returned to his own apartment and instructed Basickes to call 911. 66a—67a.

Greeley then returned to Schieber's apartment door, and "banged" on it some more, but he heard nothing further. 67a. Greeley did not attempt to forcibly enter Schieber's apartment because he "was afraid" and "thought if there's someone in there with a knife or something, what am I going to do now." Id.

Greeley returned and learned that Basickes had not called 911. 68a, 74a. Greeley repeated his request, but she refused. 68a. Greeley called 911 himself at 2:04 a.m. and reported the incident. 432a.

After calling 911, Greeley went downstairs to the first-floor apartment of Amy Reed and her boyfriend, Hooman Noorchasm. 69a. Greeley was "thinking of possibly breaking down a door," but he "wanted some other male there just in case he heard something more." Id. Greeley spoke with Reed and learned that Noorchasm was not home. Id.

Greeley then returned to Schieber's apartment and knocked on her door for a third time, but he got no response. 70a. Greeley confirmed three times during his deposition that <u>at this point, prior to the arrival of police, although he considered breaking down the door, he had decided not to</u> because he was unable to track down Noorchasm to accompany him. 71a, 73a.

Officers Scherff and Woods voluntarily responded to the call, but they were not privy to communications between Greeley and the 911 operator. 173a. Rather, they learned of the incident via a Priority 1 Police Radio dispatch of "a report of a female screaming" at "251 South 23rd." 432a—33a; 147a; 173a.

Upon arriving at the apartment building, the Officers approached the door abutting 23rd Street and interviewed a woman. 148a; 174a. She denied hearing any noises and directed the officers to the Manning Street entrance of the complex. Id. Reed and Greeley met the Officers there. 71a; 148a;174a.

While still outside the apartment complex, Greeley informed the officers that he had called 911 and led them to Shannon Schieber's apartment. 71a, 75a. Reed remained on the staircase. 134a. Greeley told the Officers that he heard his neighbor scream for help. 75a. With Officer Scherff backing him up a few feet away with his hand on his gun, Officer Woods banged loudly and repeatedly on Ms. Schieber's apartment door, announcing that police were present and asking Schieber to open the door, but there was no noise or response of any kind from her apartment. 76a; 134a—135a. At this point, Greeley expressed uncertainty regarding the location of the noise he heard prior to calling 911:

Q. Now, after there was no response to the knocking by the police with the baton, what happened next?

A. <u>That's when I said I'll be embarrassed if you break down the door and nothing's happened.</u>

Q. Tell me why you said that.

A. Because I thought they were going to break down the door, and I hadn't heard any sounds in so long that I was sort of just at this point he's probably woken up a bunch of people and I was just — let me phrase this properly. It was my ego on the line. <u>I thought he was going to break down my neighbor's door on my call, so it would be embarrassing if you break down your neighbor's door</u>

and there's nothing happening, don't you think?"

76a—77a; see also 135a.

The Officers asked Greeley whether he was sure that the noise came from inside Ms. Schieber's apartment or whether it might have come from outside, and Greeley responded that "maybe it came from the outside." 74a, 77a. Although Greeley admitted that he expressed such uncertainty about whether the noise came from inside or outside, Reed did not hear any uncertainty in Greeley's answers and she recalls that he answered "No, I don't think so," when asked whether the noise might have been people talking outside. 77a; 135a. Christian Ritter, a third-floor tenant who came over while the Officers were banging on Schieber's door, observed that Greeley's response to the Officers' questions concerning the location of the noise "was uncertain." 209a, 219a. At this point, the Officers were "still looking for anything that might indicate the necessity of continuing." 219a.

Officers Scherff and Woods also inspected the outside balcony area of Ms. Schieber's second-floor apartment. It is undisputed that, during this inspection, the Officers shined their flashlights onto the balcony area and no one observed any signs of forced entry or unusual activity. 134a; 209a; 153a—154a; 178a, 186a.

The Officers decided not to enter Ms. Schieber's apartment because they determined that they could not justify a warrantless entry under the Fourth Amendment. 152a; 189a. They correctly understood that they were required to articulate a "reasonable belief" that someone inside was in imminent danger. 55a—57a, 159a; 186a—187a, 192a. On other occasions, Officer Woods applied this exception and entered buildings without a warrant in order to protect life, but he did not believe that such conduct was warranted here. 187a—88a.

Officers Scherff and Woods left the scene and instructed the residents to "call 911 if you hear anything more." 77a; see also 154a; 179a. No one testified that they understood this instruction to prohibit them from taking action on their own if they heard more noise.

Likewise, there is no evidence in the record that anyone asked the Officers to reconsider their decision or protested when they left. 77a (Greeley said nothing to Officers as they left); 114a (Basickes made no attempt to tell

Officers they should not leave); 217a (Greeley made no comments about further action when Officers said there was nothing more they could do).

The record is also devoid of evidence that Greeley or any other neighbor expressed to the Officers a desire to break down Schieber's door. See 72a—73a (Greeley did not tell Officers he wanted to take the door himself). <u>Further, there is absolutely no evidence that the Officers instructed Mr. Greeley or the other neighbors to refrain from breaking down Ms. Schieber's door or to refrain from taking any other measures to assist her.</u>

Nor is there any evidence that neighbors discussed taking the door themselves after the Officers left. <u>See</u> 221a, 222a (neighbors "did not seem agitated" and "did not express in any way a desire to do more"). Everyone dispersed to their own apartments, and Greeley heard no additional noises and felt no desire to approach Schieber's apartment or call police. 114a—115a; 78a—79a. Greeley testified that he did not consider breaking down the door again after police left because he considered it to be "in [the Officers'] hands to break down the door" and because he did not hear any more noises, but he also stated that if he had heard more noise, he "probably" would have taken affirmative action. 86a.

The following afternoon, Schieber's brother came to Greeley's door and reported that Shannon had not met him for a scheduled lunch date. 79a. When Greeley told Schieber's brother about the noises he had heard, they forced Ms. Schieber's door open and discovered her body. 79a—80a.

VI. MISCONCEPTION NO. 6: A LONG BRIEF IS BETTER THAN A SHORT ONE. THROW IN EVERY ARGUMENT YOU'VE DREAMED UP. USE LOTS OF COMPLICATED WORDS, LONG SENTENCES, AND LEGALESE TO IMPRESS THE JUDGE.

Busy judges do not want to drag home in their briefcases the legal brief version of *War and Peace* to read at night. "From the judges' perspective, conciseness is not aspirational, it is essential." In a recent survey of members of the legal profession, including judges, "all ranked clarity and concision as the two most essential elements of good writing." Supreme Court Justice Ruth Bader Ginsburg explained that busy judges "work under the pressure of a relentless clock," and therefore "[a] kitchen-sink presentation may confound and annoy the reader more than it enlightens her."

A concise brief focuses the judge's attention on a few good arguments. The brief writer achieves that focus by editing out both weak arguments and extraneous words. "If your brief is unnecessarily long and complicated, it may not get read completely, or, worst of all, it may not be understood." Weak arguments undermine the litigant's credibility. Failing to edit out weak arguments undercuts a brief's stronger arguments by suggesting the writer cannot discern the difference and may not be a trustworthy guide to the relevant law and facts.

Further, focus the court's attention on strong arguments by editing out words that do not advance your client's argument. "Wherever you can, you should cut fluff, Latin, old-fashioned words, and useless jargon." in *Plain English for Lawyers*, Richard Wydick recommends an average sentence length below twenty-five words. Aim to reduce the length of your sentences, your paragraphs, and your brief when you revise and edit. These editing steps will improve your brief.

VII. MISCONCEPTION NO. 7: DON'T WASTE TIME SPELL CHECKING OR PROOFREADING. LAWYERS HAVE MORE IMPORTANT THINGS TO DO.

This is about your credibility with the court. If you want the court to trust you on the important steps in the analysis — like what the governing law is and how your client's facts are analogous to some cases and distinguished from others — you need to sweat the details. As one judge cautioned, "[W]e judges tend to become suspect of any argument advanced by an advocate who produced shoddy work ... I have little trust in an advocate who files a document that contains misspellings [or] poor grammar." One federal judge recently reduced a fee award by $150 per hour because the attorney's sloppy written work demonstrated disrespect for the court: "Throughout the litigation, [the attorney] identified the court as 'THE UNITED STATES DISTRICT COURT FOR THE EASTER [sic] DISTRICT OF PENNSYLVANIA.' Considering the religious persuasion of the presiding officer, the 'Passover' District would have been more appropriate."

If you do not take time to make edits that could have been done in thirty seconds, you suggest to the court that your brief is so unimportant, it was not even worth thirty seconds of you time to fix glaring errors. To illustrate, we provide three sentences below in quotations followed by an explanation of what a thirty-second edit could reveal.

Sentence One: "The plaintiff in *Smith* arrived at the injured person's side after medical treatment had begun, which the court held was too late for them to state a claim for negligent infliction of emotional distress."

Thirty-Second Edit: Here, there is a subject — pronoun disagreement between "the plaintiff" and "them."

Sentence Two: "The defendant is a corporation, it wants to file a motion to dismiss the claim."

Thirty-Second Edit: This is a run-on sentence.

Sentence Three: "In the instant case, the factual record suggests that in this particular circumstance, Ms. Kaite's complaint is likely to be able to state a claim."

Thirty-Second Edit: This sentence is wordy. A better version would read: "Ms. Kaite's complaint is likely to state a claim."

VIII. MISCONCEPTION NO. 8: IF YOUR LAW OFFICE HAS A FORM BRIEF OR THERE'S A SIMILAR BRIEF IN THE WESTLAW BRIEF BANK, JUST COPY AND FILE IT. WHY WASTE YOUR VALUABLE TIME MAKING SURE IT FITS YOUR CASE?

Brief banks can be an efficient litigation tool, if used cautiously. However, cite-check and proofread carefully when you borrow a brief from another case. Make sure the legal points made in the brief are up-to-date, accurate, and fit your facts. Citing superseded law or failing to change the litigants' names or the pronouns are all telltale signs of slipshod use of a canned brief. As Bryan Garner points out, "Besides wasting the court's time, a sloppy motion suggests that the writer is sloppy in other ways as well (in analyzing legal problems, in preserving clients' rights, and so on)."

IX. MISCONCEPTION NO. 9: MAKE IT REALLY PERSONAL. GET CAUGHT UP IN AND INFLAMED BY YOUR OPPOSING COUNSEL'S HORRIFIC MISDEEDS.

An effective brief is tailored to the needs of the reader — the court. The court does not have the time or inclination to mediate your interpersonal disputes. It wants to reach the right result, not punish a mean lawyer who has made your life miserable for the last six months.

Attorneys sometimes accuse one another of mischaracterizing or misrepresenting legal or factual information to judges. Inflammatory characterizations and adjectives mean nothing and can very easily backfire by irritating the judge. The judge wants to see for herself whether your opponent has misled the court about something or acted unfairly. Your facts should speak for themselves without inflammatory characterizations, if you present them in a compelling manner.

X. MISCONCEPTION NO. 10: TRY TO TRICK THE COURT BY IGNORING PESKY BINDING CASE LAW OR RECORD FACTS THAT UNDERCUT YOUR ARGUMENT.

According to one federal judge, most briefs "ignore or gloss over obvious weaknesses in their argument and fail to address the compelling counterpoints of the other side." There are both carrot and stick reasons for tackling the tough law and tough facts. The stick is the Rules of Professional Responsibility, which you certainly do not want to ignore. But even leaving sanctions aside, ignoring binding law or bad facts is a bad litigation strategy.

Here is the carrot: You want the opportunity to explain bad law or bad facts. If you leave it to your opponent to point them out, you may never have the opportunity to do so and you will communicate to the court that you believe that case or those facts are fatal to your client's position. As Judge Fred Parker of the U.S. Court of Appeals for the Second Circuit cautions, "[B]y failing to mention contrary precedent in the opening brief, the advocate makes that precedent more weighty than it perhaps should be." Similarly, you want to address bad facts, either to lessen or neutralize their impact on the case or, even better, to "turn the facts around [to] make them part of your case."

Keep in mind the long-term benefit of establishing a trustworthy reputation with the court. Chances are that you or your law firm will appear before this judge again. "[V]iew every brief as a chance to build your and your firm's credibility with the court." Use this opportunity to build a reputation with the court for honesty and helpfulness by showing the court how to overcome the hurdles to deciding in your client's favor.

XI. CONCLUSION

It is not easy to imagine yourself in the place of another. Yet writing effective briefs requires the writer to imagine how the reader — a judge or a law clerk — is likely to react to the unfamiliar legal and factual information set out in the brief. Recognizing some of the common misconceptions about brief writing can help the writer to appreciate the reader's position and help the writer tailor the brief to meet the reader's needs. While drafting effective briefs takes creativity and time, avoiding the common mistakes outlined in this article can help even busy lawyers managing a high volume practice to file more effective briefs.

Section 5 How to Make Technical Briefs Understandable for Judges[①]

Legal briefs on technical subjects don't have to be impenetrable. With some care aid effort, a lawyer can reduce even the most complicated subject matter to something that generalist judges — and their clerks — can understand. Doing so is important because you want the judge to be able to write an opinion in you client's favor, and a judge isn't going to be comfortable doing so if it is impossible to understand the factual reasons why your client should win.

We know that many lawyers have spent years mastering the science that underlies their special area of practice. The poor judge reading your briefs, however, likely doesn't share your passion for and mastery of, say, the biochemistry behind the development of pharmaceutical products. This disparity in knowledge can be a problem if your case involves — to continue with the same example — a drug patent. If you expect to prevail, you're going to have to simplify the science in your brief. If you don't, you risk losing the judge — and your case.

So, it should be clear from the start that your brief is not the place to show off the depths of your knowledge. Rather, it is the place to educate the judge, starting with the very basics, about the science that provides the context for the legal issues raised in your case. Judges and clerks, while adept at researching the law, are unlikely to research the science and technology independently. So your job is to give them all the knowledge they need to decide your case.

This article will help you do that. It is the product of 15 years experience

---

[①] By Hugh S. Balsam and Patrick C. Gallagher. Hugh Balsam is a partner at Locke Lord Bissell & Liddell LLP in Chicago. Patrick Gallagher is an associate at Locke Lord Bissell & l Liddell LLP in Chicago.

distilling very dense scientific matter to produce clear and understandable briefs that even a grandmother — OK, a sharp grandmother — can comprehend. We also talked to district judges and clerks to ascertain what they view as helpful — and unhelpful — in briefs in scientific and other technical subject areas.

While we refer frequently to patent cases here, this article is not limited lo patent briefs. Rather, the tips aid techniques we discuss apply equally in any case where the underlying subject matter is specialized and technical. Think medical malpractice or financial fraud, or even a case that involves a complicated statutory scheme. (Have you read through the Fair Credit Reporting Act lately?)

Our recommendations fall in a few general categories. The first is selection. Don't pack your brief with everything including the kitchen sink and let the overwhelmed judge try to sort it out to figure out what's important to YOUR argument. Your job is to include only what's important and, most critically, to leave out what isn't. The second general subject area is organization. Just as every section needs to have a place and purpose, every paragraph and sentence do too. This sounds elementary, but it's probably the hardest thing to do in a brief. The final general subject area is simplification. This is particularly important in briefs in technical areas, where the arguments by their nature, are anything but simple. Your goal is to make them less dense, and thus, more inviting, for the judge to understand ultimately rule in your favor.

A fourth recommendation is to give your brief (before you finalize it) to a lawyer who has no knowledge of the particular field you are writing about. If that lawyer can't understand what you are arguing and why, then you need to go back and improve your work. One of the authors of this article has no scientific background, yet a major portion of his practice consists of writing and improving briefs in technical subject areas. Such nontechnical lawyers can be a significant asset to the briefing process.

Step One: Select

The product — or an illustration of it-is quite helpful. In selecting what information to give the judge, don't forget the product itself. Every one of the judges and clerks we interviewed said that it is extremely helpful for them to be able to look at the article or invention in question. In fact, if possible, you should leave the article or invention in the judge's possession for the duration of your lawsuit so that the judge or clerk can refer to it as desired. Then, when writing pour briefs, you don't have to spend time explaining what the article looks like because the judge will already have a basic, macro-level understanding of the context. In this way, you can sooner get to the heart of the issues in pour brief.

Of course, sometimes it is not practical to give the judge the article itself. Your case might involve an earth-moving machine or an element of nanotechnology. In those instances, you can still be helpful by giving the judge a three-dimensional model or a picture or diagram or anything that illustrates the piece of technology in question and gives context to the technical issues.

And don't stop there. Early on in your case, whether orally or in one of your early briefs, be sure to tell the judge about the real-world application of the article or invention. In particular, be sure to explain what problem this invention solves or addresses and how it does so. This advice holds just as true if you represent a patentee or an accused infringer, for instance, if you are trying to establish that the invention was obvious, you can describe the real-world application in such a way that simplifies the problem such that the "solution" appears to be easily attained. On the other hand, if you represent the patentee, you can describe the inventor's spark of genius in such a heap that the subject matter being claimed seems truly inventive.

Be selective about your arguments. It is crucial that you resist the temptation to raise every issue for which you think you have a non-sanctionable argument. This is all the more important in cases involving complicated technology because the more you dispute, the more technology you're going to have to explain, and the greater the chance the judge will become confused. The failure to circumscribe arguments is such an acute problem that some courts have issued rules prescriptively limiting the number of claim terms that the parties can dispute or that the court will construe. See, e.g. N.D. Ill. Local Patent R. 4.1. To be sure, you have to raise an argument to preserve it for review. But if an argument is marginal in the district court, it is not likely to improve with age. So select wisely in the first instance and you, your client, and the judge will be better off for it in the long run.

That having been said, when you feel you must give the court flip-side or alternative arguments(or if your client insists on it), be sure you make it clear that you are arguing in the alternative. Lawyers sometimes overlook this, and it can be thoroughly confusing to read a brief whose arguments seem irreconcilable with each other. Further, alternative arguments should be as precise and focused as possible so as not to detract from your more important primary point.

Select only the technical facts necessary to support the arguments in your brief. The most important thing you can do in a brief involving a really technical subject is to withhold information from the judge. No, we are not advocating withholding important facts. Rather, you should strive to withhold technical information that isn't necessary to your argument or to an understanding of the general scientific context. The best way to accomplish this goal is to try to generalize the scientific or technical concepts rather than including every last supporting fact.

Consider an example. In a brief we edited recently, our client was challenging the validity of a patent that claimed to have solved the problem of a noxious black smoke forming when a certain chemical reaction occurred. There was, however, a scientific article from the 1950s that described the same type of chemical reaction and did not mention any black smoke — and the article surely would have mentioned the smoke had it occurred. Thus, tile article tended to show that the "problem" the inventors purportedly solved in the patent was not a problem at all.

The draft brief we received to work on laid out, in mind-numbing detail, the type of chemical reaction the old article described, complete with chemical diagrams and impenetrable scientific language. When we finished, however, all of that was gone. We cut it out because it was sufficient to mention the old article and tell the judge merely that it showed that the black smoke was not a problem to begin with. And we simply cited and attached the article so that the judge could go back and look at it to obtain more in-depth detail. In that way the brief was not clogged up with a maddening level of science that the judge was never going to understand from the first place. Further, in editing the excessive level of detail out of the brief, we were able to elevate, front-and-center, the

Chapter 4
Writing Briefs

excellent take-away point that the drafters of the brief were trying to make all along.

The best briefs tell a story, and this is so even when the object matter is technical.

In other words, you must always keep your take-away point in mind and present it clearly enough — which often means generally enough — that it doesn't get buried and lost in your recitation of the applicable science. Yes, you must educate the judge — but only enough for the judge to understand and resolve the issues in dispute.

Don't repeat arguments needlessly in successive briefs. The time to educate the court about the technology is your first brief where a mastery of the technology is required. Say that is your brief in support of your motion for summary judgment. If that's the case, you do not need to reeducate the court in your reply brief in support of summary judgment. Even though there might be a span of several months between when you write your initial brief and your reply brief, rest assured that the judge is not waiting for the daily mail delivery to rip open every envelope and read everything that comes in the door that day. The judge and clerics generally will wait until briefing is complete, and only then will they sit down and read the full set of briefs at once. Thus, long explanations from the initial brief need not and should not be repeated in the reply brief. Your reply brief can be more pointed and direct, because you need not waste space reeducating the court about the basic points.

That said, there is likely a need to refamiliarize with each round of new briefing.

Thus, if you educated the court primarily during a motion to dismiss, you need not repeat the whole background in your reply brief, but you might need to give a refresher course in a later brief in support of a motion for summary judgment.

Don't waste time reciting boilerplate law. The judges and clerks we interviewed advised strongly against larding briefs up with a lot of standard boilerplate law. They know that law already. It is more helpful to focus on any recent decisions that might have developed or changed the area of law you are dealing with and on cases you believe are closely analogous to the facts of your case.

213

Step Two: Organize

Don't forget to tell a story. The best briefs tell a story, and this is so even when the subject matter is technical. A patent case presents the same opportunity to narrate a story and develop a theme as any other case. Say, for example, the issue is obviousness of a patent claim. If your client is the patentee, you have the opportunity to relate how novel the claimed invention is and how surprising it was that the inventors came up with it. If your client is the alleged infringer, you can set forth a parade of prior-art references in such a way that the invention seem inevitable, and certainly not the result of some inventive spark. In most cases, therefore, you can further your argument by telling a compelling story rather than getting mired in scientific drudgery.

Build the technology piece by piece. When presenting scientific or technical subjects in your background section or your statement of facts, start with a few basic principles and then build on those principles step by step. The judge likely does not know as much as you do about the technology, but you do not know how much the judge already knows. Therefore, you should start with the very basics (probably more basic than you think you need). The judges we interviewed said that they would never complain if a lawyer spent a paragraph or two on scientific fundamentals, even if they already understand those fundamental. Far better to err on that side to start your explanation in the middle and use terms and concepts that you might incorrectly assume the judge understands.

For instance, if your case involves deciding technology, do not fear reminding the judge at the outset that, in the normal course, water freezes at 32F. While it is likely that the judge already knows this fact, when you set it out at the beginning, it establishes a common baseline of knowledge. You can then spoon-feed the judge by slowly building on that knowledge step by step until you have given the judge enough science necessary to understand your legal arguments. Be sure not to sky steps, even if they appear self-evident. And it is best (as in all writing) when you explain the steps, each sentence clearly relates to the sentence before it and the sentence after it.

Be sure your facts and argument present the science in a consistent manner. The best statements of facts are those that make it clear what the legal argument will be. This should also be your aim when writing a brief on a technical subject. To achieve this goal, it is important to use the same technical facts in the same way in both the statement of facts and the argument. It does your case no good to painstakingly teach the science in the statement of facts. Only to use, in the argument section, a different vocabulary or more advanced concepts than you set forth in your fact statement. Be sure your brief is a unified, harmonious whole.

A technology tutorial is a session where the parties educate the court about the science and technology involved in the case.

Use headings liberally. All the advice we offer in this section is easier to apply if you make liberal use of headings and subheadings, especially in your statement of facts. While most lawyers blow to break LIP their argument using section headings, fewer lawyers use headings in their statements of facts. That is the reader's loss, because a logically thought-out statement of facts lends itself perfectly to headings and subheadings that not only make the brief look less intimidating but actually make it easier to understand.

Use topic sentences. It is always a good practice to use a topic sentence for each paragraph, and never more important than when you are writing an argument based on complicated technology. When the writer fails to use a topic sentence, the reader begins reading the paragraph unsure of the point the writer is trying to make. And a writer who fails to use topic sentences probably hasn't thought out the structure of tile brief and how the various paragraphs fit together. Just as one sentence should build on the previous sentence, each paragraph should build on the paragraph before it. In this way, the argument has a logical structure and readers aren't at a loss for what point they are supposed to be getting from the paragraph.

While lawyers often start their paragraphs by talking about a case and its facts, this doesn't help their arguments, because their readers don't know how the facts fit into the overall argument.

Thus, a very bad first sentence to a paragraph is something like: "In Smith v. Jones, the defendant sped through a red light and hit the plaintiff's car." A far better practice is to tell the reader at the start of the paragraph what the point of the paragraph is. Then the case discussion will make more sense. Thus, it is more effective to start the paragraph by saying "Courts in this jurisdiction consistently hold that the defendant's violation of a traffic law is persuasive evidence of negligence," and then proceed to explain how Smith v. Jones illustrates that point. In other words, don't assume the court knows where you are going when you start reciting the facts to Smith v. Jones. The court might be able to guess, but it might not.

Step Three: Simplify

Offer a technology tutorial. Even if the court does not ask for one, you should consider offering the court a technology tutorial. This is a session where the parties educate the court about the science and technology involved in the case. If you hold a tutorial, you can refer back to the concepts and terminology used at the session in your briefs to jog the judge's memory. That said, don't assume that the judge has automatic and immediate recall of complicated concepts introduced months or years earlier. Further, there is turnover among the judge's clerks, so a clerk who sat in on a tutorial might no longer be working for the judge when you are submitting your briefs. There may be a new clerk who hasn't had the benefit of your tutorial. In this regard, it might also be helpful for you to offer the videotape to the tutorial if the judge does not beat you to the punch and suggest it in the first instance.

Eliminate or define technical terms. Becoming proficient in a technical area like engineering, chemistry, or medicine entails learning a new vocabulary, in which like learning a foreign language. But, just as you wouldn't write a brief in French, so you shouldn't write a brief in the technical language of the field you are dealing with. Rather, you should try your best to strip your brief of as many technical terms as possible.

Of course, it will usually not be possible to parse all the technical jargon out of your brief; it is likely that some technical terms will be necessary to your argument. That's OK — the court is an intelligent audience. But they may not have the technical background and scientific understanding that you have or that your client has. You should tell the court what the technical terms mean, and you should take a step back and explain how these terms relate to your argument and the larger scientific context.

Say, for example, you are dealing with a patent that claims a faster way to

Chapter 4
Writing Briefs

release a drug from a tablet so it gets into the body more quickly. A key concept in this area is dissolution testing, which, in the pharmaceutical context, consists of dropping a pill into a solution and measuring how fast it dissolves. It will probably be unavoidable for you to refer often to dissolution testing. So, you just need to be sure that the first time you mention this potentially off-putting phrase, you explain it in a manner that is friendly enough that the judge can capture a mental image and be comfortable with the concept each time you use the term.

Don't try to obscure a bad argument in a thicket of impenetrable science. If your argument is weaker than you would like it to be, resist the temptation to obscure your position in a morass of unexplained science. First of all, a judge who can't understand our position is unlikely to rule in your favor. Judges are aware of the obfuscation trick, and they do not reward it. Second, your opponent might well explain the science and take the time to translate your argument into something understandable, exposing its flaws. In that event, you will simply wind up looking foolish and unhelpful.

Avoid acronyms and odd specially defined terms. Acronyms frequently make a brief more difficult to follow and should generally be avoided unless the acronym is universally known (e.g. IBM). A brief we recently were asked to edit had the following sentence: "During this time period, FIE compensated ZSC for the PPO access provided and its other bill-review services, and ZSC paid CCN for access to the PPO." Huh? Some lawyers flunk acronyms are a convenient shorthand, but if you use more than just one or two of them in a brief, they quickly wear out their welcome and become overwhelming. If a party's name is Zippo Service Corporation, call it Zippo in your brief, not ZSC.

Similarly, there is no need to ascribe shorthand nicknames to selected terms you use in a given brief. Say your case involves a certain seven embezzled checks. You might be tempted to define these initially as "the Checks" and then invariably refer to them in this artificial manner throughout the rest of the brief. Avoid the temptation. There are many other perfectly natural-sounding ways in which you can refer to the checks and still leave no doubt in the judge's mind which checks you are referring to — "the checks at issue" or "the embezzled checks," and so on. Better to use these general terms interchangeably (making sure the context makes it clear you mean the seven checks) than to set forth madeup terms of art that you have endowed with special meaning for purposes of this one brief only.

Along these same lines, you should avoid the practice of advising the judge that Sarah Smith will henceforth and forevermore be known in your brief as "Smith." Or that Honda Motor Co, will be referred to as "Honda." Provided there are no other. Smith or Honda entities in your case, you can safely just go ahead and use the person's surname, or the shortened form of the company's name.

Don't forget to simplify the non-science, too. Not only is it important to simplify the science in your brief, but you must also strive to pare down or eliminate unnecessary nonscientific details. This is another fix that is important in technical briefs because you plainly cannot remove all the science. Therefore, eliminating other unnecessary details becomes that much more important. These unnecessary details come in a variety of different forms — all equally disagreeable.

You can start with dates. Lawyers love to include them, not just in procedural histories, but in any and all other factual recitations. Sometimes, of course, exact dates are important — as in a case involving the statute of limitations or any number of patent-invalidity defenses — and we are not advocating eliminating those dates from your brief. But most other dates are truly superfluous. Unless relevant to some issue, no one really cares what date you filed your answer or the date so-and-so moved for summary judgment. If you feel compelled to use dates, general mileposts are usually fine, e.g. "a few months later" or "in 2007."

Lawyers also obsess about setting forth precise dollar figures, right down to the cents. In some contexts, of course, you need to be precise. But if not, it is much more reader-friendly to write more than $89 million instead of $89,235,702.55. And it is always preferable to write $89 million instead of $89,000,000.00. The judge knows that $89 million is a lot of money, so including all the zeroes — especially the .00 — to try to put it up further is transparent pilling on. And while we're talking about numbers, it is insulting — and unnecessary — to put a numeral in parentheses after writing out a number. There seems to be little doubt that the judge will understand what the word thirty means even if you don't put (30) after it.

There are also certain lawyerisms that you should avoid in any brief, and especially in a technical brief that is already difficult for the reader to plow through. It makes for far more pleasant reading if you write in plain English, and not in legalese. So, do your judge a favor aid avoid not only the usual suspects, such as hereinbefore, hereinafter, and their many ugly, but also other more innocent-sounding words and phrases that only lawyers use, like prior to ("before" is preferable), pursuant to (use "under" instead), attempt ("try" works better), and instant ("this").

Also, it is almost always preferable to call a party by its name, or at least a reasonable shorthand of its name. The use of party labels like "plaintiff" and "defendant" can be confusing intellectual property cases, because sometimes the plaintiffs the party accused of, "fringing" L and is seeking a declaratory judgment that exonerates it from liability.

Avoid footnotes. As long as you have had this far, will stay on our soapbox just a moment longer and exhort you to avoid footnotes in your brief. Many judges don't read them, and many courts hold that substantive arguments presented only in footnotes are waived. Thus, our briefs are generally devoid of footnotes. If the material you wish to put in a footnote is substantive, there should be a logical place for it in your argument. Sticking it in a footnote is just lazy and risks disrupting the logical organization you have worked so hard to create. If, on the other hand, the material you propose to include in the footnote is not substantive, you and your reader can probably do quite well without it.

And last, always have a conclusion. You have done a lot of work to select the important facts, organize your brief in a logical manner, and simplify the complicated concepts to the best of your ability. When you are finished with all that, don't forget to tell the court precisely what you want. We hope that if you follow the advice in this article, you stand a better chance of getting it.

Section 6   Preparing and Delivering an Appellate Oral Argument[①]

For law students, the prospect of delivering an appellate oral argument for a law school assignment or during a moot court competition can be disquieting. The reason for this unease is simple: law students have no experience in appellate advocacy. Students may, however, ease their anxiety if they understand the purposes of oral argument and if they thoroughly prepare for oral argument. Therefore, in this article, I will discuss how you, as a law student, may sufficiently prepare and effectively deliver an oral argument, particularly if you are giving an oral argument for the first time.

A. The General Format of an Oral Argument

In general, the format of an appellate oral argument is as follows: each party is allotted a set number of minutes to argue its side of the case. Typically, each party has from fifteen to thirty minutes to present its argument. The party appealing the lower court's ruling, usually called the appellant or the petitioner, proceeds first with an opening argument. The appellant/petitioner is also given the opportunity to reserve a few minutes of his or her total time for a rebuttal argument. The appellant/petitioner may choose not to reserve rebuttal time if he or she wishes. After the appellant/petitioner's opening argument, the party who is not appealing the lower court's ruling, usually called the appellee or the respondent, gives his or her argument. After the appellee/respondent's argument concludes, the appellant/petitioner gives his or her rebuttal argument. After the rebuttal, the oral argument is over.

B. Preparing an Oral Argument

Although the delivery of the oral argument should be of great concern to a student advocate, it is absolutely critical that the advocate first thoroughly prepare for the argument. It is simply not possible to give a good appellate oral argument by "winging" it. Since the key to oral argument is meticulous

---

[①] James D. Dimitri, professor of law at Indiana University, Robert H. McKinney School of Law.

Chapter 4
Writing Briefs

preparation, I recommend that you take the following steps to prepare for your argument:

1) Understand the two main purposes of appellate oral arguments.

2) With those purposes in mind, conduct a brainstorming session where you think of (a) the important points you need to make to the court and (b) the questions that the judges may ask you.

3) Prepare a short outline to remind you of the points you must get across to the court and to provide you with a safety net regarding key facts and legal authority.

4) Practice and refine your argument.

(1) The Purposes Behind Oral Argument

As a student advocate, you should first understand the main purposes of oral argument. You need this understanding because student arguments, of course, possess the same dynamics as real appellate court arguments. If you understand the two primary purposes behind real appellate oral arguments, then you will be better prepared to handle a moot court argument.

The first purpose of oral argument relates to your role as an advocate before the court. As an advocate, it should be your goal to share your side of the case with the court. You should have done this when you wrote the brief, and you should do this again during your oral argument. Thus, the first and primary purpose underlying oral argument is a purpose driven by your role as an advocate: to get across to the court the key points of your case.

The second purpose of oral argument is a function of the court's role in the appellate process. Appellate courts do not set every case for oral argument. Often, appellate courts decide cases without oral argument, on the briefs that the parties submit to the court. Thus, in those cases where the court does hear oral argument, the court must have possessed an important reason for calling the lawyers before it to argue the case. In most cases, the main reason that the court sets oral argument is to ask questions about the case. This is contrary to the mistaken impression that many unseasoned advocates hold: that they are called before the court to give an uninterrupted speech. An oral argument is not a monologue where the advocate gives a rhetorical account of his side of the case; rather, it is a *dialogue* between the bench and the advocate, where the advocates are advisors to the court.

In the judge/advocate dialogue that is an oral argument, appellate courts ask the advocates questions for different reasons. First, and very commonly, the judges want to identify the most important issue or issues in a case. This may be necessary because the parties may have presented multiple issues in their briefs, some of which are fairly simple and can easily be disposed of by the court, and others that are intricate and require further and more involved discussion. In other words, the court may desire a dialogue with the lawyers to separate the wheat from the chaff.

Sometimes, the parties' briefs only peripherally touch on issues that the court deems central to a case and about which the court wants to learn. Similarly, the briefs may not thoroughly discuss very complex issues about which the court needs more information. Therefore, the court may want the advocates to clarify the facts, law, and public policy implications involved with those issues.

Finally, an appellate court's decision in a case inevitably has consequences outside of that case. For instance, appellate courts often set forth rules of law that will be applied in future cases. Thus, the court may wish to question the advocates about the impact of its decision on future cases. For example, if the appellant urges the court to adopt a particular rule of law, the court may ask the advocates questions about how that rule will operate in a case with facts different from the case at bar.

So, as a student advocate, keep in mind that the second main purpose behind oral argument is for the court to have a dialogue with you and your opposing counsel. Because it is a dialogue, the court will be asking you questions, which you should answer to the court's satisfaction. Therefore, preparing to answer questions should be a major thrust of your preparation for your moot court argument.

(2) Brainstorming

With the purposes of oral argument in mind, you are now ready to begin your actual preparation. The initial stage of preparation should involve a brainstorming session, which you can divide into two sub-stages: (a) identifying the two or three critical points that you must share with the court to win your case, and (b) anticipating and preparing to answer questions from the court.

i. Identifying Your Main Points

You will have a limited time period within which to present your moot court argument. In most student moot court arguments, each advocate is allowed fifteen minutes to present his or her side of the case. Because your brief should cover all of the issues involved in the case, it is unlikely that you will be able to present during your oral argument every single point that you made in your brief.

Since you will have a short amount of time to present your side of the case, you should concentrate on presenting to the court the two or three most important points underlying your argument. The most important points, of course, are those points that you would have to present to the court to win your case if your argument were before a real appellate court. I recommend two or three points because in fifteen minutes, you will not be able to present more than that. You will find that your time will go by very quickly.

To identify the crucial points that you must make during your oral argument, review your brief carefully and ask yourself, "If this were a real appellate oral argument, what two or three points from this brief would I need to make to the court during oral argument to convince the court that I should win this case?" Then, highlight those two or three critical arguments in your brief. If you do not like to use a highlighter, jot down each critical point on a separate piece of paper. Then, set these points aside, but keep them in mind when you prepare to answer the court's questions and when you begin to prepare an outline for your argument.

ii. Supporting Your Major Points and Preparing to Answer Questions

Next, you need to consider how you will support the two or three main points in your argument. You also need to ponder the questions that the court may ask you during oral argument. So, try to view the case through the judges' eyes. Put yourself in the judges' shoes and ask yourself, "If I were a judge in this case, what would I want to know about the case from the advocates?" In nearly every oral argument, the judges will ask questions about the governing legal authorities and the facts appearing in the record of proceedings that support your oral argument. Therefore, you should be prepared to answer questions about the facts and law. Additionally, judges commonly wish to address the weaknesses of the parties' cases. Be especially prepared to answer questions about the weaknesses of your case.

To put yourself in a judge's frame of mind, start by reviewing your brief a second time. Reviewing the brief will direct you to the crucial legal authorities and facts for the case, particularly those authorities and facts that you must use to support the two or three critical points that you will be making to the court during oral argument.

Next, review the legal authorities that govern the case. It should go without saying that you must know well the law applicable to your case. An important function of appellate courts is to determine the outcome of legal issues. In most cases, appellate courts are required to say what the law is, how it applies to the case before it, and how it should or may apply in future cases. As a consequence, you can be certain that the court will ask you questions about the law. Therefore, make sure that you thoroughly review the legal authorities that are crucial to your argument, especially the authorities that directly relate to the key points of your oral argument. For instance, if your argument centers on an issue of federal constitutional law, you should definitely commit to memory the important facts, holding, and reasoning of any United States Supreme Court cases addressing that issue.

You should also reacquaint yourself with the facts of your case. To do this, you should revisit the record of proceedings in the case. As you review the record, concentrate on the portions of the record that contain information crucial to your argument. Specifically, look for facts that you need to support the key points of your argument. Then, take a piece of paper and jot down the page numbers of the record that contain information critical to your case. Keep these record citations on hand for use when you put together an outline for your oral argument.

During your review of your brief, the law, and the record, the weaknesses of your case should become apparent to you. To further identify the weaknesses of your case, you should review your opponent's brief to see which issues your opponent emphasizes in support of his or her argument. Focus on the legal authorities and facts that your opponent cites in his or her brief. Then, conduct a brainstorming session, during which you consider how you can minimize the impact of the weaknesses in your case. For example, think of how you can distinguish unfavorable case law or explain why the court's reasoning in an unfavorable case is inapplicable. Similarly, think of ways to explain why facts unfavorable to your case are not critical to deciding the core legal issues before the court. During this brainstorming session, jot down concise and assertive answers to the court's possible questions regarding the weaknesses of your case. Keep these answers for reference when you practice your oral argument later in the preparation process.

The standard of appellate review is another area about which the court may question the advocates. The standard of review is a statement of the level of deference that the appellate court must afford to the lower court decision under review. In general, appellate courts give great deference to the lower court's determination of the facts and little deference to the lower court's determination of the applicable law. Because an appellate court needs to be informed on the level of deference it must afford to the lower court's findings, you can be virtually certain that your judges will ask you about the standard of review. Know the standard of review and be prepared to discuss it, especially if the standard of review is favorable to you.

More importantly, make sure that you understand what the standard of review means. Frequently, I see student advocates who can state the standard of review during oral argument, but who do not understand what it really means; therefore, they cannot explain the standard's meaning to the judges.

This is not uncommon among student advocates because they have little or no litigation experience, and hence, do not fully understand the process that lower courts use to arrive at decisions. If you do not understand the standard of review, speak to someone who does, such as a professor or an experienced appellate practitioner.

(3) Preparing an Outline

The next step in your preparation should be to write an outline for your oral argument. This outline serves several purposes. First, as I stated previously, your oral argument should focus on the two or three most important points supporting your side of the case. Therefore, your outline should serve to remind you of those points. Second, your outline should serve to remind you of critical legal authorities and portions of the record of proceedings about which the court may question you during oral argument.

For student oral advocates, I recommend the preparation of a short and concise outline rather than an outline that is long and detailed. Many beginning advocates tend to prepare very extensive and detailed outlines because they believe that they will be giving a speech to the court and that they will be unprepared without a detailed outline. In judging moot court arguments, I have even noticed a few students who prepared a verbatim text of the oral argument that they then delivered like a speech.

Remember, however, that an oral argument should be a dialogue between the bench and the advocate, not an uninterrupted speech. Therefore, an extensive outline is something that you should strive to avoid. Do not think of your outline as a "crutch" upon which you must lean to deliver your argument. Instead, endeavor to prepare an outline that functions as a "safety net," which is there to catch you if you forget to bring up a critical point that you must make to support your side of the case or if you forget to mention a crucial legal authority or fact.

From the standpoint of format, you should begin by typing an outline that contains the two or three key points that support your argument. Place your most important point first. Use bullets or numbers to set each point apart from the others. Use buzz phrases or key words to describe each point rather than long, detailed sentences. By doing this, you will not be tempted to read your argument, which you want to avoid, and you will seem more natural and conversational as you deliver your argument to the court. Moreover, the more extensively you prepare for and practice your argument, the less likely you will need a detailed outline.

If there is a constitutional provision, statute, or administrative regulation at issue in the case, you might also want to place in your outline the relevant portions. Include also the citations to key portions of the record that you compiled while reviewing the record.

Next, gather a set of small note cards. After reviewing the key judicial decisions in support of your argument, use a separate note card to write down the citation for each case. In addition, write a very short synopsis of the case, including the critical facts, holding, and reasoning. While the most important judicial decisions should be fresh in your mind through your thorough review of them, these note cards will permit you to jog your memory during oral argument should you forget certain details about a case.

Finally, obtain a manila folder, preferably one that is legal-sized, and open it like a book. On the left side of the folder, tape your outline. On the right side of the folder, tape your note cards in a fashion that will allow you to flip through and easily locate the citations and case synopses. Now you should be ready to begin practicing your oral argument.

(4) Practicing Your Argument

The final stage in preparing to deliver your student oral argument is to practice it. Aside from the initial stage of preparing to answer questions by reviewing the briefs, law, and record, practicing your argument is the most important stage of preparation because it enables you to hear criticism and to revise and refine your oral argument. Practicing your argument will also help you to anticipate questions that the judges may ask you during your actual oral argument.

If you are competing in a national moot court competition, the best way to practice before your argument is to have practice moot court arguments during which you are questioned by panels of volunteer judges. National moot court competitors should try to schedule at least four to six practice arguments before the competition. Depending upon the difficulty of the case that you will argue, you might want to schedule more than six practice arguments.

Each panel of practice judges for competitors preparing for a national competition should consist of at least two judges. Three is the optimal number. Vary the types of judges that you have on the panel for each practice argument in terms of their background, knowledge, and experience. Practice judges should come from varying backgrounds; practitioners, actual trial or appellate court judges, students, and professors will normally suffice. Practice judges should also have varying levels of knowledge about the case and/or experience in the area of law in which the case is set. You may be surprised at the insightful questions that come from practice argument judges who have little or no experience in the area of law that you are arguing. Similarly, judges who are unfamiliar with the facts and law governing the case will help you prepare for more basic questions and permit you to simplify your presentation because you will have to learn how to explain simply and concisely the facts and the law.

In addition, vary the time limit for the practice arguments. During the first practice argument, do not set a time limit so the judges can ask as many questions as possible. The more questions that the judges ask during practice, the more likely you will be prepared to field a wide array of questions during your actual argument. Depending upon the number of practice arguments that you have scheduled, you might want to have no time limit on the second practice argument. From thereon out, practice your argument using the time limit required by the moot court competition's rules.

If you are going to deliver an oral argument for your legal writing course or for an intramural moot court competition, your practice methods should be slightly different from those used to prepare an argument for a national moot court competition. Practice your oral argument with the student who has been assigned as your partner, the students who have been assigned as your opponents, and other classmates. Each student should take turns delivering his or her oral argument. The students who are not arguing should serve as judges and ask questions of the student who is presenting the argument.

Additionally, you can practice your argument in front of a mirror. If you do this, take the answers that you thought of during your brainstorming session and rehearse them. You might also present your argument to a friend, your spouse, or a significant other. Permit your listener to ask you questions.

Your listener may certainly be someone who does not have any knowledge of the case or the law. That way, your answers to any questions will need to be much more concise and simple.

After practicing, you should revise and refine your argument. For example, you may find that your practice judges focused their questioning on an issue that you did not anticipate in your preparation. If that is the case, you will want to be prepared to discuss that issue the next time that you practice your argument.

One final note about practicing: do not over-practice. While you should be well versed in the facts, law, and public policy of your case, you can get to the point of being so saturated with the case that you lose your zeal for it. It is important that you show enthusiasm for your case to the court during your oral argument. If you lose your eagerness to discuss the case with the court, you will detract from the persuasiveness of your argument.

(5) Other Considerations During Preparation

There are a few other considerations to be mindful of when preparing for oral argument that do not neatly fit into the steps that I just described. To begin, make sure that you are familiar with the rules or guidelines for the assignment or competition of which your oral argument is a part. Read those rules before you prepare for your argument, read them during your preparation, and read them again shortly before you actually give your oral argument. Do not risk losing points on your argument because you violated the rules.

Scout your argument location before your argument, including the building and courtroom where you will argue, if that is possible. If you know where the courtroom is, you will not risk being late for your argument. Also, you will be familiar with the layout of the courtroom, such as the location of the podium, the bench, and the tables for the advocates. I have coached several teams during national moot court competitions. We always arrive for the competition at least a day before the competition so we can locate the courthouse and the courtrooms where we will argue the next day.

Put yourself in a confident frame of mind about your case. Oral advocates who project confidence at the podium are more impressive to the judges than advocates who are meek. The best way to instill self-confidence is to prepare thoroughly during each step of preparation that I have described. Good preparation fosters confidence.

Keep in mind the "big picture" of the case. Although the court before which you will argue is not a real appellate court, it will function like one and ask questions like one. Appellate courts are always interested in the consequences of their decisions beyond the case at bar. In other words, they are always thinking of the "big picture" implications of the case. Therefore, you should think of those implications, too.

Finally, know the remedy that you are seeking. Do you want the court to affirm? To reverse? To remand for further proceedings? I am always surprised to see student advocates who are able to deliver a great oral argument on the facts and the law, but who are unfortunately unable to tell the court what result they desire. Again, even though you are not appearing before a real appellate court, treat your moot court as a real court. A real appellate court will certainly want to know the remedy that you seek.

C. Delivering the Oral Argument

You have prepared for your oral argument. You have practiced it for several times. You have reached the day on which you will actually deliver your oral argument. If you are competing in a moot court competition, you will have to deliver your argument several times, and you will probably have to argue both sides of the case. So how do you proceed?

(1) Getting Started

When you enter the courtroom for your argument, you should seat yourself at the appropriate counsel table. In most appellate courts, counsel for the appellant/petitioner sits at the table on the left side as the parties face the bench, and the appellee/respondent sits at the table on the right side. Despite this customary placement of the parties, I have seen courtrooms that seat the parties in the opposite manner — the appellant/petitioner on the right and the appellee/respondent on the left. If you have any doubt regarding where to sit, make sure that you find out which table is yours before your argument.

After the bailiff has called the court to order and the judges have taken their places on the bench, the appellant/petitioner will proceed first. If you are the appellant or petitioner, you should wait to approach the podium until the chief judge of the panel tells you that you may proceed. When you reach the podium, you should not begin speaking until you have the attention of all of the judges on the panel. In other words, you know that you may begin when all of the judges are looking at you.

As you begin speaking, it is critical that you treat your oral argument as a dialogue with the bench rather than an uninterrupted speech or monologue. You should refrain from reading your argument to the court and should attempt to

Chapter 4
Writing Briefs

maintain as much eye contact with the judges as possible. Indeed, the most important time to maintain eye contact with the judges is at the beginning of your oral argument. Therefore, you may want to memorize the opening to your argument.

In your opening, it is customary to begin by greeting the judges ("Good morning" or "Good afternoon" will suffice) and stating, "May it please the court." You should also introduce yourself, tell the court which party you represent, and inform the court how much time you have reserved for rebuttal. After introducing yourself, you should give the court what is typically called a "roadmap." Your roadmap is your explanation of which issue or issues the case involves and which specific points you will discuss in your argument. Just as you did in your brief, you should frame your statement of each point persuasively and assertively, in terms that favor your client. Finally, you should tell the court what remedy you are seeking.

In a national moot court competition in which I served as a coach, one of the issues that the students argued was whether a criminal defense attorney who slept through parts of his client's trial should be presumed to have prejudiced his client in violation of the Sixth Amendment's right to the assistance of counsel. The advocate for the United States, which had lost the case in the lower court and was appealing that ruling, could have begun his presentation as follows.

> Good afternoon, and may it please the court. My name is James Dimitri, and I represent the Appellant, the United States of America. With the court's permission, I have reserved two minutes for rebuttal.
>
> Your Honors, the issue before this court is whether a criminal defendant must prove prejudice under the Sixth Amendment to the United States Constitution when his counsel sleeps during portions of the defendant's trial. The United States respectfully asks this court to reverse the judgment of the district court, which presumed prejudice, for the following reasons. First, the Sixth Amendment is not violated when defense counsel sleeps through portions of the defendant's trial that are not critical to the defendant's interests. Here, defense counsel slept through portions of the trial that were peripheral to or inconsequential to the defendant's guilt. Second, prejudice is normally presumed only when the government is responsible for causing

> the prejudice. Here, the United States did not engage in conduct that caused the defendant's prejudice. Finally, a presumption of prejudice in cases where counsel sleeps might encourage unscrupulous attorneys to feign sleep in order to secure a reversal of a conviction on appeal.

Following your introduction, if you are the appellant, you may provide the court with a brief recitation of the relevant facts in the case. In real appellate arguments, many appellants dispense with a recitation of the facts. An appellant may do this because the time allotted to the parties for argument is normally quite brief and because most judges have already read the briefs and are familiar with the facts. Whether you, as a student oral advocate, give a statement of the facts is up to you. Most judges in moot court competitions expect to hear a recitation of the facts, so you probably should talk about the facts. If you do explain the facts, do so very briefly. If you take up more than ninety seconds discussing facts, you will be using time that is better devoted to discussing the issues. Therefore, when reciting the facts, focus only on those facts that are relevant to the points you will be making in your argument.

After reciting the relevant facts for the court, you should begin arguing the most important point in your argument, provided that you have not already received questions from the bench. As I explained previously, your most important point is the point that gives you the best chance of success on appeal. Argue the most important point first so you do not get sidetracked from conveying your message to the court.

Follow your most important point by discussing the one or two other points that you need to make during your argument. Many novices believe that you should support each point in your argument with many references to citations and legal precedent. I recommend that you avoid this approach because dwelling on citations and precedent will bore the court and cause your argument to become unfocused. Moreover, I have heard a few judges remark that an advocate who dwells on reciting case law to answer questions from the bench appears to be too evasive.

Limit your references to citations and legal precedent. Support your argument by explaining why your argument presents the most logical approach to solving the issues before the court. Do this in terms of the facts, governing legal concepts, and public policy involved in the case. Weave some equitable concepts into your argument by explaining why you should win in terms of common sense and fairness.

(2) Answering Questions from the Bench

It is a rare occasion when your argument will be uninterrupted by questions from the bench. Remember that one of the primary reasons courts set cases for oral argument is to ask questions about the case. Hence, you should not treat questions from the bench as an intrusion upon your presentation. Rather, you should welcome questions from the bench and strive to answer them to the court's satisfaction.

Learning how to properly answer questions from the bench takes time and practice. Jon Laramore, a former colleague of mine who has argued scores of cases before state and federal appellate courts, has suggested five steps for answering questions that I have found helpful. Those steps are:

1) Listen to and understand the question;
2) Pause to digest the question and think about an answer;
3) Answer directly;
4) Explain the answer;
5) Relate the answer to your argument.

First, you should listen carefully to the question. This means that you must stop talking immediately when a judge asks a question. If you talk over the judges, you may miss part of the question, and you may appear to be giving too little deference to the judges. Make sure that you listen to the entire question, not just part of it. If you do not listen to the entire question, you may supply the judge with an answer to only part of the question, not all of it. More importantly, make sure that you understand the judge's question. If you do not understand the question, ask the judge politely to repeat it. For example, you may say, "I'm sorry your honor, but I didn't understand your question. Could you please ask it again?"

Second, after listening to and understanding the question, take a brief moment to pause to digest the question in your mind and to think about an answer. Pausing is important because it gives you the opportunity to really ponder the question and to formulate a complete answer. Do not be frightened by a brief moment of silence in your presentation. Your oral argument does not have to be continuously filled with your speaking. Most judges will expect the advocates to momentarily pause.

Third, and most importantly in the five steps that I have listed above, you should provide a direct answer to the question. If you can answer the question with a "yes" or a "no," then do so. If you do not know the answer to the question, do not try to bluff the judges or evade the question by failing to answer it. Rather, be honest with the court and tell the judges that you do not know the answer to the question and then move on. If the question is not about a critical area of your case, the judges will appreciate your candor. Of course, there will be critical areas of your case about which you should know, such as the record of proceedings and controlling law. If you are questioned about facts from the record or the controlling law and do not know the answer, refer to your outline. If you cannot find an answer in your outline, tell the court that you do not know the answer, apologize to the court, and move on.

After you have given a direct answer to the question, the fourth step is to explain your answer to the court. If you have given a "yes" or "no" answer to the court, tell the court why you have provided it with that answer. For instance, if you had to concede a negative point in your case through your answer to a question, explain why that concession should not prevent the court from deciding the case in your favor.

The fifth and final step in answering questions is the most difficult task and requires a lot of practice. The fifth step is to find a way to relate your answer to one of the main points that you intend to make in your argument, particularly to a point that you have not yet addressed. In other words, try to use your answer to segue to the next point in your argument if you are ready to begin discussing that particular point.

As I noted before, many of the questions coming from the bench will focus on the weaknesses of your case. Sometimes, a judge may ask you to concede or admit to a point, particularly a weakness in your case. If a judge asks you to concede to a weakness in your case, it may be appropriate to make the concession, particularly if admitting to the weakness will not affect the ultimate outcome of the case or the strength of your argument. Making a concession in this instance will permit you to gain credibility because of your candor with the court, which will strengthen your argument in the long run. Nonetheless, you do not want to be too conciliatory with the court, especially if a judge insists that you concede to a point that will result in defeat.

Do not assume that all questions from the bench will be about the weaknesses in your case. In real appellate arguments, a judge who agrees with one advocate's position in the case will often ask favorable questions of that advocate. Usually, judges ask friendly questions to convince their colleagues on the bench that the advocate the judge is questioning has a valid position and should probably win the case. You should expect to be asked some friendly questions during your argument. Thus, try to recognize friendly questions so you can provide a direct and strong answer to them.

You should also expect to encounter hypothetical questions from the bench. Judges ask hypothetical questions to test the bounds of the positions put forth by the advocates because the court's decisions will affect similar cases in the future. Of course, a court in a moot court argument will not be making an actual decision in the case. Nonetheless, it is not out of the ordinary for moot court judges to ask hypothetical questions. Whatever you do, do not brush off a hypothetical question by responding, "That's not the case before the court." Instead, try to answer the question directly. If you are not sure of the answer to a hypothetical question, there is nothing wrong with admitting that you do not know the answer.

On rare occasions, you may encounter a moot court judge who is quite hostile with his or her questioning. For instance, there may be a judge who persists in pressing you to concede to what he or she perceives to be a weakness in your case. Or, you may have a judge who simply tells you that your argument is stupid. Unfortunately, not all judges are civil with their questioning. No matter how hostile statements or questions from the bench may become, you should be graceful and poised. Tell the judge posing a hostile question or comment that you respectfully disagree and move on with your argument.

If you are participating in a moot court competition, you are probably a member of a team in which your partner is arguing another issue to be addressed in the case. When you prepare for your oral argument, you should at least be generally familiar with your partner's issue and argument. Occasionally, a judge may ask you a question regarding the issue that your partner is arguing. I would caution against answering such a question by merely saying, "My co-counsel will address that point." Instead, try to answer the question to the best of your ability. Respond briefly to the question, then say, "Co-counsel will develop this discussion further, with the court's permission, since she has prepared to address the answer to the court's question."

Sometimes you may encounter questions from the bench that are tangential or irrelevant to the issues before the court. Resist the temptation to characterize the question as irrelevant or unimportant. Do not act as if the judge is creating an inconvenience to you with the question. Rather, be patient with the court and try to answer all questions from the bench, even if they take you off on what you consider to be a tangent. To avoid being sidetracked, keep your answer to such a question concise and direct. Then, move on to whatever relevant points you need to discuss with the court.

(3) Wrapping up Your Argument

After you have made the points you need to make and have answered all of the court's questions, you should conclude your argument. In real appellate oral arguments, the parties are not required to use up the entire time that has been allotted for argument. Therefore, most good appellate lawyers will "quit while they're ahead" and conclude their argument before their time is up if the lawyer has made all of the necessary points during the argument and has answered all of the court's questions. Some moot court competitions, however, require the advocates to use a minimum number of minutes to make their presentations. If you are arguing in a moot court competition, make sure that you check the rules of the competition to determine if there are a minimum number of minutes that you must argue. Otherwise, you may conclude before your time has expired, provided that you have sufficiently answered all of the court's questions and have made to the court all of the points that you must make.

Your conclusion should be brief. I suggest that you briefly summarize the points that you made during your argument and that you repeat the remedy you are seeking from the court. Sometimes, you may be in the middle of answering a question from the court when your time for argument expires. If this occurs, acknowledge that your time is up and ask the court for permission to continue your answer. I have never seen a court refuse this request. Then, after you have finished your answer, say, "Thank you," and sit down. Do not launch into a prepared conclusion in which you reiterate the points you have made and repeat your prayer for relief.

(4) Rebuttal

After the appellee has presented his or her argument, the appellant has an opportunity to give a short rebuttal. If you are giving a rebuttal, reserve no more than two or three minutes to do so. If you reserve more time than this, you will probably take away time that you will need to address the issues during your opening argument. You should reserve time for rebuttal, regardless of whether you use that time. If you do not, you will be unable to correct any factual or legal misrepresentations that opposing counsel has made during his or her argument.

To "rebut" something means to refute it or to respond to it. If you represent the appellant, you should keep this meaning in mind because you should use your rebuttal only to respond to points that the appellee raised in his or her argument. For example, you might use your rebuttal to clarify or correct factual misrepresentations or misstatements of legal doctrine that your opposing counsel made in his or her argument. *Never* use rebuttal to raise new issues or to raise points that you were unable to cover in your opening argument. This is not the purpose of rebuttal, and the judges will not be pleased if you use rebuttal to cover points that you neglected in your opening argument.

Because the time allotted for rebuttal will be brief, you should cover no more than two points in your rebuttal. Be concise and direct in discussing these points. In addition, listen carefully and closely to your opposing counsel's argument. Otherwise, you will not have anything to talk about on rebuttal. For example, you may fail to address a critical misrepresentation made by opposing counsel.

If you are counsel for the appellee, you may believe that you are at a disadvantage because the appellant has the last word with rebuttal. This, however, is a mistaken belief. Indeed, the appellee's argument is, in part, a rebuttal of the appellant's opening argument. A good advocate arguing on the appellee's behalf will not be a slave to her outline. Rather, the good advocate will be flexible; she will listen closely to the appellant's opening argument and will take note of any incorrect or unclear characterizations of the facts or the law. She will then incorporate into her argument a rebuttal to those mischaracterizations. In sum, if you represent the appellee, you should "go with the flow" and modify your argument according to what the appellant says during her opening argument.

(5) Appearance, Mechanics and Miscellaneous Advice

Your physical appearance when you appear for an oral argument should be business-like and conservative. Both male and female advocates should dress in a dark, conservative business suit. Avoid flamboyant ties, shirts, or blouses. I have heard some judges state that they prefer to see women wearing skirts, but I do not believe that most judges would be offended to see a female advocate wearing pants with a suit. If you do wear a skirt, make sure that it is of a conservative length. Don't show up for an argument wearing a mini-skirt.

Your posture at the podium should be even. Stand up straight and face the bench. Do not stand leaning on one leg, and do not shift your weight from one leg to the other. Rather, remain stationary. You should also bend your knees slightly.

Eye contact with the judges is extremely important during your presentation. Remember, you want to maintain a conversational tone with the judges, and eye contact with the bench will aid you in that goal. When a judge asks you a question, you should focus on keeping eye contact with the whole bench, not just the judge who asked you the question.

Your delivery of your argument should be simple and deliberate. Use simple, concise sentences to promote comprehension. Do not speak too quickly or rush through your argument, because you will be hard to understand. Furthermore, avoid a monotonous or meek delivery. Chief Justice William Rehnquist of the United States Supreme Court suggests that you have a "controlled enthusiasm" for your case. This means that you should use some vocal inflection for emphasis to show the court that you believe in your case. It also means that you should avoid being overly dramatic with your argument. For example, do not pound on the podium or raise your voice too loudly. You may gesture with your hands, but do not overdo it to the point that it becomes distracting. I have a tendency to gesture a lot when I speak. To prevent myself from gesturing distractingly during oral argument, I typically fold my hands in front of me.

Avoid verbal pauses and verbal filler. Verbal pauses are the "uhs" and "ums" that some people use when speaking. Speakers often use verbal pauses when they are thinking of what to say. Instead of using verbal pauses, simply pause silently. Verbal filler is language that a speaker unnecessarily uses to preface a point that he or she is making. For example, an advocate may say, "*It is the Appellant's position that* the court should reverse the decision of the trial court," or, "*We would submit that* the case mentioned by opposing counsel is not controlling." Using verbal filler is unnecessary because it lengthens your argument and weakens the impact of your advocacy. Therefore, eliminate it from your argument completely.

Your demeanor should be deferential but firm. Refer to each judge as "your honor" or by the judge's title and name, such as "Justice Souter." Refer to the judges collectively as "this court" or "your Honors." As my legal writing professor used to remind me, an oral argument is not a military exercise, so the judges should not be called "ma'am" or "sir." Further, do not take a defensive tone with the judges. One of the worst things that you can do during an oral argument is to fight with a judge regarding a point about which you do not agree. This may make the judge upset at you and will unquestionably cause you to lose credibility with the court. It is certainly permissible to disagree with a judge as long as you do so respectfully. If you do not agree with a judge's assessment of an issue or point, say, "I respectfully disagree, your honor," and then use the facts and the law to give the reasons why you disagree. Logic is your best ally in this situation.

If you are making a point in response to a judge's question that you made before in your argument, avoid prefacing your statement with "As I said before," or, "As I said earlier." Some judges may be offended by these prefatory comments because to them they may mean, "Why weren't you listening to me before?" Similarly, avoid prefacing statements with the words "clearly" or "obviously," especially if you are making a key legal point in your argument. For instance, you would not want to say, "*Clearly* the trial court incorrectly decided this case." If this were "clear," then there would be no need for oral argument. Moreover, judges tune out this sort of language because lawyers have overused it over time.

Avoid reading long quotations from the record or the case law you are using in support of your arguments. You will bore the judges if you do so.

This does not mean that you may never quote from the record or the law. If you do so, keep the quote short.

Finally, be yourself during oral argument. Everyone has a different style of speaking, so you should not try to mimic the speaking style of other advocates. If you have prepared well for your oral argument, then you can afford to be yourself because you will give a good oral argument.

Exercises

1. Suppose you were Marie Lin, an associate with ABA Law Firm in Indiana, U.S.A. Arnold Jones was your client and you have filed a motion with the trial court to dismiss the charge. Please write a brief to a trial court.

On May 16, 2008, Arnold Jones, the driver of a fuel oil truck, was convicted of driving on the left side of a two-lane highway. He said that he did so to avoid a large and unexpected patch of ice. It was rush hour. No one was forced off the road.

State Law §117.01 provides:

> It shall be a misdemeanor for any person to drive in the left lane of a two-lane highway.

The following four cases from the state court of appeals interpret this statute.

Cain v. State (1969)

The defendant was convicted of driving on the wrong side of the road. The defendant was joyriding with friends and was intoxicated. Two cars were forced off the road. We reject his appeal. Traffic safety is of paramount concern. There can be no exceptions, for exceptions would undermine any confidence the reasonable person would have in highway safety.

Mckinney v. State (1975)

The defendant was convicted of driving on the wrong side of a two-lane highway when he swerved to avoid hitting a child. There was little traffic, and the incident occurred during the day. We reverse. Although every reasonable person has a right to expect other cars to stay in their appropriate lanes, it would be intolerable for the law to put a driver in this kind of dilemma.

Shoop v. State (1981)

The defendant was convicted of driving on the wrong side of a two-lane highway when he swerved to avoid hitting a pothole. The defendant is a mechanic, and he testified that the pothole was clearly visible. He also testified that the pothole was likely to have irreparably damaged a tire and bent the tie rod on his car. The road was generally rough, and there was light traffic. We affirm. Financial self-interest is not enough to outweigh highway safety.

Gordon v. State (1991)

The defendant, a volunteer fireman driving to a fire station for an emergency call, was convicted of violating State Law §117.01. He was not using flashing lights or a siren, and there was nothing about his car to distinguish it as an emergency vehicle. The defendant was passing long lines of cars to get to the station. We affirm the conviction. An exception to §117.01 would be permissible when there is a clear public necessity, but this is not the proper case for such an exception.

2. Suppose you are Marie Lin, an associate with ABA Law Firm in Indiana, U.S.A. Dr. Richard Farmer is your client and you have filed a motion

for summary judgment with the trial court, claiming that Farmer's negligence did not proximately cause the death of Mary Lee's son. Please write a 500-to 600-word brief to a trial court.

On May 6, 2009, fourteen-year-old Andrew Lee was struck by a truck while riding his bicycle. Although his injuries seemed slight, his mother, Mary Lee took him to the hospital. His sole complaint was a headache. After Mary described the accident, Dr. Richard Farmer ordered X-rays. The X-rays did indicate a skull fracture. Farmer did not examine the back of the boy's head, where there was a red mark, nor did he use the other diagnostic procedures that are standard in such cases. Farmer sent the boy home and asked his mother to observe him. Andrew died early the next morning. The coroner concluded from an autopsy that the boy died from hemorrhaging due to a basal skull fracture.

Mary Lee has sued Dr. Farmer for the negligent death of her son. All of the facts above-mentioned were brought out during discovery and they are not in dispute. There is no dispute that Farmer was negligent. There are two relevant cases in Indiana State:

Moulton v. Ginocchio (1966)

Craig Moulton, who is the administrator of the decedent's estate, brought this action against Samuel Ginocchio, a physician, for negligence in treating the decedent's illness. The trial court dismissed the complaint on the ground that doctor's negligence did not proximately cause her death. We disagree and reverse. The decedent, a diabetic, went to Ginocchio's hospital with intense abdominal pain, which Ginocchio diagnosed as a stomach "bug". He gave her pain medication and released her. She died several hours later from massive hemorrhaging caused by an intestinal obstruction. Ginocchio claims that there is no basis for concluding with certainty that his negligent diagnosis and treatment caused her death. The law does not require certainty, however; a physician is answerable if he prevents a substantial possibility of survival. Moulton's experts testified categorically and without contradiction that the decedent would have survived had she undergone prompt surgery. Moulton, therefore, satisfied the "substantial possibility" requirement.

Chapter 4
Writing Briefs

Mallard v. Harkin (1969)

Eleanor Mallard brought suit against Joseph Harkin, a physician, for Harkin's allegedly negligent failure to immediately diagnose and perform surgery to arrest a degenerative disease that has now left Mallard paralyzed. The trial court found that Harkin breached this duty of reasonable care but that his actions did not proximately cause Mallard's condition. Only the latter ruling has been appealed. We agree with the trial court and affirm.

We held in Moulton v. Ginocchio (1966) that a doctor is liable when his negligence "prevents a substantial possibility of survival" for the decedent. In that case, there was testimony that the decedent would have survived. Traditional standards of proximate cause similarly require evidence that the result was more likely than not caused by the act. Mallard does not meet that standard. Mallard's expert witness testified that prompt surgery would have given Mallard "a possibility" of recovery but that she "probably would not have recovered."

It is an attractive and emotionally appealing idea that physician should be held liable for the loss of even a remote chance of full recovery from a debilitating disease or injury. But such a rule would result in an unjust situation in which the physician would be held accountable for harm that he did not cause and may not have been able to prevent. We refuse, as a matter of public policy, to hold a physician liable on a mere possibility.

3. Suppose you were Martin Harrison, an associate with ABC Law Firm in Indiana, U. S. A. Maria Jones was your client. The trial court made a proper judgment. However, the defendant filed a suit to an appellate court. Please write a brief to the appellate court in Indiana to affirm the judgment of the trail court.

The defendant Juvenile, fifteen (15) years old and the victim both were students of Emma Donnan Middle School in Indianapolis. On the afternoon of December 8, 2005, Juvenile got on the bus, while the victim already sitting in front of the bus. Juvenile called the victim "bitch" when he went by. The victim went to the back of the bus where Juvenile was sitting to ask why he called her names. But Juvenile responded with calling the victim a "black bitch" and a "nigger" again. Juvenile started fighting by hitting the victim on her face which was painful. When the fight was stopped by others, the victim's nose was bleeding.

The trial court properly dealt with the evidence. There is sufficient evidence to prove beyond a reasonable doubt that Juvenile hit the victim and caused victim's nose bleeding thereby establishing Battery, Class A Misdemeanor. You are going to argue that the evidence is sufficient to prove that Juvenile hit the victim and caused bodily injury.

According to *Smith v. State*, 809 N. E. 2d 938 (Ind. Ct. App. 2004), you can know that the Court will neither reweigh the evidence nor judge the credibility of the witness when reviewing a claim of sufficiency of the evidence; rather, the Court will consider the evidence and reasonable inferences drawn therefrom that support the verdict and will affirm the conviction if there is probative evidence from which a reasonable person could have found the defendant guilty beyond a reasonable doubt.

4. Suppose you were Martin Harrison, a law clerk in the State of Indiana, U. S. A. The trial court made a proper judgment. However, the defendant filed a suit to an appellate court. Please write a brief to the appellate court in Indiana to affirm the judgment of the trail court.

On September 14, 2005, Defendant was walking past the Metro Park in Marion County, Indian. Defendant came across several gas cans, he looks around and took a can and moved quickly to the front of the building. Defendant went quickly through the gate toward the end of the building and went around the building. The owner of the park was observing Defendant's movements through a wooden fence. This owner followed Defendant for a while and started saying "Hey" to him to his attention. Defendant turned and threw the gas can at the owner and field. The owner dialed 911 and police found Defendant in dry creek bed and arrested him with the help of a canine unit.

On September 15, 2005, Defendant was charged with Court I, Theft, a Class D Felony; Court II, striking a Law Enforcement Animal, a Class A Misdemeanor and Court III, two counts of Resisting Law Enforcement by force, a Class A Misdemeanor. Defendant waived his right to a jury trial and a bench trial was conducted on January 10, 2006, at which Defendant was judged of theft, resisting of law enforcement and one count of resisting law enforcement by force; he was acquitted of the remaining counts.

A sentencing hearing was held on January 10, 2006. Defendant was sentenced to 545 days for Theft, 365 days for Resisting Law Enforcement and 365 days for Resisting Law by force. The court ordered all of the counts to run concurrently.

According to *McClendon v. State.* 671 N. E. 2d 486, 488 (Ind. Ct. App. 1996), you know that the court will neither reweigh the evidence nor judge the credibility of the witnesses, when reviewing the sufficiency of the evidence. In the contrary, the Court will consider the evidence most favorable to the judgment together with all reasonable interferences to be drawn therefrom. According to the case *Newman v. State.* 677 N. E. 2d 590, 593 (Ind. Ct. App. 1997), the Court will affirm a conviction if it is supported by substantial evidence of probative value.

The statute **IND. CODE SECTION 35-43-4-2** provides:

(a) A person who knowingly or intentionally exerts unauthorized control over property of another person, with intent to deprive the other person of any part of its value or use, commits Theft, a Class D Felony.

There are three relevant cases in Indiana State:

Brant v. State (1989)

PROCEDURAL POSTURE: Defendant sought review of a judgment of the Lake Superior Court (Indiana), which convicted him of theft in violation of Ind. Code Section 35—43—4—2 (Supp. 1985).

OVERVIEW: Defendant worked as a car salesman. Defendant's employer agreed to sell him a car and that he would pay for the car by performing certain specified mechanical repairs on other cars at the lot and earning sales commissions. Pursuant to the agreement, defendant took his employer's check to the car's seller and returned with the car and title, which had been endorsed with him as the purchaser, but was not notarized. Defendant's employer kept the title on his desk. Defendant came to work one day and after speaking with his employer took the title and left. The court rejected defendant's contention that he lacked the requisite criminal intent. The court also held that there was evidence that the title had value as required under Code Section 35—43—4—2, and that defendant knew he had no right to take the title. The court determined that the State did violate a discovery order to disclose the criminal history of the complaining witness, the employer. The court found that there was no evidence or contention that the employer had been convicted of or even charged with any crime.

OUTCOME: The court affirmed the judgment.

Hart v. State (1996)

PROCEDURAL POSTURE: Defendant appealed his convictions by the jury in the Clay Circuit Court (Indiana) for intimidation with a deadly weapon in violation of Ind. Code Section 35—45—2—1, escape while using a deadly weapon under Ind. Code Section 35—44—3—5, and theft in violation of Ind. Code Section 35—43—4—2.

OVERVIEW: Pursuant to a tip off of defendant's erratic driving, a deputy town marshal (deputy marshal) followed defendant. After stopping defendant, the deputy marshal conducted sobriety tests and tried to disarm defendant and take him to a local hospital for urine test. As deputy marshal reached into his police car for brass knuckles, defendant pointed a gun at him and later escaped. Defendant argued, inter alia, that the trial court erred in giving instruction on "lawful detention" and in rejecting his tendered instruction on the same and that the trial court's instruction was misleading; that the trial court erred in denying his motion for directed verdict as to the escape and theft charges; that the trial court erred in allowing the state to amend information after the parties had rested; and that his conviction for escape while using a deadly weapon and intimidation with a deadly weapon violated the prohibition of double jeopardy. The court held that defendant was not prejudiced by the instructions and that the directed verdicts were not appropriate because the evidence was sufficient to support defendant's convictions and that double jeopardy was not violated.

OUTCOME: The court affirmed defendant's convictions for intimidation with a deadly weapon, escape while using a deadly, and theft.

Brown v. State (1990)

PROCEDURAL POSTURE: Defendant appealed from a judgment of the Martin Circuit Court (Indiana), which convicted him of attempted murder and resisting law enforcement.

OVERVIEW: After a bank robbery, defendant's car was stopped at a roadblock. Defendant shot at the policeman who was approaching the car. He was convicted of attempted murder and resisting law enforcement. He claimed that the evidence was insufficient, that he should have been granted a change of venue and individual sequestered *voir dire*, and that the trial judge was biased. The court affirmed his conviction. The requisite intent for attempted murder could be inferred from the use of a deadly weapon in a manner likely to cause death or great bodily harm. There was ample evidence from which the jury could conclude that defendant used his gun in a manner reasonably calculated to cause severe injury or death. Defendant did not show evidence of pretrial publicity sufficient to create community bias or prejudice or that the potential jurors were unable to set aside preconceived notions of guilt. Defendant had no absolute right to separately question prospective jurors and failed to show highly unusual or potentially damaging circumstances. Defendant did not move for a change of judge on the basis of impartiality.

OUTCOME: The court affirmed defendant's conviction.

Chapter 5

Drafting Contracts

Contracts are promises that the law will enforce. The law provides remedies if a promise is breached or recognizes the performance of a promise as a duty. Contracts arise when a duty does or may come into existence, because of a promise made by one of the parties. To be legally binding as a contract, a promise must be exchanged for adequate consideration. Adequate consideration is a benefit or detriment which a party receives which reasonably and fairly induces them to make the promise/contract. For example, promises that are purely gifts are not considered enforceable because the personal satisfaction the grantor of the promise may receive from the act of giving is normally not considered adequate consideration. Certain promises that are not considered contracts may, in limited circumstances, be enforced if one party has relied to his detriment on the assurances of the other party.

Contracts are mainly governed by state statutory and common (judge-made) law and private law. Private law principally includes the terms of the agreement between the parties who are exchanging promises. This private law may override many of the rules otherwise established by state law. Statutory law may require some contracts be put in writing and executed with particular formalities. Otherwise, the parties may enter into a binding agreement without signing a formal written document. Most of the principles of the common law of contracts are outlined in the Restatement of the Law Second, Contracts, published by the American Law Institute. The Uniform Commercial Code, whose original articles have been adopted in nearly every state, represents a body of statutory law that governs important categories of contracts. The main articles that deal with the law of contracts are Article 1 (General Provisions) and Article 2 (Sales). Sections of Article 9 (Secured Transactions) govern contracts assigning the rights to payment in security interest agreements. Contracts related to particular activities or business sectors may be highly regulated by state and/or federal law.

A contract in its most basic form is a legally binding agreement between two parties. The subject matter and terms of a contract are almost limitless as long as they are not illegal, impossible to fulfill or entered into by a minor or someone without the mental capacity to contract. Contracts do not have to be in writing; however, enforcement of an oral contract can be difficult. A valid contract must contain three elements: an offer, acceptance and consideration. In addition, a written contract must be signed by both parties and dated. Please take the following five steps to draft a simple contact[1]:

(1) Gather the full names and contact information for the parties along with any necessary legal descriptions, if applicable.

(2) Identify the parties to the contract in the first paragraph as well as the subject matter of the contract. The date should also be included in the first paragraph.

(3) Explain the terms of the contract in more detail in the succeeding paragraphs. Include precise terms such as a description of any property involved, dates of any payments to be made and amounts written out as words, not numbers.

(4) Provide a section for default terms and choice of law in the event of a dispute. Although the hope is that there will not be a need to address a breach of the contract, it is best to plan ahead. If specific steps are to be followed in the event of a default, include them in this section. In addition, specify which state law shall apply in the event of a breach.

(5) Sign and date the contract. You can also choose to sign in front of a notary public or impartial witnesses, although it is not required to be legal and valid.

---

[1] By Renee Booker http://www.ehow.com/how_5058814_draft-simple-contract.html

1. How to Draft a Notice of a Breach of Contract[①]

In any type of business arrangement, contracts and written agreements are often required to set forth the terms of a working relationship between an employer and employee, or between a business and contractors hired on behalf of the business. A breach of contract occurs when one or more parties subject to the terms of a specific contract fails to abide by those terms. A breached contract results in nullifying the original agreement and often requires that a notice of breach of contract be sent to the offending party.

(1) Enter the date on which you create and print the breach of contract notice at the top of the page. It should be emphasizes the importance of creating a record to show when the offending party is notified of the contract breach. Include the delivery method by which you are sending the notice to the breaching party. State the name of the other party along with your own name, or the business name, and the name of the agreement, if applicable. Include the effective date of the contract, or when the contract was signed.

(2) Describe in clear, concise language how the agreement was breached. Provide a brief explanation regarding how the breaching party's actions have either hindered the other party's ability to live up to the contract terms, or how the breaching party has failed to perform according to the terms set forth in the agreement. Indicate how you would like to remedy the situation going forward. You may provide the breaching party with a deadline during which the breach can be rectified. Alternatively, you may notify the breaching party that the contract is void and that appropriate legal action is to follow.

(3) Type your breach of contract notice using a computerized word processing program, and have the document professionally printed in a clear, legible font. Send your notice to its intended recipient through certified mail or document courier. Retain a copy of the letter in addition to a record of the delivery notice. If legal action is required now or in the future, you may need to furnish these documents to the court.

[①] http://www.ehow.com/how_12130705_draft-notice-breach-contract.html

2. How to Draft a Contract Clause Dealing with Delay in Performance

Some contracts require performance to be performed by a specific date or have services or outcomes that will be impacted negatively if delay occurs. When drafting a clause to deal with delay, here are some things to consider.

(1) Be aware that the limitations in contractual remedies make dealing with delays of performance difficult.

- It can be difficult to assess the? costs? arising from a delay.
- A breach of time stipulation is not a serious breach without more actionable breaches being attached to it.

(2) Ensure that the clause drawn up makes it clear that time is of the essence.

- If it is made clear that time is of the essence, any delay will justify termination of the contract. You may wish to guide the client into raising this specifically in oral discussions with the other party if you consider it would emphasize the importance of not delaying and the termination outcome.
- If time has not been made of the essence, it may be possible to send a notice to the non-performing party to remedy the delay within a reasonable time and to stipulate that time is now of the essence. However, to try and insert this into a contract after it has been signed off, you will need to read the conditions set out in the contract's termination clause, which usually determines how to deal with breaches.

(3) Require that payment will be withheld during a delay. This withholding should occur until the delay is remedied. This is the best method for dealing with delay as part of drafting the contract.

Consider what will happen if it is you or your client who delays. You may need to add something into the contract to cover this possibility. Be aware of the consequences on yourself if delay is caused by your end.

3. How to Draft a Contract for a Catering Business[①]

For most people, hiring a caterer is not a common event and only occurs during a major life change or event — such as a wedding or graduation party.

---

① by Michelle Hogan, Demand Media

When drafting your contract for your catering business, make sure you understand that most people are unfamiliar with the process caterers develop to make events successful; therefore, ensure that each aspect of the event is clearly and concisely presented to your client within a formal contract.

(1) Write a list of all of the items you want to cover in your contract. This can include the customer's name and address; the type of function; the location of the function; how many guests are expected; whether you or the client will be responsible for dining service, dinnerware, tables and chairs and other items, as well as the suggested menu for the event.

(2) Include clear language about the amount of the deposit and date reservation. The client must understand that by reserving a certain date, you are now unable to book that date for anyone else should they cancel. The date reservation deposit is usually 50 percent of the total bill. State when final payment is due. Many catering businesses expect payment in full a few days ahead of the scheduled event if costs exceed a certain dollar amount.

(3) Present a clear cancellation policy. The policy can give a flexible refund, depending on how far in advance the cancellation is made. If a client cancels three months in advance of the original reserved date, you have a good chance of rebooking that date, so a larger refund can be given than if the client cancels only two weeks before the reserved date.

(4) Create a clear liability policy. You should not be held responsible for any damage to rented equipment or property as well as any loss caused by guests at the event. Consult a lawyer to make sure this language is very clear in the contract. Also make clear what you will be liable for, such as damage caused by your own employees.

(5) Write down your policy for leftovers when the event is over. In some states, health regulations prevent the caterer from giving the leftovers to the client, so this must be stated clearly, otherwise there could be a dispute over who owns the leftovers. If you are able and willing to leave the leftovers with the client, negotiate this with them at the contract signing.

(6) Leave space at the bottom of the contract for your signature and that of your client(s) as well as the date. Always include a paragraph before signing that states your guarantee for quality service as well as a direct number to reach

you if any issues arise or changes are needed.

(7) Write a paragraph that offers help for your clients, includes a direct number for reaching you and guarantees your service.

(8) Write down the exact procedures for any breach of contract as well as what constitutes a breach of contract and make sure all parties understand who is responsible for legal fees or other procedures should they become necessary.

(9) Leave ample room for both your signature and the signature(s) of your clients at the bottom as well as the date.

4. How to Draft a Contract for the Purchase & Sale of a Business

Small business owners can get into trouble buying or selling a business as much for what's not in the contract as for what is. Leaving important items out of a contract, including hard and intangible assets and liabilities, can cause problems months after the sale goes through. Payment terms are another critical aspect of a contract. When you draft a contract for the sale of a business, make sure both parties know exactly what they are getting at the time of signing, as well as in the future.

Parties Involved

When drafting a contract, it's important to correctly list the parties involved to avoid confusion or allow one party to escape from the contract. List the seller and buyer by full name and address, as well as any business affiliation. For example, write, "The following is a contract between Joseph A. Smith, of Smith & Associates, LLC, 123 Main St., Anytown GA, 30066, and Deborah L. Jones, of Deb's Floral Shop, 222 S. 50th St., Springfield, MA 00233." When signing the contract, the signatories should use their titles after their names to protect them from a lawsuit. For example, use "Joseph A. Smith, Owner, Smith & Associates, LLC." Include the names of all parties involved, including partners of the buyer and seller who may hold an interest in either business.

Sale Items

List the items that will be included in the sale. This would include all physical assets, business records, cash, name of the business, logos, goodwill, licenses, patents, royalties, trademarks, recipes, trade secrets, formulas, databases, inventory and any other items the company used to conduct business.

If possible, list the assets by item and count. For example, if you are selling a restaurant, include the number of tables and chairs, ovens, refrigerators and other items a seller might try to take before he leaves. Include liabilities such as loans or other debt, including accounts payable. Include any non-compete clauses that go with the sale in this section to prevent the seller from competing with you after you buy the business.

Disclosure

Include a disclosure agreement that requires both parties to state they have disclosed any legal obligations, debts, lawsuits, fines or other encumbrances. This will make the seller responsible for any undisclosed liabilities the buyer discovers after the sale, or protect a seller who is financing a sale from a buyer with undisclosed bad credit or partners. Include a statement from the buyer and seller that each is legally the owner of the business they are representing and allowed to make the purchase or sale.

Sale Terms

Include the terms of sale, including how payment will be made and the date or dates of any payment. This would include whether the payment will be made in installments; if the payments will be made by cash, check, credit card or electronic transfer; if the seller will finance all or part of the sale and at what interest rate; if a deposit is required; and other details involved with the payment process. List any brokers or agents involved in the sale, as well as any financial companies facilitating the transaction. Add a clause detailing where and how disputes will be adjudicated. For example, include the state where any lawsuit must be brought and/or whether you wish disagreements to be handled by an arbitrator.

Signing

Require all parties involved in the sale to sign and date the document. Once you've drafted your contract, have an attorney review it before anyone signs it. Tell them to sign with their full names and titles. Have each party provide a witness signature. Have each signatory sign multiple copies so both parties can have an original copy. Have the documents notarized by a notary public.

5. How to Draft Sales Contract Forms

Drafting sales contract forms can be difficult, but doing them yourself can save thousands of dollars and the process is not that complicated. Attention to detail and slow, careful consideration needs to go into these legal-binding contracts, but almost anyone can learn to draft sales contract forms.

Sales Contract Form

These forms need to state several things. First, it must state that you, the seller, previously owned the item and has a right to sell. Next, the agreed price or compensation must be listed, along with a description of the sold item. Name and location of the transaction along with the date is also routine. Finally, you must state that you have agreed to accept ownership of the item. All of these may seem obvious, but many sales contracts do not include this information, which can lead to disputes.

Creating the Forms

Anyone can write their own legal contract, and many do. Just be sure to include the above information. However, collecting professionally drafted forms can save time because they require you to only fill in the blanks. These sales contract forms can be found online at several legal form websites, sometimes for free, although they are generally generic and may not fit your needs. Several software programs also create drafts more suited to individual needs. These sites allow you to type in information and save it. These sites offer a professional, but moderately priced solution. The most expensive and best way of drafting your own sales contract forms is by getting professional help. An hour's guidance with a lawyer can teach you how to write airtight contracts. Although it may cost hundreds for the advice.

6. Samples
Sample 1

SALES CONTRACT

Contract NO:
Signed at:
Date:

  The Buyers:
  The Sellers:
The Buyers agree to buy and the Sellers agree to sell the following goods on terms and conditions as set forth below:

(1) Name of Commodity, Specifications and Packing	(2) Quantity	(3) Unit Price	(4) Total Value
	(Shipment Quantity ％more or less allowed)		

  (5) Time of Shipment:

  (6) Port of loading:

  (7) Port of Destination:

  (8) Insurance: To be covered by the _____ for 110％ of the invoice value against _____ .

  (9) _____ payable at sight with TT reimbursement clause/_____ days'/sight/date allowing partial shipment and transshipment. The covering Letter of Credit must reach the Sellers before _____ and is to remain valid in _____ . China until the 15th day after the aforesaid time of shipment, failing which the Sellers reserve the right to cancel this Sales Contract without further notice and to claim from the Buyers for losses resulting therefrom.

  (10) Inspection: The Inspection Certificate of Quality/Quantity/Weight/Packing/Sanitation issued by _____ of China shall be regarded as evidence of the Sellers' delivery.

  (11) Shipping Marks:

OTHER TERMS:

1. Discrepancy: In case of quality discrepancy, claim should be lodged by the Buyers within 30 days after the arrival of the goods at the port of destination, while for quantity discrepancy, claim should be lodged by the Buyers within 15 days after the arrival of the goods at the port of destination. In all cases, claims must be accompanied by Survey Reports of Recognized Public Surveyors agreed to by the Sellers. Should the responsibility of the subject under claim be found to rest on the part of the Sellers, the Sellers shall, within 20 days after receipt of the claim, send their reply to the Buyers together with suggestion for settlement.

2. The covering Letter of Credit shall stipulate the Sellers's option of shipping the indicated percentage more or less than the quantity hereby contracted and be negotiated for the amount covering the value of quantity actually shipped. (The Buyers are requested to establish the L/C in amount with the indicated percentage over the total value of the order as per this Sales Contract.)

3. The contents of the covering Letter of Credit shall be in strict conformity with the stipulations of the Sales Contract. In case of any variation thereof necessitating amendment of the L/C, the Buyers shall bear the expenses for effecting the amendment. The Sellers shall not be held responsible for possible delay of shipment resulting from awaiting the amendment of the L/C and reserve the right to claim from the Buyers for the losses resulting therefrom.

4. Except in cases where the insurance is covered by the Buyers as arranged, insurance is to be covered by the Sellers with a Chinese insurance company. If insurance for additional amount and /or for other insurance terms is required by the Buyers, prior notice to this effect must reach the Sellers before shipment and is subject to the Sellers' agreement, and the extra insurance premium shall be for the Buyers' account.

5. The Sellers shall not be held responsible if they fail, owing to Force Majeure cause or causes, to make delivery within the time stipulated in this Sales Contract or cannot deliver the goods. However, the Sellers shall inform immediately the Buyers by cable. The Sellers shall deliver to the Buyers by

registered letter, if it is requested by the Buyers, a certificate issued by the China Council for the Promotion of International Trade or by any competent authorities, attesting the existence of the said cause or causes. The Buyers' failure to obtain the relative Import Licence is not to be treated as Force Majeure.

6. Arbitration: All disputes arising in connection with this Sales Contract or the execution thereof shall be settled by way of amicable negotiation. In case no settlement can be reached, the case at issue shall then be submitted for arbitration to the China International Economic and Trade Arbitration Commission in accordance with the provisions of the said Commission. The award by the said Commission shall be deemed as final and binding upon both parties.

7. Supplementary Condition(s) (Should the articles stipulated in this Contract be in conflict with the following supplementary condition⟨s⟩, the supplementary condition⟨s⟩ should be taken as valid and binding.)

(Sellers):　　　　　　　(Buyers):

Chapter 5
Drafting Contracts

Sample 2

PURCHASE CONTRACT

This contract was made on the _____ day of _____ 2010, between Mr. _____ of _____ Ltd. (hereinafter referred to as the Seller) and Mr. _____ of _____ Company (Hereinafter referred to as the Buyer). Whereas the Seller has agreed to sell and the Buyer has agreed to buy _____ (hereinafter referred to as Contracted Products). The quality, specifications, quantity of the contracted products have been confirmed by both Parties and this contract is signed with the following terms and conditions:

1. Contract Products: _____
2. Quantity: _____
3. Origin: _____
4. Price: _____ F.O.B.
5. Shipment:

First shipment to commence within 30-45 days from date of receipt of Letter of Credit, and all shipments are to be completed within twelve (12) months from date of first shipment.

6. Grace Period:

Should last shipment have to be extended for fulfilment of this contract, the Buyer shall give the Seller a grace period of thirty days upon submitting evidence by the Seller.

7. Insuracne:

To be effected by the Buyer.

8. Packing:

In new kraft paper bags of _____ kg/bag or in wooden cases of _____ kg/case, free of charge.

9. Payment:

The Buyer shall open a 100% confirmed, irrevocable, divisible and negotiable and partial shipment permitted Letter of Credit in favor of the Seller within 5 calendar days from date of the agreement through the Issuing Bank. The L/C shall be drawn against draft at sight upon first presentation of the following documents:

(1) Full set of Seller's Commercial Invoices;

(2) Full set of clean, blank, endorsed Bill of Lading;

(3) Inspection Certificates of quality and weight.

10. Notice of Readiness:

The Buyer shall advise the Seller by fax the scheduled time of arrival of cargo vessel at least seven days prior to the arrival of the vessel at the loading port.

11. Performance Guarantee:

(1) Upon reciept of Buyer's Irrevocable L/C by the Advising Bank, the Seller shall perform a Performance Guarantee representing _____% of the L/C value.

(2) The Performance Guarantee shall be returned in full to the Seller after completion of shipment and delivery of the contracted goods. In case of non-delivery of (all or part) of the goods for reasons other than those specified in Clause 12, the Performance Guarantee shall be forfeited in favor of the Buyer in proportion to the quantity in default.

(3) Should the Buyer breach the contract or fail to open the L/C in favor of the Seller within the period specified in Clause 9, (except for Clause 12), the Buyer has to pay the Seller the same value as the Performance Guarantee.

(4) The Letter of Credit must fulfill all the terms and conditions of this contract. The terms of the L/C should be clear, fair and made payable to the Seller. Upon acceptance of L/C by the advising bank, the Advising Bank shall send the Performance Guarantee to the Issuing Bank.

12. Force Majeure:

The Seller or the Buyer shall not be responsible for non-delivery or breach of contract for any reason due to Force Majeure which may include war, blockade, hostility, insurrection, strike, lockout, civil strife, commotion, governmental import/export restriction, riot, severe destruction by fire or flood or other natural factors beyond the control of human beings.

In case the time of delivery for shipment has to be extended, the Buyer or the Seller shall have to provide evidence for such event.

13. Arbitration:

All disputes or divergences arising from the execution of the contract shall be settled through friendly discussion between both Parties. In case no settlement can be reached, the disputes shall be submitted to Arbitration. The Arbitration shall take place in _____ and be conducted by the Arbitration Committee of _____ in accordance with the Statutes of the said Committee.

The decision of Arbitration by the said Committee shall be final and binding upon both Parties. The Arbitration fee shall be borne by the losing Party. In course of Arbitration, the contract shall continuously be executed by both Parties except for the part under Arbitration.

14. Currency Devaluation:

In the event of any official devaluation of U. S. Currency, the Selller reserves the right to readjust the contract price in proportion to the devaluation ration.

15. Valid Period:

This contract will automatically become null and void should the buyer fail to open a L/C in favor of the Seller within seven days after signing of this contract. However, the Buyer shall still be responsible for the payment of compensation in accordance with the terms in Clause 11, Items 2 and 3.

This contract is made in duplicate, both Parties have read carefully and agreed to abide by all the terms and conditions stipulated. The contract is signed by both Parties in the presence of witnesses.

Seller:

_____

Buyer:

_____

Winesses:

_____

Sample 3

GAS PURCHASE AND SALES CONTRACT

This Gas Purchase and Sale Contract ("this Contract") is made as of and effective April 1, 2000, between Tenaska Marketing Ventures, a Nebraska partnership ("TMV") and Warren Resources, Inc., a _____ corporation("Company"), individually referred to as "Party" and collectively referred to as "the Parties."

ARTICLE I
PURPOSE AND PROCEDURES

1.1 Agreement. This Contract establishes mutually agreed and legally binding terms governing purchases, sales and exchanges of Gas between TMV and Company made during the term of this Contract. The transactions encompassed by this Contract will be designed on transaction-specific Confirmation(s) in the form of Exhibit "A" and, if relevant to a particular transaction, a Trigger Price Confirmation in the form of Exhibit "B." This Contract consists of the provisions set forth herein and, with respect to a particular transaction, the provisions contained in the Confirmation(s). More than one Confirmation may be in effect at the same time. As used herein, the term "Buyer" refers to the Party purchasing and receiving Gas and the term "Seller" refers to the Party selling and delivering Gas.

1.2 Confirmation Procedure. If the Parties come to an understanding regarding the sale and purchase of Gas, the transaction will be communicated in a Confirmation that will reflect the Transaction Type, Contract Quantity, Delivery Period, Contract Price, Delivery Point(s) and any other special terms to which the Parties have agreed. Each Confirmation shall be sent by TMV to Company via facsimile and shall become a part of this contract. If a Confirmation is not objected to or returned to TMV by Company via facsimile within two (2) Business Days of the successful transmittal thereof, then that Confirmation shall be accepted by both Parties.

1.3 Transaction Types. The terms and conditions incorporated in this

Chapter 5
Drafting Contracts

Contract are intended to facilitate the entering into by Buyer and Seller of the following Transactions Types as further defined in this Contract: i) Swing Transactions; ii) Firm Transactions; and iii) EFP Transactions.

1.4 Tape Recordings. Each Party hereby consents to the recording of telephone conversations by the other in connection with this Contract or any potential Transaction, and agrees to obtain any necessary consent of, and to give notice of such recording to, its affected personnel. Any tape recordings may be submitted into evidence to any court or in any legal proceeding for the purpose of establishing any matter, whether relating to this Contract, any Transaction or otherwise.

ARTICLE II
DEFINITIONS

2.1 "Business Day" means a period of eight (8) consecutive hours, beginning at 8:00 a.m., Central Clock Time ("C.C.T."), on any day except Saturday, Sunday or federal bank holidays and ending at 4:00 p.m. C.C.T., on the same calendar day.

2.2 "Buyer's Deficiency Quantity" means the difference between the Contract Quantity and the actual Gas quantity received by Buyer for each Day on which Seller's failure occurred pursuant to Section 7.1(a).

2.3 "Contract Price" means the price to be paid for Gas as set forth in the Confirmation.

2.4 "Contract Quantity" means the quantity of Gas to be delivered by Seller and received by Buyer as set forth in the Confirmation.

2.5 "Contract Value" means the amount of Gas remaining to be delivered or purchased under a Transaction multiplied by the Contract Price per unit.

2.6 "Day" means a period of twenty-four (24) consecutive hours, as defined in the tariff of the Transporter receiving Gas at the Delivery Point.

2.7 "Delivery Period" means the period of time during which Gas shall be delivered and received under a transaction as set forth in the Confirmation.

2.8 "Delivery Point" means the specific point(s) at which the Parties have agreed to make and take delivery of Gas, as specified in the Confirmation.

2.9 "Early Termination Date" means any date on or after a default designated by the Performing party as the time at which any or all Forward Contracts (including any portion of a Forward Contract not yet fully delivered) will be liquidated.

2.10 "EFP Transaction" means a Firm Transaction to purchase, sell or exchange Gas and the concurrent obligation to buy or sell natural gas futures contracts pursuant to the Exchange of Futures for Physical (EFP) procedures of an Exchange in accordance with an applicable Confirmation. Failure to buy or sell such quantity(ies) of Gas or futures contracts shall subject the failing party to the damages set forth in Article VII.

2.11 "Exchange" means any United States commodity exchange that trades natural gas futures contracts.

2.12 "Firm Transaction" means Buyer shall have an absolute obligation to purchase and receive, and Seller shall have an absolute obligation to sell and deliver one hundred per cent (100%) of the Contract Quantity in the applicable Confirmation. Failure to buy or sell the Contract Quantity shall subject the failing party to the damages prescribed in Article VII.

2.13 "Forward Contract" means any agreement constituting a "forward contract" within the meaning of the United States Bankruptcy Code, including, without limitation, a Transaction or any other agreement for the sale, purchase or transfer (including a swap) of Gas which has a maturity date or delivery period more than two days after the date the Forward Contract is entered into.

2.14 "Gas" means any mixture of hydrocarbons and non-combustible gases in a gaseous state consisting primarily of methane.

2.15 "Imbalance Charge" means any scheduling, imbalance or similar penalties, fees, forfeitures, cashouts, or charges (in cash or in kind) assessed by a Transporter for failure to satisfy the Transporter's balance and/or nomination requirements.

2.16 "Market Value" means the amount of Gas remaining to be delivered or purchased under a Transaction multiplied by the market price per MMBtu determined by the Performing Party in a commercially reasonable manner.

2.17 "MMBtu" means one million BTU's, equal to one dekatherm.

2.18 "Payment Date" means the twenty-fifty (25th) day of the calendar month in which the invoice was rendered, or ten (10) days after the date of receipt of the invoice, whichever is later; provided that if the twenty-fifth (25th) day is not a Business Day, payment is due on the next Business Day following that date.

2.19 "Replacement Price" is the price at which Buyer is able, acting in good faith, to obtain comparable Gas supplies at the lowest reasonable price.

2.20 "Sales Price" is the price at which Seller is able acting in good faith, to make comparable Gas sales at the highest reasonable price.

2.21 "Schedule" or "Scheduled" means the acts of Seller, Buyer, and the Transporter(s) of notifying, requesting, and confirming to each other the quantity of Gas to be delivered hereunder on any given Day.

2.22 "Seller's Deficiency Quantity" means the difference between the Contract Quantity and the actual Gas quantity delivered by Seller for each Day on which Buyer's failure occurred pursuant to Section 7.1(b).

2.23 "Swing Transaction" means that deliveries and receipts of Gas will be on a swing or interruptible basis. The Contract Quantity may be reduced, interrupted or terminated by either Party for any reason upon the other Party's receipt of notice given prior to its Transporter's nomination deadline for the requested change. Any failure to provide such notice by either Party shall subject that Party to the damages prescribed in Article VII.

2.24 "Transaction" means a particular purchase, sale or exchange of Gas evidenced in a Confirmation.

2.25 "Transporter(s)" means all Gas gathering or pipeline companies, or local distribution companies, acting in the capacity of a transporter, transporting Gas upstream or downstream of the Delivery Point pursuant to a particular Transaction Confirmation.

2.26 "Trigger Price" means a Contract Price that is determined in part by the natural gas futures price on any Exchange.

ARTICLE III
TERM

This Contract shall be in force as of the date first above written and shall extend month-to-month thereafter until terminated by either Party upon giving thirty (30) days' prior written notice; provided, however, that if one or more

Confirmation(s) are in effect, termination shall not be effective for any such Confirmation until the expiration of the Term of such Confirmation.

ARTICLE IV
SCHEDULING

Buyer and Seller shall provide each other and all necessary third parties, including Transporter(s), with the information necessary to Schedule the Contract Quantity for each Day as agreed to for a specific Transaction hereunder. The Parties will provide each other with timely nomination information or of any changes to nominations prior to the Transporters' nomination deadline.

ARTICLE V
QUANTITY AND DELIVERY

5.1 Obligations. Seller agrees to Schedule and to sell and deliver, and Buyer agrees to Schedule and to purchase and receive the Contract Quantity each Day at the Delivery Point(s) for a particular Transaction. Seller shall be responsible for transportation to the Delivery Point(s) and the Buyer shall be responsible for transportation from the Delivery Point(s). Title to and possession of all Gas shall pass from Seller to Buyer at said Delivery Point(s).

5.2 Imbalance Notification. Both parties hereto shall promptly notify each other as soon as possible of any Transporter notification of imbalances that are occurring or that have occurred, and the Parties shall cooperate to eliminate any such imbalances, including the use of make-up or balancing rights that either Party may have, within the time prescribed by the Transporter.

5.3 Imbalance Charges. The Party causing an Imbalance Charge shall be responsible for paying the charge. Buyer shall assume all liability for and reimburse Seller within thirty (30) days of presentation of invoice and substantiating documentation, for any Imbalance Charge resulting from Buyer's failure to comply with balancing or notification requirements of Seller's Transporter. Seller shall assume all liability for and reimburse Buyer within thirty (30) days of presentation of invoice and substantiating documentation, for any Imbalance Charge resulting from Seller's failure to comply with balancing or notification requirements of Buyer's Transporter.

ARTICLE VI
PRICE

6.1 Buyer agrees to pay Seller the Contract Price for each MMBtu of Gas delivered by Seller to Buyer in accordance with the terms of this Contract and the relevant Confirmation.

6.2 Trigger Price. If the Parties agree to a Trigger Price, the Trigger Price Confirmation will define the factors to be used in the calculation. The Company may request that TMV execute trades through an Exchange in order to establish the Trigger Price. Following execution of such trades, TMV will transmit to Company a Trigger Price Confirmation no later than the close of business on the Business Day following execution of such trade(s). Company will have one Business Day after receipt of the Trigger Price Confirmation to object to any of the terms contained therein. If no objection is received by TMV within the prescribed time, the Trigger Price Confirmation will be deemed to have been accepted by both Parties and will be considered part of the Contract and will be used to calculate the Trigger Price.

ARTICLE VII
FAILURE TO PERFORM

7.1 If either Party fails on any Day to Schedule and receive or deliver the Contract Quantity, as provided in Section 5.1, that Party shall be liable for, and shall pay the other party, the following damages:

(a) Buyer's Failure. If the quantity Buyer receives and purchases on any Day is less than the applicable Contract Quantity and the Sales Price is less than the Contract Price, then Buyer shall be liable for and shall pay to Seller a dollar amount equal to the product of (i) the difference between the Contract Price and the Sales Price, and; (ii) Buyer's Deficiency Quantity. In addition, Buyer shall pay Seller an amount equal to ten percent (10%) of the amount calculated pursuant to the first sentence of this subsection (a) to cover Seller's administrative and operational costs and expenses.

(b) Seller's Failure. If the quantity Seller sells and delivers on any Day is less than the applicable Contract Quantity and the Replacement Price is greater than the Contract Price, then Seller shall be liable for and shall pay to Buyer a dollar amount equal to the product of (i) the difference between the Replacement Price and the Contract Price and; (ii) Seller's Deficiency Quantity. In addition, Seller shall pay Buyer an amount equal to ten percent (10%) of the amount calculated pursuant to the first sentence of this subsection (b) to cover Buyer's administrative and operational costs and expenses.

(c) Failure to Replace. If Seller or Buyer does not make a replacement purchase or sale, the failing Party shall still be liable in accordance with the provisions of Section 7.1 and the Sales Price or Replacement Price shall be deemed to be the daily price as posted in BTU's Daily Gas Wire for Gas for each day to failure at the location which most closely reflects the relevant Delivery Point(s); provided, however, if the non-failing party does not learn of the failure until after the fact, then in lieu of the remedy provided in this subsection (c), the non-failing party may calculate its damages as of the date(s) on which replacement purchases or sales are actually made.

7.2 EFP and Trigger Price Transactions. If the Transaction is an EFP Transaction, any Party failing to offer and complete the purchase or sale of Exchange futures contracts from or to the other Party shall be liable to the other Party for actual losses incurred by it due to such failure. If either Party fails to complete the purchase or sale of gas after the other Party has executed trades pursuant to Section 6.2 Trigger Price, then the failing Party shall be liable to the non-failing Party for an actual losses incurred for the reversal of trades so executed. Calculation of any damages pursuant to this Section 7.2 shall be incorporated as necessary in the calculation of damages set forth in Section 7.1 to assure that the non-failing Party will be fully compensated for its actual loss incurred because of the other Party's failure.

ARTICLE VIII
BILLING AND PAYMENT

8.1 Invoice and Payment Dates. Seller shall invoice Buyer by the tenth (10th) day of the calendar month for Gas delivered to Buyer during the preceding month. If Seller has not received Transporter notification of the actual quantity delivered, the statement shall be based on the Scheduled quantity, and the Parties agree that the next statement shall be adjusted to reflect the actual quantity delivered. Buyer shall remit to Seller the amount due by wire transfer, pursuant to Seller's invoice instructions, on or before the Payment Date. If Buyer, in good faith, disputes the amount of any such invoice or any part thereof, Buyer will pay to Seller such amount as it concedes to be correct; provided, however, if Buyer disputes the amount due, Buyer must provide supporting documentation acceptable in industry practice to support the amount paid or disputed. In the event any payments are due Buyer hereunder, payment to Buyer shall be made in accordance with this Section.

8.2 Late Payment. If either Party owing an amount to the other Party fails to pay in accordance with this Contract, that Party shall pay interest on any overdue amount at a rate equal to the lesser of: (i) the posted prime rate in The Wall Street Journal as listed under "Money Rates", plus two percent (2%), or (ii) the maximum rate allowed by law, from the due date until such principal amount and interest thereon are paid.

8.3 Audit Rights. Each Party shall have the right, at its own expense, upon reasonable notice and at reasonable times, to examine the books and records of the other Party only to the extent reasonably necessary to verify the accuracy of any invoice, statement, charge, payment, or computation made under the Contract. This examination right shall not be available with respect to proprietary information not directly relevant to transactions under this Contract. All invoices and billings shall be conclusively presumed final and accurate unless objected to in writing, with adequate explanation and/or documentation, within two years after the month of Gas delivery. All retroactive adjustments under this Article shall be paid in full by the party owing payment within 30 days of notice and substantiation of the inaccuracy.

ARTICLE IX
NETTING PROCEDURES

9.1 If the Parties to this Contract participate in multiple Transactions in a given month whereby each party sells Gas to and purchases Gas from the other in individual Transactions, then in lieu of the procedures set forth in Article VIII, the Parties may agree to a net settlement procedure as follows:

(a) By the tenth (10th) day of each calendar month following the month in which such Transactions occurred, each Party shall determine the sales price for the Gas sold to the other Party and issue an invoice reflecting the amount due for Gas sold. No fewer than three (3) days prior to the Payment Date, the Parties will confer by telephone and compare/confirm invoice amounts and total amounts owed. Any difference resulting after offsetting the total amount each party owes to the other Party shall be paid by the Party owing the greater amount, no later than the Payment Date.

(b) If either Party, in good faith, disputes the amount of any invoice or portion of any invoice in the current billing month, then only the non-disputed portion of the invoice(s) will be subject to netting according to this Article IX. The disputing Party must provide supporting documentation acceptable in industry practice to support the amount paid or disputed. Upon resolution of such dispute, any amounts owing will be included in netting procedures in the subsequent month.

ARTICLE X
FINANCIAL RESPONSIBILITY AND EARLY TERMINATION

10.1 Events of Default. Either Party (the "Defaulting Party") will be in default under this Contract if it:

(i) makes an assignment or any general arrangement for the benefit of creditors;

(ii) files a petition or otherwise commences, authorizes, or acquiesces in the commencement of a proceeding or cause under any bankruptcy or similar law for the protection of creditors, or has such petition filed against it and such proceeding remains undismissed for 30 days;

(iii) otherwise becomes bankrupt or insolvent (however evidenced);

(iv) is unable to pay its debts as they fall due;

(v) fails to pay or perform, when due, any obligation to the other Party (the "Performing Party"), whether under this Contract or any other contract between the Parties, including a contract(s) in connection with credit support obligations or otherwise, if such failure is not remedied on or before the third Business Day after notice of such failure is given to the Defaulting Party;

(vi) fails to give adequate security for or assurance of its ability to perform its further obligations under this Contract within forty-eight (48) hours of a reasonable request by the other Party, or

(vii) fails to deliver any volumes of gas which it is obligated to deliver to the other Party and such failure is not remedied within a 48-hour period.

10.2 Default Remedies. If a Party is in default, then the Performing Party shall have, in addition to any and all other remedies available hereunder or pursuant to law, the right to withhold or suspend deliveries/receipts or payment and/or to specify an Early Termination Date and to liquidate any or all Forward Contracts (including any portion of a Forward Contract not yet fully delivered) then outstanding at any time or from time to time thereafter by:

(i) closing out each Transaction being liquidated at its Market Value so that each such Transaction is canceled and a settlement payment in an amount equal to the difference between such Market Value and the Contract Value of such Transaction shall be due to the Buyer under the Transaction if such Market Value exceeds the contract Value and to the Seller if the Contract Value exceeds the Market Value;

(ii) discounting each amount then due under subsection (i) above to present value in a commercially reasonable manner as of the time of liquidation to take into account the period between the date of liquidation and the date on which such amount would have otherwise been due pursuant to the relevant Transaction; and

(iii) netting or aggregating, as appropriate, any or all settlement payments under this Contract (discounted as appropriate). The net amount due any such liquidation shall be paid by the close of business on the Business Day following the Early Termination Date. The rate of interest used in calculating net present value shall be determined by the Performing Party in a commercially reasonable manner.

10.3 Set-off. If a Party is in Default, at the election of the Performing Party, any or all other amounts owing between the Parties under any contract may be set off against amounts owing under this Contract so that all such amounts are aggregated and/or netted to a single amount payable by one Party to the other.

ARTICLE XI
TAXES

Seller shall pay or cause to be paid all taxes lawfully levied on Seller applicable to the Gas delivered hereunder prior to its delivery to Buyer. Buyer shall pay all taxes lawfully levied on Buyer applicable to such Gas upon and after delivery to Buyer or for the account of Buyer. If Seller is legally obligated to collect any taxes from Buyer, Seller shall have full authority to do so. If Buyer is exempt from any taxes, Buyer shall furnish Seller with a valid and properly completed resale or exemption certificate upon request by Seller.

ARTICLE XII
FORCE MAJEURE

12.1 Excuse for Force Majeure. Except with regard to a Party's obligation to make payments due under this Contract, in the event either Party hereto is rendered unable, wholly or in part, by Force Majeure to carry out its obligations, then upon notification by telephone with a subsequent written notice setting forth the specifics within a reasonable time, but not in excess of six (6) days after the commencement of the failure to perform due to Force Majeure, the obligations of the Party giving such notice, insofar as they are affected by such Force Majeure, from its inception, shall be excused during the entire period of any inability so caused but for no longer period.

12.2 Inclusions. The term "Force Majeure" as employed in this Contract will mean any event that prevents delivery or receipt of Gas at the Delivery Point, including acts of God, strikes, lockouts, or industrial disputes or disturbances, civil disturbances, interruptions by government or court orders, necessity for compliance with any court order, law, statute, ordinance, or regulation promulgated by a governmental authority having jurisdiction, acts of the public enemy, events affecting facilities or services of non-affiliated third parties, or any other cause of like kind not reasonably within the control of the Party claiming Force Majeure and which by the exercise of due diligence such Party could not have prevented or is unable to overcome.

12.3 Exclusions. The term Force Majeure specifically excludes the following occurrences or events:

(i) The curtailment of interruptible or secondary firm transportation unless primary, in-path, firm transportation is also curtailed;

(ii) increases or decreases in Gas supply due to allocation or reallocation of production by well operators, pipelines, or other parties;

(iii) changes in market conditions or economic curtailment;

(iv) loss of markets or Gas supply unless such loss would also constitute an event of Force Majeure under this Contract;

(v) failure of specific, individual wells or appurtenant facilities in the absence of a Force Majeure event broadly affecting other wells in the same geographic area; and

(vi) regulatory disallowance of the pass through of the costs of Gas or other related costs.

ARTICLE XIII
WARRANTIES AND LIABILITY

13.1 Seller Warranties. Seller warrants that all royalties, taxes and other sums due on production and transportation of the Gas to the Delivery Point(s) are paid, and that it will have the right to convey and will transfer good and merchantable title to all Gas sold hereunder and delivered by it to Buyer, free and clear of any and all liens, encumbrances and claims.

13.2 Indemnity. Subject to Section 16.8, each Party assumes full responsibility and liability for and shall indemnify and save harmless the other Party from all liability and expense on account of any and all damages, claims or actions, including injury to and death of persons, arising from any act or accident occurring when title to the Gas is vested in the indemnifying Party unless the act or accident was the result of the willful misconduct or gross negligence of the indemnified Party, its agents or assigns.

ARTICLE XIV
QUALITY, MEASUREMENT AND DELIVERY PRESSURE

All Gas delivered by Seller hereunder shall conform to the heat, quality and delivery pressure specifications of Buyer's Transporter(s).

ARTICLE XV
NOTICES

15.1 All billings, payments, statements, notices and communications made pursuant to this Contract shall be made as follows:

Notices, statements and invoices:	Payments to Tenaska Marketing Ventures:
Tenaska Marketing Ventures	Tenaska Marketing Ventures
11235 Davenport Street	First National Bank of Omaha
Omaha, NE 68154	Omaha, NE 68154
Notices: Manager, Administration	Account No.:
Invoices: Gas Accounting	ABA Routing No.:
Gas Control: Director—Throughput Mgmt.	Federal Tax I.D. #: —
Phone: (402) 758-6128	Duns #:
Fax: (402) 758-6250	

Notices, statements and invoices:	Payments to:
Warren Resources, Inc.	Big Basin Petroleum, LLC
c/o Millennium Gas Marketing, LLC	LX CBM Operating Account
513 East Bismarck Expressway, Suite 6	First National Bank of Gillette
Bismarck, ND 58504	Account No.:
Notices: Claudia Bender, Vice President	ABA Routing No.:
Invoices: Gas Accounting	Federal Tax I.D. #:
Phone: (701) 250-8585	Duns #: — —
Fax: (701) 250-8511	

15.2 All notices required hereunder may be sent by facsimile or mutually acceptable electronic means, a nationally recognized overnight courier service, first class mail or hand delivered.

15.3 Notice shall be given when received on a Business Day by the addressee. In the absence of proof of the actual receipt date, the following presumptions will apply. Notices sent by facsimile shall be deemed to have been received upon the sending party's receipt of its facsimile machine's confirmation of successful transmission, if the day on which such facsimile is received is not a Business Day or is after 4:00 p.m. C.C.T. on a Business Day, then such facsimile shall be deemed to have been received on the next following Business Day. Notice by overnight mail or courier shall be deemed to have been received on the next Business Day after it was sent or such earlier time as is confirmed by the receiving party. Notice via first class mail shall be considered delivered five Business Days after mailing.

ARTICLE XVI
MISCELLANEOUS

16.1 Transfer or Assignment. This Contract shall be binding upon and inure to the benefit of the successors, assigns, personal representatives, and heirs of the respective Parties hereto, and the covenants, conditions, rights and obligations of this Contract shall run for the full term of this Contract. No assignment of this contract, in whole or in part, will be made without the prior written consent of the non-assigning party, which consent will not be unreasonably withhold or delayed; provided, however, either Party may transfer its interest to any parent or affiliate by assignment, merger or otherwise without the prior approval of the other Party. Upon any transfer and assumption, the transferor shall not be relieved of or discharged from any obligations hereunder unless such assumption is made in the transfer/assumption agreement.

16.2 Severability. If any term, provision, covenant, or condition of this Contract or the application thereof, to any party or circumstance, shall be held to be invalid or unenforceable (in whole or in part) for any reason, the remaining terms, provisions, covenants, and conditions hereof shall continue in full force and effect as if this Contract had been executed with the invalid or unenforceable portion eliminated.

16.3 Applicable Law. The Contract shall be governed in accordance with the laws of the State of Nebraska except for such laws concerning the application of the laws of another jurisdiction.

16.4 Entire Agreement. THE TERMS CONTAINED IN THIS CONTRACT CONSTITUTE THE ENTIRE CONTRACT OF THE PARTIES, AND THERE ARE NO CONTRACTS, UNDERSTANDINGS, OBLIGATIONS, PROMISES, ASSURANCES OR CONDITIONS, PRECEDENT OR OTHERWISE, EXCEPT THOSE EXPRESSLY SET OUT HEREIN.

16.5 Confidentiality. The terms of this Contract, including but not limited to the price paid for Gas, the identified Transporter(s), the quantities of Gas purchased or sold and all other material terms of this Contract shall be kept confidential by the Parties hereto, and shall not be disclosed to any third party except to the extent that any information must be disclosed to a third party for the purpose of effectuating transportation of the Gas delivered hereunder or as may be required by law or regulation.

16.6 Non-Waiver. Any waiver of any default under this Contract shall not be construed as a waiver of any future defaults, whether of like or different character.

16.7 Conflict of Terms. In the case of conflict between the terms of any Confirmation and the terms of this Contract, the terms of the Confirmation shall control.

16.8 Limitation on Liability. EXCEPT AS OTHERWISE SPECIFICALLY PROVIDED HEREIN, IN NO EVENT WILL EITHER PARTY BE LIABLE UNDER THIS CONTRACT, WHETHER IN CONTRACT, IN TORT (INCLUDING NEGLIGENCE AND STRICT LIABILITY) OR OTHERWISE, FOR INCIDENTAL, CONSEQUENTIAL, SPECIAL OR PUNITIVE DAMAGES.

16.9 Non-Recourse. Without limiting the Company's ability to enforce its rights under any guaranty provided to it by an affiliate of TMV, the obligations of TMV under this Contract shall have recourse only to the assets of TMV and no recourse to the personal assets of any partner in TMV or any affiliate of any partner in TMV, any individual controlling person or any officer, director, employee or stockholder thereof, or any successor thereto.

IN WITNESS WHEREOF, this Contract has been executed as of the date first abovewritten:

TENASKA MARKETING VENTURES

By: Tenaska Marketing, Inc.
    Managing General Partner
By: /s/ Fred R. Hunzeker

_____

Fred R. Hunzeker
President
Date: 3-28-00

WARREN RESOURCES, INC.

_____

Title: Ops Manager

Date: 4-5-00

Exercises

1. Review the following contract, not an agency agreement between two firms (names, products, and countries have been changed). The native language of the drafters of the contract was not English.

2. As you read the contract, try to determine exactly what the parties intended. Some of the provisions are confusing, due in part to improper language use.

3. Divide into groups and rewrite the contract if you are attorneys from the law firm representing the principal. Hints to aid in your revision are provided in bold.

In the real world, when confusion about the terms of an agreement arises, the attorney can ask management what was intended and write the provision to fit the law and management's expectations. In this contract, you don't have that option. So make equitable choices, but don't forget that you represent the principal in this case.

AGENCY AGREEMENT

THIS AGREEMENT, made and entered into as of 15 June, 1998 by and between Dominican Manufacturing, Inc., (hereinafter referred to as "Principal"), a company incorporated under the laws of France and with its principal place of business at Toulouse, France and Singh Engineering, Inc., (hereinafter referred to as "Agent"), a company incorporated under the laws of India and with its principal place of business at Mumbai, India. [**Is all this information necessary? Check the punctuation.**]

WITNESSETH:

WHEREAS, the Principal produces and exports mineral drilling equipment and other products as set forth and specified in Appendix I (hereinafter referred to as "Products"); and WHEREAS, the Agent desires and possesses the capacity, knowledge and capability to market and sell the Products in India and Sri Lanka (hereinafter referred to as "Territory").

NOW, THEREFORE, the Parties have agreed as follows:

[**Review the information in the Legal Thumbnail. Some of the language above is unnecessary.**]

1. APPOINTMENT

1.1 The Principal appoints the Agent as the exclusive sales agent in the Territory to promote the sales of the Products.

[**Is a duty or a right being created here? Use "shall" when creating a duty; "is entitled to" when creating a right.**]

1.2 The Agent shall have no right to [**Can you shorten this?**] solicit or negotiate contracts for sale of the Products with customers situated outside the Territory or to customers who are likely, directly or indirectly, to reexport the Products outside the Territory.

[**What happens if the products are reexported?**]

1.3 Should the Agent receive an inquiry for the Products destined for use outside the Agent's Territory, the Agent shall forward such inquiries for the Principal's handling through its [emphasis added] regular marketing channels in the country of use. [**Does "its" refer to the Agent or the Principal? Would the Agent have regular marketing channels in a country outside its Territory?**] However, in particular cases, where there is no legal or business reason to the contrary, the Principal may extend to the Agent its written approval to handle such business. In this connection, the Agent undertakes, in respect of such inquiries, to ascertain the ultimate destination of the Products, and agrees that it will neither quote nor furnish any information received under this Agreement to its prospective client without prior receipt of the Principal's approval.

[**Is a second approval necessary? Is a telephonic approval acceptable? Is a duty created?**]

1.4   The Principal reserves to itself at its sole discretion the right to anytime revise its list of Products [**word order**] by adding items thereto or subtracting items therefrom said revisions to be effective in each case upon receipt of Principal's notice thereof by the Agent. Exception to the above is when the Principal stops production totally or the production of a product or production line. [**unnecessary, old-fashioned language**]

1.5   While the Principal reserves the right not to accept an order at its sole discretion [**word order**], the Principal shall assist the Agent in the performance of its duties by informing, [**object missing**] on a continuous basis of current delivery terms and of changes in expected delivery dates.

1.6   The Principal will furnish the Agent with price lists and catalogues and shall promptly notify the Agent of any changes thereto [**"Will" is future tense, not a duty.**]

1.7   The Principal shall without delay inform the Agent whether it accepts orders forwarded by the Agent. [**What does "without delay" mean?**]

1.8   The Principal shall promptly pay to the Agent the commission having accrued to him as provided in Article 5.2 hereunder. [**Do you need this here?**]

...

5. COMMISSIONS

5.1   The Agent is entitled to the commission provided for in Appendix 2, on all sales of the Products which are made during the term of the contract to customers established in the Territory and to which the Agent has contributed or which are the permanent customers of the Agent in the Territory. The Agent is not entitled to the commission for other sales of the Products to the Territory included but not being limited to such sales. [**Are you creating a duty or a right here? What does the last line mean? The phrase is most often seen as "including but not limited to."**]

5.2   The Agent's right to commission shall become due and the commission shall be calculated quarterly (bases on the calendar year) for the Products delivered to and paid in full by the customer during the period in question pursuant to this Agreement. Payment of the commission shall be made by the Principal within thirty (30) days following the full payment of the invoice of the products or services subject to commission. [**When is the Agent to be paid?**]

Appendix 2
COMMISSIONS

In cases where sales of the Products dealt with in this Agreement are effected by the Agent alone, or as a result of the combined efforts of the Principal and the Agent, the Agent shall be paid commissions varying with the type of sales involved and determined in accordance with the following schedules. [**Can you simplify this language?**]

With respect of sales of the Products listed in Appendix 1 following commissions of the ex works price shall be paid: 10%. [**Check prepositions and articles.**]

In cases where sales into the Agent's Territory of the Products dealt with in this Agreement are effected by the Principal. its Affiliate Companies, or its regularly appointed agents or representatives, the Agent's commission will amount to 50% of the compensation payable to the Principal by its Affiliate Companies or its Appointees on such transactions. [**Is this consistent with Section 5?**]

In cases where the Principal obtains orders from third parties outside the Agent's Territory for the delivery of the Products into the Agent's Territory, the Agent's commission will be reduced to 1/3 of the normal rates. [**Is this consistent with Section 5?**]

Chapter 6

Understanding Legal Citations

Legal citations permit readers to find the sources that you cite. This critical function demands a high degree of accuracy on the part of the writer. If your citation is inaccurate, you reader will question your research abilities, suspect that you may have plagiarized the work, or consider your work to be sloppy and untrustworthy. To write legal citations accurately, and to later understand their function in legal writing, we must first understand the parts of a legal citation. This section reviews some of the basic elements of common legal citations.

1. How to Read a Case Citation

In all types of legal writing, whether by scholars or by practitioners, it is customary to cite an authority or authorities to show support for a legal or factual proposition or argument. An author may cite an authority that identifies the source of a quotation or an authority referred to in the text; authority that directly or clearly states his or her legal or factual proposition; authority that less directly supports the author's proposition but from which one can infer the proposition; authority that contradicts the author's proposition; and authority that provides background material that the reader might find useful in understanding the proposition.

The "basic purpose of a legal citation is to allow the reader to locate a cited source accurately and efficiently." American legal citations follow certain conventions that have arisen over the years. Correct case citations will generally show the names of parties, the court that made the decision, and the year of the decision. The citation will also include information about where to find the decision: a volume number, the name of the case reporter, and the page where the case is found. The citation must allow the reader to find the authority in a law library.

The best way to understand a legal citation is to look at an example. Consider this first citation. The number under each part of the citation refers to the explanatory paragraphs which follow the case citation.

> Krys v. Lufthansa German Airlines, 119 F.3d 1515, 1518—19 (11th Cir. 1997).
>   1   2   3   4   5   6   7

(1) The Parties

Many cases have more than one plaintiff or more than one defendant. A case citation, however, will usually show only the first named plaintiff and the first named defendant. Unless you are writing footnotes for a law review article, the case name should be underlined or italicized. Many people assume that the first name is the plaintiff-appellant, and the second name (after the "v" for "versus") is the defendant-appellee. That is not always the case. In this example, Krys is the plaintiff-appellee (having prevailed in the lower court, here the U.S. District Court for the Southern District of Florida) and Lufthansa is the defendant appellant.

Readers must also know that a case citation will give the name of only the first appellant and only the first appellee. Thus the following example:

> Honduras Aircraft Registry, Ltd., a Honduran Corporation, and Honduras Air Register Bureau, Limited, a Bahamian Corporation, Plaintiffs Appellees, and Omega Air Sociedad de Reponsibilidad Limitada, Intervenor Appellee, versus the Government of Honduras and Guillermo Chineros, Director General of Civil Aeronautics of the Repubic of Honduras, individually, Defendants Appellants, 119 F.3d 1530 (11th Cir. 1997).

Becomes:

> Honduras Aircraft Register, Ltd., v. Government of Honduras, 119 F.3d 1530 (11th Cir. 1997).

Chapter 6
Understanding Legal Citations

Only the first name of the appellant and the first name of the appellee appear in the citation.

(2) Volume Number

The first number is the volume number of the reporter where the decision is found. The volume number in the Lufthansa example is "119."

(3) Reporter (and Series)

The symbol "F. 3d" indicates that this case is reported in the *Federal Reporter, Third Series*, which is published by the West Publishing Company. The symbol "F. 2d" *refers to the Federal Reporter, Second Series.*

(4) First Page of the Case

This first number is the first page of the reporter where the case is found. This first page number is used not only to find the case in the reporter but also to "Shepardize" the case. To "Shepardize" a case means to use a private service offered by the Shepard's Company. The service tracks later court decisions that cite this court decision. By using this service, researchers can learn whether the case has been cited by other courts and whether the decision has been explained, followed, reversed, or distinguished.

(5) Pages Where the Cited Material Is Found

Some cases can be exceptionally long — even 100 pages or more. Yet, even with shorter decisions, the time of readers and researchers is better spent when they can go directly to the pages or pages where the cited material can be found. Page 1515 is the first page of the case in the Lufthansa example. The pages where the cited material is found are pages 1518 and 1519. These pages are abbreviated here as 1518—1519.

(6) Court

Unless the name of the court is obvious from the citation, you must include the name of the court in the parenthesis. With this information, the reader will know, for example, whether the case is binding or persuasive. The Lufthansa example is from the U. S. Court of Appeals for the Eleventh Circuit. (Additionally, the Federal Reporter in which this case appears reports only cases from the U. S. Courts of Appeals for the various circuits. If the case were from a United States District Court, the decision may be reported in the Federal Supplement instead of the Federal Reporter.)

283

(7) Year of the Decision

The reader must also know the year of the decision. The year is the one in which the decision was issued, not when the case was argued. With this information, the reader will know which case is the most recent expression of the law.

2. Subsequent Case History

A writer must also include "subsequent case history" when a case is affirmed or reversed on appeal. Subsequent case history citations are also common when a state appellate court refuses to hear an appeal or when the U.S. Supreme Court denies a writ of certiorari to have a case heard by the highest court in the nation.

In the following example, the citation shows that a decision from the U.S. Court of International Trade was affirmed on appeal by the U.S. Court of Appeals for the Federal Circuit.

> Hasbro Indus., Inc. v. United States, 703F. Supp. 941 (Ct. Int'l Trade 1988), aff'd, 879 F.2d 838 (Fed. Cir. 1989).
>
> Depending on the purpose of the citation, the writer may also chose to cite only to the appellate court's decision and not refer at all to the lower court.
>
> Hasbro Indus., Inc. v. United States, 879 F.2d 838 (Fed. Cir. 1989).

Do you remember our first example with Lufthansa German Airlines? That case was appealed to the U.S. Supreme Court, but the Court refused the writ of certiorari. Here is how the case should now be cited:

> Krys v. Lufthansa German Airlines, 119 F.3d 1515, 1518—19 (11th Cir. 1997), cert. denied, 118 S. Ct. 1042(1998).

The "S. Ct." is an unofficial reporter of U.S. Supreme Court decisions. The official reporter is the *United States Reports*, abbreviated as "U.S."

3. Parentheticals

Readers are often assisted by the use of "parentheticals" that explain why the writer is citing to a particular page or pages. A "parenthetical" is the information contained in parenthesis after the case citation. As Professor Linda Edwards has noted, a writer can use parentheticals with case citations to "quote a nugget of language or to highlight examples of relevant facts from the cited case." The following example, using the *Lufthansa* case once again, explains to readers that the case is cited for its discussion of the Warsaw Convention, an international treaty that limits liability to airplane passengers on international flights.

Krys v. Lufthansa German Airlines, 119 F. 3d 1515, 1518—19 (11th Cir. 1997) (discussing the applicability of the Warsaw Convention), *cert. Denied*, 118 S. Ct. 1042 (1998).

Parentheticals may also describe the facts of the case:

Regensburger v. China Adoption Consultants, *Ltd.*, 138 F. 3d 1201 (7th Cir. 1998) (unsuccessful lawsuit by prospective adoptive parents alleging that the adoption agency gave them a child who "was not three years old but was in fact between six and eight years old and mentally and physically delayed").

Parentheticals may be used for sources other than judicial decisions, as demonstrated in these two examples:

63 Fed. Reg. 27,112 (1998) (requesting by the Secretary of State's Advisory Committee on Private International Law for pubic comment on a draft UNCITRAL Legislative Guide).

Maureen Bezuhly, David Fidler, Mark E. Wojcik, and Lane Porter, *International Health Law*, 31 Int'l L. 645, 647 (1997) (reviewing legal developments in the emergency measures to protect against "mad cow" disease).

4. Parallel Citations

There are official and unofficial reporters of judicial decisions. This means that a court decision can be found in more than one place. It also means that in some instances it will be necessary to provide a "parallel citation" to both the official and unofficial reporters.

A case reporter may be official or unofficial. The official reporter for case from the United States Supreme Court, for example, is the *United States Reports*. Unofficial reporters for Supreme Court decisions include the *Supreme Court Reporters* and the *Supreme Court Reports, Lawyers Edition*. U.S. Supreme Court decisions are published in other sources as well, including *United States Law Week*, newspapers such as the *New York Times* or the *Chicago Daily Law Bulletin*, and electronically on several Internet sites. The official reporter is the version published or authorized by the court. The official version will control if there is a discrepancy with a version published by an unofficial (private) publisher. The official version usually takes much longer to publish, however. The unofficial reporters are available much more quickly and often contain additional features (such as summaries and headnotes) that make information in the court decisions more accessible to readers.

Parallel citations also exist for certain other courts. Decisions of the United States Court of International Trade will be published in the official reporter of that court, but many of the decisions will also appear in the *Federal Supplement*. Decision of the highest court of the State of New York, the New York Court of Appeals, will be published in the official reporter for that court and in the *Northeastern Reporter*. Decisions for lower courts in New York will be published in the state reporters (such as A.D.2d) and in West's *New York Supplement*. Decisions for courts in California will appear in the California state reports and in West's *California Reporter*.

Here are examples of parallel citations for a state court decision from California and another from New York:

> *Philippine Export and Foreign Loan Guarantee Corp. v. Chuidian*, 218 Cal. App.3d 1058, 1099, 267 Cal. Rptr. 457, 480(1990).
>
> *Sigmoil Resources, N.V. v. Pan Ocean Oil Corp.* (Nigeria), 234 A.D.2d 103, 105, 650 N.Y.S.2d 726, 727(1996), *appeal denied*, 89 N.Y.2d 1030, 680 N.E.2d 619, 658 N.Y.2d 245(1997).

Chapter 6
Understanding Legal Citations

5. The Functions of Legal Citations

Legal citations serve three important purposes in legal writing. They avoid problems of plagiarism; they provide a source of legal bibliography that readers can consult to confirm that legal authorities are not distorted; and, when used effectively, they enable writers to write shorter sentences.

(1) Citation Avoid Plagiarism

Legal citations provide authority for statements of law that the writer may make in a memorandum, a court pleading, a law review article, or any other legal document. The use of a citation avoids potential problems of plagiarism when the write acknowledges the original source of a statement or an idea. To avoid plagiarism, the write must cite to any material used from a court decision, a legal encyclopedia, a law review article, or any other source relied upon.

Most American educational institutions take a strict stand against plagiarism, and many students are surprised at how strict these rules can actually be. In some instances, students have been expelled from law school for plagiarism. Citations must be used whenever you use a source or an idea of another person. To avoid plagiarism problems, you should follow these rules:

a) You must acknowledge direct use of another person's words. To avoid plagiarism problems, you must use "quotation marks" around words, phrase, and sentences that are quoted directly. You must also include a citation to the source, even if you are not quoting directly.

b) You must acknowledge any words that you paraphrase from any source. You must always give citations to the sources of your ideas. If you change a few words or change the order of the source sentence, you must still give a citation to the source.

c) You must acknowledge direct use of another person's idea. You must cite when you are using another person's thoughts or research. Not to do so may be considered theft of that idea or work. If you are ever in doubt about whether to cite, you should always err on the side of giving credit to the other person. Use of a citation increases the persuasiveness of your idea. Use of a citation does not diminish your own work — your job is to analyze and express meaningful commentary about the work of others.

(2) Citations Allow Readers to Consult the Original Source and to Find

Additional Information

Legal citations provide an important source of legal bibliography. Readers can find the original source material and check the accuracy of quotations. Readers can consult the source or sources cited to confirm that information from those sources is presented in an accurate and fair context. A proper citation will also allow trained readers to judge for themselves the answers to several questions, including:

a) Whether the rule of law comes from a binding, primary law source or is merely persuasive within the jurisdiction;

b) Whether the rule comes from a court decision, statute, or agency regulation;

c) Whether a proposition based on statutory authority comes from a "plain reading" of the statute itself or from its legislative history;

d) Whether the year of the court or agency decision indicates anything about how strong the rule may currently be; and

e) Whether the level of a court decision means that a higher court may reach a different result.

Readers can also consult the legal sources cited to obtain additional information about a particular issue. Cases will provide additional information about the issue then before the court; statues will provide the general guidelines applicable to all cases. For readers who require additional background information, the writer may wish to citations to other authorities, such as scholarly treatises.

Example: Pursuant to the antidumping laws, the United States Department of Commerce will impose duties on imported products sold, or likely to be sold, in the United State at less than their fair value if such sales harm, or pose the potential to harm, domestic industry. See 19 U.S.C. §1673(1988); *Zenith Elecs. Corp. v. United states*, 77 F.3d 426,428 (Fed. Cir. 1996); see also Ralph H. Folsom & Michael W. Gordon, *International Business Transactions* §6.5, at 130—31(1995) (discussing the evolution of U.S. antidumping law).

The additional citation to a scholarly treatise will provide the readers with a secondary source of additional information that may help them better understand the primary sources cited.

Chapter 6
Understanding Legal Citations

(3) Effective Citation Make for Stronger, More Concise Writing

Legal citations, when used effectively, will enable writers to write more concise sentences. This is true because a legal citation can convey a great deal of information to a trained reader. For example, you may want to discuss a case that was decided by the U.S. Court of Appeals for the Federal Circuit. The abbreviation "Fed. Cir." Including in the parenthesis will inform readers that the case was decided by the U.S. Court of Appeals for the Federal Circuit.

Example: the United State Court of Appeals for the Federal Circuit held in 1989 that to determine the common meaning of a tariff provision, a court "may consult dictionaries, scientific authorities, and other reliable information sources to ascertain that common meaning." *Hasbro Indus. v. United States*, 879 F. 2d 838, 840 (Fed. Cir. 1989).

In the example above, the reader can see from the citation that the source of authority is the United States Court of Appeals for the Federal Circuit. Because that information is obvious to the reader, the sentence can be edited as follows:

Example (as revised): to determine the common meaning of a tariff provision, a court "may consult dictionaries, scientific authorities, and other reliable information sources to ascertain that common meaning."

Hasbro Indus. v. United States, 879 F. 2d 838, 840 (Fed. Cir. 1989).

In yet another example, all of the information contained in the sentence is obvious from the citation:

Example: the decision in *Hasbro Industries, Inc. v. United States* was decided by the United States Court of International Trade in 1988 and affirmed by the United States Court of Appeals for the Federal Circuit in the following year. *Hasbro Indus., Inc. v. United States*, 703 F. Supp. 941 (Ct. Int'l Trade 1988), *aff'd*, 879 F. 2d 838 (Fed. Cir. 1989).

The writer could have easily eliminated the information from the above sentence and instead have substituted meaningful analysis about the substance of the court decision.

6. Understanding "*ID.*"

The "*id.*" in American legal writing has nothing to do with the psychology of Dr. Sigmund Freud. The term is used to avoid repeating citations in full when the previous citation was to the same source. *Id.* is preferred over ibid. in

American legal writing. This section explains "*id.*" and gives several examples of how to use "*id.*" correctly.

The Latin term *ibidem* (abbreviated as *ibid*) has been defined to mean: "in the same place; in the same book, chapter, passage, etc.: used to avoid the repetition of a reference." Although *ibidem* would seem to be the preferred abbreviation for repetitive legal citations, writers in the United States use *id.* rather than *ibid*. The term *idem* is "used to indicate a reference previously made." According to *The Bluebook*, the term *id.* is used "when citing to the immediately preceding authority." If the previous authority is a "sting" citation with more than one source, the use of "*id.*" with multiple sources may confuse readers.

Here are some examples of the correct uses of "*id.*" and "*see id.*"

> *Adler v. Federal Republic of Nigeria*, 107 F. 3d720, 726(9th Cir. 1997)
> Id.
> Id. at 723

Under the *Bluebook's* rules for citing material that is on more than one page, only the last two digits will generally be used.

> *In re estate of Ferdinand Marcos Human Rights Litigation*, 94 F. 3d 539, 542—43(9th Cir.1996)
> See id. at 542
> 19 C.F.R. §141.31(1997)
> See id. §141.32.
> 63 Fed. Reg. 4682, 4683 (1998)
> Id. §63, at 404

7. Using "*ID.*" with Parallel Citations

A parallel citation is a citation to another source that reprints the same material found in another place. Attorneys from other countries, for example, are often surprised by the number of different places that the same court case can be found. In other countries, the legal market is simply too small to support multiple publication of the same material.

The term "*id.*" can also be used with sources that have parallel citations and subsequent legal history on appeal. Here are some correct examples using reported judicial decisions from California, Illinois and New York.

California

Philippine Export and Foreign Loan Guarantee Corp. v. Chuidian, 218 Cal. App. 3d 1058, 1099, 267 Cal. Rptr. 457, 480 (1990).
Id. at 1098, 267 Cal. Rptr. at 480.

Illinois

Doe v. Roe, 289 Ill. App. 3d 116, 129, 681 N.E. 2d 640, 649, 224 Ill. Dec. 325, 334 (1997), *appeal denied*, 174 Ill. 2d 558, 686 N.E. 2d 1160, 227 Ill. Dec. 4 (1997).
Id. at 128, 681 N.E. 2d at 639, 224 Ill. Dec. at 333.

New York

Sigmoil Resources, N.V. v. Pan Ocean Oil Corp. (Nigeria), 234 A.D. 2d 103, 105, 650 N.Y.S. 2d 726, 727 (1996), *appeal denied*, 89 N.Y. 2d 1030, 680 N.E. 2d 619, 658 N.Y.S. 2d 245 (1997).
Id. at 104, 650 N.Y.S. 2d at 727.

8. Short Citations

A short citation form may be used if it identifies a case that was previously cited in the same document. Short cites may be appropriate to use when you cannot use "*id.*" The following paragraph illustrates a proper use of *id.* and a short citation form.

The Foreign Sovereign Immunities Act (FSIA) establishes a "comprehensive framework" for determining whether a federal or state court in the United States "may exercise jurisdiction over a foreign state." *Republic of Argentina v. Weltover*, 504 U.S. 607, 610 (1992); *Adler v. Federal Republic of Nigeria*, 107 F. 3d 720, 723 (9th Cir. 1997). Under the FSIA, a foreign state, as well as its agents and instrumentalities, "shall be immune from the jurisdiction of the courts of the United States" unless one of several statutory exceptions applies. 28 U. S. C. §1604（1994）. The FSIA confers original jurisdiction to the district courts over any nonjury civil action against a foreign state where the foreign state is not entitled to immunity under the Act. *Id*. §1330; *Adler*, 107 F. 3d at 723. These provisions of the FSIA provide the only basis to obtain jurisdiction over a foreign state in the courts of the United States. *Argentine Republic v. Amerada Hess Shipping Corp.*, 488 U. S. 428, 443 (1989); *Adler*, 107 F. 3d at 723. If the claim against the foreign country does not fall within one of the exceptions, the court will lack subject matter jurisdiction and must dismiss the case against the foreign country. *Greenpeace, Inc. (U. S. A.) v. State of France*, 946 F. Supp. 773, 780(C. D. Cal. 1996).

9. General Abbreviations:

The following abbreviations are commonly accepted in legal citation:

- §Section*
- USC United States Code
- ¶ Paragraph*
- Const. Constitution
- art. Article
- amend. Amendment
- Cir. Circuit (referring to Circuit Courts)
- ann. Annotated
- cl. Clause
- 2d, 3d Second Series, Third Series (second or third set of volumes for a particular Reporter)

Note: If you need to say "section" at the beginning of a statement, spell it out, but if it's within a sentence, you may use the §symbol, available on most word processors.

- In Word Perfect on a PC, these characters can be accessed under the "Insert" menu → Characters → Typographic Symbols. On a Macintosh Computer, the key combination option-6 produces the §symbol for most word processing programs, option-7 produces ¶.

Chapter 6
Understanding Legal Citations

Exercises

Edit the following paragraphs to eliminate information that is obvious from the citation. It is not necessary to rewrite the entire sentence; you may just strike the unnecessary language. You may also edit the paragraphs for grammar and style where appropriate.

1. Under section 2 of article 3 of the United States Constitution, the U.S. Supreme Court has original jurisdiction over all cases affecting ambassadors, other public ministers, and consuls. U.S. Const. art. III, §2.

2. As stated in section 441(1)(a) of the *Restatement (Third) of the Foreign Relations Law of the United States*, a federal court may not try a person in a criminal case "unless he is before the court at the time the trial begins." *Restatement (Third) of the Foreign Relations Law of the United States* §441(1)(a) (1987). As explained further in the comments to that section, however, if the person flees after trial has begun, the accused person "will be deemed to have waived his right to be present" and the trial may continue even in his absence. *Id.* cmt. C(iii).

3. Under Rule 44.1 of the Federal Rules of Civil Procedure, the court may determine matters of foreign law by considering any relevant material or source, including testimony. Fed. R. Civ. P. 44.1

4. Pursuant to the antidumping laws as promulgated in the *Unites States Code* and as interpreted by the United States Court of Appeals for the Federal Circuit, the U.S. Department of Commerce must impose duties on imported products sold, or likely to be sold, In the United States at less than their fair value if such sales harm, or pose the potential to harm, domestic industry. See 19 U.S.C. §1673 (1988); *Zenith Elecs. Corp. v. United States*, 77 F.3d 426, 428 (Fed. Cir. 1996).

5. According to Sutherland's treatise on statutory construction and at least one federal appellate court decision, identical words used twice in the same statute are presumed to have the same meaning. 2A *Sutherland Statutory Construction* §46.06 (4th ed. 1984); *See also ICC Indus., Inc. v. Unites States*, 812 F.2d 694, 700 (Fed. Cir. 1987).

Appendix

Law Office Memo (1)

Memorandum on How to Write Memoranda

To: International Lawyers
From: Mark E. Wojcik
Date: April 22, 2001
Re: Parts of an Office Memorandum
File: LS-ESL (M) 1

FACTS

This is a memorandum about writing a memorandum. A law office memorandum "is usually written by a [law] clerk or junior attorney for a more experienced attorney to predict what effect application of the relevant law will have on the client's situation." John C. Dernbach, A Practical Guide to Legal Writing and Legal Method 187(2d ed. 1994). "There is no required format that all lawyers use or that all law schools use for a legal memorandum." Helene S. Shapo et al., Writing and Analysis in the Law 75 (3d ed. 1995). This memorandum describes one common format that includes a fact section, the issue and brief answer, a section for the relevant statute or contract provision, the discussion section, and a conclusion. It is by no means, however, the only model for an office memorandum. Because there are different types of legal problems, there are different types of office memoranda.

Office memoranda may begin with a section that sets forth the relevant facts of a client's case. The section may be labeled "facts" "relevant facts" or "statement of facts." Although the fact section may be the first part of an office memorandum, it may also follow the issue and brief answer sections in some memoranda.

The fact section will set forth legally relevant facts of a dispute and exclude the irrelevant facts. In a dispute between two parties, for example, the memorandum should contain all of the facts that favor the plaintiff and all of the facts that favor the defendant. The statements of facts must also contain all of the other facts necessary to keep the story together. These additional facts may turn an otherwise adversarial presentation of the facts into an objective presentation of facts. They make the fact section tell a story that readers can understand more easily. When a reader understands the factual stories that each side wants to tell, it makes it easier to compare the facts of this case to the facts of earlier cases.

All of the facts that will appear later in the discussion section of the memorandum must appear first in the statement of facts. Introducing new facts in the discussion section of the memorandum will cause readers to suspect that the memorandum is sloppy or untrustworthy. Readers may suspect that a writer is "holding out" on adverse facts that mat help the other side. These adverse facts will come out at trial: it is better to disclose them first in an office memorandum.

The best approach for writers will be to assume that readers have no prior knowledge of the factual situation. The statement of facts must therefore tell a story in complete detail. In reality, some readers may be more familiar with the facts than the writer. Readers, for example, may include clients, witnesses, and technical advisors who may conduct factual investigations for the law firm. If they note errors in the statement of facts, these readers can correct those errors so that the legal analysis is not built upon erroneous factual assumptions.

ISSUES

Should an office memorandum include issues that combine the relevant law and the relevant facts?

1. Can this section include sub issues?
2. Can the memorandum discuss more than one issue?

BRIEF ANSWERS

The "brief answer" or "short answer" section should relate directly to the issues or questions presented. Each answer should provide readers with a prediction of how a court, agency, or other tribunal would rule if the case proceeds to trial. The answer should give the predicted result and a summary of the facts and law that support the writer's prediction. If it is necessary to base the prediction upon any assumed facts, the writer should advise the readers that the decision is subject to certain assumed facts, the writer should advise the readers that the decision is subject to certain assumed facts.

The issue section can contain sub issues or multiple issues. Readers need to know the issues and sub issues that the memorandum will discuss. An effective issue section will allow readers to know immediately what these issues are.

RELEVANT STATUTE

If more than one statute is cited here, the section would be labeled "**Relevant Statute.**" The section can also be used, with appropriate modification, to set forth quotations from relevant provisions of a contract or insurance policy, or from other sources of law, such as an administrative regulation or regulation or the terms of a binding treaty. A section quoting relevant statutes and regulations, for example, could be labeled "**Relevant Statute and Regulations.**"

It will often be necessary to quote the provisions of a statute, regulation, constitutional provision or treaty. When the quoted section is more than 50 words long, it should be single-spaced and indented on each side. You must also take special care to quote accurately. A misplaced comma may be enough to cause confusion in some cases. If you find that part of a statute or other material is not necessary to quote in full, you may use a series of three dots known as an "ellipsis"... to show that some of the words from the quoted material are missing. You may also place a word in [brackets] to show that language from the original text has been altered or added.

If you are quoting a statute, regulation, or treaty, you should include a proper Bluebook citation on a separate line after the quoted text. See Editor of the Columbia Law Review et al., *The Bluebook: A Uniform System of Citation* (16th ed. 1996).

DISCUSSION

The discussion section may begin with a thesis paragraph. The thesis paragraph can highlight claims made by the parties and briefly summarize the controlling law. The thesis paragraph may also be a simple roadmap of issues that will appear in the discussion section. If the discussion section has two issues, for example, the thesis paragraph may tell the reader that the discussion section will discuss: (1) the first issue; and (2) the second issue.

(1) The First Issue

This section will discuss the first issue. The use of a short headline helps readers identify that this section will be limited to discussion of the first issue.

The first issue section may be organized to follow a small-scale format such as "IRAC." The term "IRAC" refers to an "Issue, Rule, Application, and Conclusion." It is one of many possible models for the small-scale discussion of an office memorandum. See, e.g., Mark E Wojcik, The Death of IRAC, in Legal Writing Institute, The Second Draft, Vol. 10, No. 1, at 16 (Fall 1995) (special issue on teaching IRAC in legal writing classes). There are other possible models as well that set forth the issue to be discussed, the controlling rule of law, a definition or other explanation of that rule of law, factual and legal arguments for each of the parties, and a prediction of how the court or other tribunal will rule on this single issue.

(2) The Second Issue

This section will discuss the second issue. The use of a short headline again helps the reader identify that this section will be limited to discussion of the second issue. Both the first and second section will set forth the issue to be discussed, the controlling rule of law, an explanation of that rule, arguments for each of the parties, and a prediction of how the court or other tribunal will rule on this issue. The conclusion for this section should relate only to the second issue. The overall conclusion for a paper with multiple issues can appear in the following "conclusion" section.

CONCLUSION

The conclusion section of the memorandum will present an overall conclusion to the issue (or issue) in dispute. If there are two issues (as is suggested in this memorandum), the conclusion section will show the reader how those two issues relate to one another. Additional advice for the client or law partner may also appear in this section, such as a recommendation for further research on an alternative remedy or a related issue not covered in this memorandum.

Law Office Memo (2)

MEMORANDUM[①]

To: Assigning Partner
From: Lov Kumar Goel
File: Potential Client Kenny Aoki (v. World Industries Skateboards)
Re: Negligence claim for skateboard accident during hired commercial filming

QUESTION PRESENTED

Whether Mr. Aoki's (Aoki) cause of action for negligence is barred by the doctrine of primary assumption of risk.

BRIEF ANSWER

There is a strong case for Aoki that World Industries Skateboards Inc. (World) will be liable to him under the doctrine of contributory negligence. The director, an agent of World, had an ordinary duty of care to Aoki. By making the sport inherently more dangerous, the director violated his duty of care to Aoki and opened himself up to contributory negligence liability. By fundamentally altering the nature of skateboarding, World will likely be liable Aoki.

STATEMENT OF FACTS

Aoki, our prospective client, has achieved notoriety in the skateboarding community by appearing in the "X games" (a widely televised extreme sports competition sponsored by ESPN) and competing in several national skateboarding competitions. He was commissioned by World to be featured in a 2008 Super bowl commercial. He was to perform a rather complicated skateboarding trick ("varial heelflip") which he assured World industries he would be able to perform without incident.

On the morning of the filming, however, Aoki was told by the director that he was to wear a large helmet camera during the filming. Despite protest

---

[①] http://lovgoel.googlepages.com/OfficeMemoWritingSample.pdf

from Aoki and other skateboarders that the camera would interfere with the trick, the director insisted he try anyway. After one unsuccessful attempt, Aoki continued his protests saying that, in fact, the camera had prevented him from successfully executing the trick. Despite this initial fall, the director insisted Aoki try again. This second attempt resulted in Aoki dislocating his collarbone.

Aoki also contends that, although he physically recovered, he missed significant class time at UC Davis School of Law. This lost time will prevent him from taking the California Bar Exam on time.

DISCUSSION

Aoki would like to know whether his cause of action for negligence would be barred by the doctrine of primary assumption of risk. The short answer is probably not. There is a strong argument to be made that he did not assume risk unilaterally, but that World contributed to his accident by negligently requiring him to wear a bulky helmet camera. If we can show that the director was partially at fault for Aoki's injuries by encouraging his attempt, he can likely recover partial damages. By arguing that the risk taken (attempting the skateboarding trick while encumbered) was a reasonable implied risk, Aoki will likely recover part of the damages he feels he is owed by World.

First, we argue that Aoki does not consent to attempting the trick. If we establish a lack of consent, we negate a critical element of primary assumption of risk. It can be argued that the protests of Aoki and his fellow skateboarders show an apprehension on his part to undertake the challenge, and that he was compelled to attempt the trick against his will. He clearly expressed trepidation towards attempting the complex skateboarding trick while wearing the device, but was nevertheless coaxed into attempting the trick anyway. This line of reasoning affords us a complete negation to primary assumption. Even if we don't establish complete lack of consent, case law suggests that even consent does not establish primary assumption of risk per se.

The risk posed by the helmet camera is not necessarily a risk inherent within the realm of those risks skateboarders traditionally assume. Aoki, a talented skateboarder, who has performed the required maneuver many times, has a strong argument for direct and proximate cause for his injury due to the camera. It has also been decided that "although defendants generally have no legal duty to eliminate... risks inherent in the sport itself, it is well established that defendants generally do have a duty of care not to increase the risks to a participant over and above those inherent in the sport." *Knight v. Jewett*, 3 Cal. 4th 296, 315 (1992). In this case, the plaintiff sought recovery for injuries sustained during a consensual game of touch football. The court rejected defendant's motion for summary judgment because the defendant failed to establish primary assumption of risk under traditional consent. *Id* at 338. Like the instant case, the actions of the plaintiff were consensual (assumed). She was free to leave the "super-bowl halftime" football game whenever she felt threatened. In fact, it can be argued that the surrounding circumstances of Aoki's case suggest that he was less free to exercise his own discretion than the plaintiff in Knight: He was under contract to perform the trick; he presumably had to travel to the commercial site, which incurred some expense and time, etc. Even without these circumstances, the Knight decision cuts in favor of finding a secondary assumption of risk for Mr. Aoki because recovery was granted for injuries sustained during a purely consensual activity. We can also argue a classic violation of duty of care by World.

The director's ordinary duty of care was breached when he made the sport more dangerous. Even though skateboarding involves an inherent risk of falling for which Aoki might be liable, primary assumption of risk would not bar recovery in a situation where the director made it more likely that he would fall. [Citation omitted] *Huffman v. City of Poway*, 84 Cal. App. 4th975, 994 (2000). Huffman finds the plaintiff bringing action for injuries sustained during a rehearsal of a musical that had recently switched theaters. The plaintiff was aware of the danger of the trapdoor that he fell through. Moreover, he was a professional actor hired to perform in a production who also expressed trepidation towards the actions his director instructed him to carry out. Id at 980—981. Like the instant case, he was well aware of the risk that he was taking and allowed to recover under a secondary assumption of risk action. It should also be noted that the court barred the primary assumption of risk claim because "it concluded [Defendant's] acts and omission increased the risks of injury to Huffman." *Id* at 993.

Conversely, the defense will likely argue that the controlling rule is that "there is no duty of care to protect another from the risks inherent in the activity." Knight, 3 Cal. 4th at 314. Aoki, they will likely say, having achieved such a high level of skateboarding skill should have been aware of the inherent risks and thus been aware of the fact that serious injury could have resulted from undertaking the act encumbered by a foreign device. He should be barred from recovery under the doctrine of primary assumption of risk as previously described because he implicitly agreed to sustain the risk when he contracted to perform the trick for the company. Again, citing Knight, "In some situations, however, the careless conduct of others is treated as an 'inherent risk' of a sport, thus barring recovery [under primary assumption] by the plaintiff." *Id* at 316. They are also likely to claim that after the first failed attempt, Aoki was solely negligent for attempting the trick again after realizing the extent of the risk because he was unable to perform a rather ordinary trick for someone of his outstanding abilities. Our answer would be that Mr. Aoki only consented to the known risks of skateboarding. By adding the helmet camera, there was a uniquely dangerous aspect added to the activity that distinguishes Knight from the instant case. Aoki did not claim to be an expert in skateboarding while encumbered with heavy equipment, but in skateboarding alone.

Additionally, World is likely to argue that the requirement to wear the helmet camera does not expose them to liability because it does not deter "vigorous participation in the sport" or "fundamentally alter" the nature of skateboarding. *Freeman v. Hale*, 30 Cal. App. 4th 1388, 1389 (1994). In that case, an inebriated Freeman collided with Hale tragically causing her to become a quadriplegic. It was argued that Hale did not assume the additional risk of skiing on a slope with a drunken skier because the consumption of alcohol is not critical to the sport of skiing. If the additional act can be removed without altering the fundamental nature of the sport, then it is shown to not be an inherent risk, and thus one not primarily assumed. The ultimate upshot of Freeman is that we can access a vacuum test; by removing the camera, we do not fundamentally alter the nature of skateboarding (see above; indeed we revert back to its true nature). This analysis can be used to show that the additional risk posed by the camera is not one that is inherent to skateboarding, and therefore not one that is primarily assumed. *Id* at 1393—1394. It cuts against finding for the World Industries because primary assumption of risk doctrine requires no change in the fundamental nature of the activity.

CONCLUSION

Based on the previous discussion, I feel as though Aoki, our prospective client, has a valid claim that primary assumption of risk does not bar recovery for his injuries. There is a strong argument to be made for secondary assumption/comparative negligence based on the conduct of the director of the commercial shoot, remonstrations of Aoki and the other skateboarders at the time of the accident, and the fundamental change in the nature of skateboarding that the camera entails.

Should Aoki decide to pursue litigation, we should immediately obtain clarification and begin discussion with Aoki as to the intending circumstances will be required, as well as possibly interviewing the other skateboarders. Additionally, it would be prudent to have experts review the helmet camera apparatus and site of filming to see if there were any precautions the filming crew or World could have taken to prevent harm from befouling Aoki.

A Brief to a Trial Court (1):

SUPERIOR COURT OD THE STATE OF CALIFORNIA
IN AND FOR THE COUNTY OF SAN FRANCISCO

TIMOTHY TYLER,	CASE NO. 1122-a
Plaintiff,	MEMORANDUM OF POINTS AND
vs.	AUTORITIES IN OPPOSITION TO
EASTERN PACIFIC UNIVERSITY	EASTERN PACIFIC UNIVERSITY'S
Defendant.	MOTION FOR SUMMARY JUGEMENT

I. INTRODUCTION

Plaintiff, Timothy Tyler, submits this memorandum in opposition to Defendant Eastern pacific University's motion for summary judgment. The statute of limitations was tolled in this action because Tyler had no reason to suspect fraud or to inquire further until he discovered the fraud in March 1993. This action therefore has been timely filed and is not barred.

II. STATEMENT OF FACTS

Timothy Tyler was a member of his high school's varsity soccer team and was named to the state's All Star team. (Joint Stipulation of Facts 2.) In 1988, during the fall of his senior year, Tyler was recruited to play soccer for Eastern Pacific University (Eastern) by Richard Cramer, a recruiter for Eastern. Tyler had already accepted a full athletic scholarship to attend Yosemite College after graduation. (Joint stip. ¶¶ 3, 5.)

In the course of their discussion, Cramer learned of Tyler's desire to obtain a graduate degree from the Global policy studies (GPS) program at E astern. Cramer told Tyler that Eastern had a policy of giving priority to its own graduates in admission to the GPS program. Cramer admits that he had no idea whether the GPS program had such a policy and made this statement only to induce Tyler to play soccer for Eastern. (Joint Stip. ¶ 9.) Tyler had previously spoken with the staff of the GPS program and on such policy had been mentioned. That discussion with GPS staff had concerned the excellence of the program and the high caliber of student the program was able to attract. (Joint stip. ¶ 10.)

Tyler subsequently declined the scholarship to Yosemite College and enrolled at Eastern. Since no scholarships were available, he financed his education by working part time and taking out substantial loans. Tyler was able to obtain a position as a student assistant in the GPS program. (Joint Stip. ¶ 5.) Although he assisted the admissions secretary during his freshman year, his responsibilities for applications and mailing letters as he was instructed by the secretary. Tyler was not involved in admissions decisions or aware of how they were made. The priority admissions policy was never mentioned during the course of his employment. (Joint stip. ¶ 6.)

In October 1992, Tyler applied for admission to the GPS program. When his application was denied in March 1993, Tyler discovered for the first time that Cramer had deceived him regarding the admissions policy. (Joint Stip. ¶ 11.) Tyler promptly filed this action in October of 1993 to recover the damages incurred as a result of Cramer's deception.

III. ARGUMENT

TYLER'S ACTION FOR FRAUD WAS FILED WITHIN THE THREE-YEAR PERIOD ALLOWED BY THE STATUTE OF LIMITATIONS BECAUSE HE DID NOT DISCOVER UNTIL MARCH 1993 THAT HE HAD BEEN MISLED AND COULD NOT REASONABLY HAVE DISCOVERED THE FRAUD EARLIER.

The statute of limitations for fraud does not begin to run until "the discovery, by the aggrieved party, of the facts constituting fraud." Cal. Civ. Proc. Code 338. (d) (West 1985 & Supp. 1994). Discovery occurs when the plaintiff obtains information "sufficient to make a reasonably prudent person suspicious of fraud, thus putting him on inquiry." *National Auto. & Casualty Ins. Co. v. Payne*, 261 Cal. App. 2d 403. 409, 67 Cal. Rptr. 784, 788 (1968). When a plaintiff has no reason to suspect fraud, however, the statute of limitations does not begin to run. Seeger v. Odell, 18 Cal. 2d 409, 115 P. 2d 977 (1941); *Hobart v. Hobart Estate Co.*, 26 Cal. 2d 412, 159 P.2d 958 (1945).

Seeger and Hobart are controlling here. In Seeger, an elderly couple was misled about an execution sale of their real estate by the defendants' attorney, who as an attorney, he knew all the pertinent facts about the sale. 18 Cal. 2d at 412, 115 p. 2d at 979. Similarly, in Hobart, the plaintiff was misled about the market value of his stock by the attorney who had represented his family's business for a long time. In both cases, the plaintiffs had no reason to suspect that they had been misled. And in both cases, the court held that the statute was tolled until the plaintiffs obtained information indicating that the attorneys had lied. Hobart, 26 Cal. 2d at 441, 159 p. 2d at 974; Seeger, 18 Cal. 2d at 418, 115 p. 2d at 982.

Tyler was similarly misled by someone who held himself out to be an expert. Tyler, a high school senior, had no reason to suspect that a recruiter employed by Eastern would lie to him about its admissions policy, just as the plaintiffs in Seeger and Hobart had no reason to suspect that the attorneys would lie to them. Thus, the statute did not begin to run until Tyler discovered Cramer's fraud in March of 1993.

Eastern's reliance on *Bedolla v. Logan & Frazer*, 52 Cal. App. 3d 118, 125 Cal. Rptr. 59 (1975), and *National Automobile & Casualty Insurance Co. v. Payne* is misplaced. In these cases, the plaintiffs were either aware of other wrongdoing by the defendants that should have aroused suspicion or were in a position to know the information that disclosed the fraud. In Bedolla, the court held that the plaintiff general partners should have suspected more wrongdoing on the part of the defendant accounting firm when the partners were already aware of other discrepancies in the books kept by the firm. 52Cal. App. 3d at 130, 125Cal. Rptr. At 68. And in Payne, the court held that members of a board of directors had a duty to discover a fraudulent sale of stock options that was contained in the corporate books. 261 Cal. App. 2d at 414, 67Cal. Rptr. At 791.

Tyler, on the other hand, had no reason to suspect that Cramer had lied to him. His previous discussion with the staff of the GPS program had disclosed only that many of its students were honor graduates from major universities. There was no discussion regarding the preferential admissions policy. Unlike the defendants in Bedolla, Tyler had no information that should have led him to suspect fraud.

Tyler's situation is also very different from that of the directors in Payne, who had a fiduciary responsibility to know the contents of the corporation's books. Tyler, a part-time student worker, had no responsibility to learn how admissions decisions were being made. His job was to complete the various clerical tasks assigned to him by the secretary in the GPS program.

Tyler has been harmed by the deliberate deception Cramer used to induce him to attend Eastern for the benefit of its soccer team. He should not be barred from recovering for the damages he has incurred because it took four years for the truth to come to light. As observed by the court in *Twining v. Thompson*, 68 Cal. App. 2d 104, 113, 156 p. 2d 29, 34 (1945):

The courts do not lightly seize upon small circumstances in order to deny an award to an innocent victim of a fraud upon the ground that he did not discover the fraud sooner.

Since Tyler had no reason to suspect the lack of a priority admissions policy before his application was rejected, the statute of limitations began to run only in March 1993. This action therefore is timely.

IV. CONCLUSION

For the reasons stated herein, Eastern's motion for summary judgment should be denied.

Dated: March 17, 1994

                                          HERNANDEZ & CRUZ
                                          By _____
                                          Maria Hernandez

                                          Attorneys for Plaintiff
                                          Timothy Tyler

A Brief to a Trial Court (2):[1]

UNITED STATES DISTRICT COURT FOR THE DISTRICT OF COLUMBIA

PUBLIC CITIZEN, INC.
1600 20th St., NW
Washington, D.C. 20009
    Plaintiff,
      vs.
OFFICE OF MANAGEMENT AND BUDGET
725 17th Street, N.W.
Washington, D.C. 20503
    Defendant.

C. A. No. _____

COMPLAINT FOR DECLARATORY AND INJUNCTIVE RELIEF
INTRODUCTION

This is an action under the Freedom of Information Act (FOIA), 5 U.S.C. §552, to compel the production of records identifying which agencies can submit budget-related materials, legislative proposals, reports, and testimony to Congress without first seeking clearance from the Office of Management and Budget (OMB).

JURISDICTION

This Court has subject matter jurisdiction under 28 U.S.C. §1331 and 5 U.S.C. §552(a)(4)(B).

---

[1] http://www.citizen.org/documents/ombcomplaint.pdf

PARTIES

Plaintiff Public Citizen, Inc. is a national non-profit public interest organization. Since its founding in 1971, Public Citizen has worked before Congress, regulatory agencies, and the courts to advance the interests of its members and educate the public on a wide range of consumer protection issues. In particular, Public Citizen works to promote openness in government and collects and disseminates information related to agency accountability.

Defendant OMB is an agency of the United States and has possession of and control over the records Plaintiff seeks.

STATEMENT OF FACTS

On December 8, 2006, Public Citizen submitted a FOIA request to OMB for lists of agencies that are allowed to transmit legislative and/or budgetary materials to Congress without first submitting them to OMB for coordination and clearance. In particular, Public Citizen requested

1) All records listing agencies that may directly submit legislative proposals, reports, or testimony to Congress without receiving OMB clearance;

2) All records listing agencies that may directly submit budget-related materials to Congress without receiving OMB clearance; and

3) All records explaining that agencies or an agency may directly submit legislative or budget-related materials to Congress without receiving OMB clearance or providing statutory authority for agencies or an agency to directly submit legislative or budget related materials to Congress without receiving OMB clearance.

By letter dated January 10, 2007, and signed by Lauren E. Wright, Deputy Assistant Director for Administration, OMB partially denied Public Citizen's request. Ms. Wright informed Public Citizen that OMB had found two documents that were "potentially responsive" to its request, but that she had decided that the documents are exempt from mandatory disclosure under FOIA

Exemptions 2 and 5, 5 U.S.C. §§552(b)(2) & (5), because the "documents relate to OMB's internal personnel rules and practices and, to the extent that they contain information that extends beyond such rules and practices, the documents contain pre-decisional and deliberative information, the disclosure of which would harm the decision making process." Ms. Wright enclosed a document that contained a list of "Statutes that Address the Direct Submission of Legislative Materials (and the agency concerned)" and a list of "Statutes that Address the Direct Submission of Budget Materials (and the agency concerned)."

By letter dated January 18, 2007, Public Citizen appealed OMB's denial. It explained that FOIA Exemptions 2 and 5 do not apply to the requested records. It also appealed the adequacy of OMB's search for records, noting that it had requested any record explaining that any agency can submit legislative or budgetary materials to Congress without receiving OMB clearance, and that it was difficult to believe that an adequate search for records responsive to the request would turn up only two records.

By letter dated February 26, 2007, and signed by Kimberley Luczynski, Acting Deputy General Counsel, OMB denied Public Citizen's appeal, asserting that its search was sufficient and that "the two documents referenced in our January 10, 2007 letter have been properly withheld pursuant to FOIA Exemptions (b)(2) and (b)(5)."

Plaintiff has a statutory right to the records it seeks, and there is no legal basis for Defendant's failure to disclose them to Plaintiff.

CLAIMS FOR RELIEF

WHEREFORE, Plaintiff requests that this Court

A) Declare that Defendant's failure to disclose records requested by Plaintiff is unlawful;

B) Order Defendant to make all the requested records available to Plaintiff;

C) Award Plaintiff its costs and reasonable attorneys' fees pursuant to 5 U.S.C. §552(a)(4)(E); and

D) Grant such other and further relief as this Court may deem just and proper.

Respectfully submitted,

s/

Adina H. Rosenbaum

(DC Bar No. 490928)

Brian Wolfman

(DC Bar No. 427491)

Public Citizen Litigation Group

1600 20th Street, N.W.

Washington, D.C. 20009

(202) 588-1000

(202) 588-7795 (fax)

Attorneys for Plaintiff

Dated: February 28, 2007

A Brief to a Trial Court (3):[①]

UNITED STATES DISTRICT COURT
FOR THE DISTRICT OF COLUMBIA

INTERFAITH WORKER JUSTICE 1020 West Bryn Mawr Ave., 4th Floor Chicago, IL 60660 　　　　Plaintiff, 　　v. UNITED STATES DEPARTMENT OF LABOR 200 Constitution Ave., NW Washington, DC 20210 　　　　Defendant.	C. A. No. _____

COMPLAINT FOR DECLARATORY AND INJUNCTIVE RELIEF
INTRODUCTION

This is an action under the Freedom of Information Act ("FOIA"), 5 U.S.C. §552, to compel the production of records relating to workers owed back wages under federal back-wage settlements whom the Department of Labor has been unable to locate. In particular, Plaintiff seeks records reflecting the names of the unlocatable workers, the companies for whom they worked, and the period of time covered in the settlement.

JURISDICTION

This Court has subject matter jurisdiction under 28 U.S.C. §1331 and

---

① http://www.citizen.org/documents/DOLcomplaint.pdf

5 U.S.C. §552(a)(4)(B).

PARTIES

Plaintiff Interfaith Worker Justice is a national non-profit organization concerned with improving the wages, benefits, and working conditions of workers.

Defendant Department of Labor is an agency of the federal government of the United States and has possession of and control over the records Plaintiff seeks.

STATEMENT OF FACTS

By letter to Defendant dated April 4, 2005, and signed by Plaintiff's Executive Director, Kim Bobo, Plaintiff requested "a copy of the following records: The names of all workers owed back wages from federal DOL back-wage settlements (who are unlocatable and still within the eligible time period for claiming and receiving back wages); the name of the company each potential claimant worked for and the period of time covered in the settlement."

By letter dated April 22, 2005, and signed by Nancy M. Flynn, Director, Office of Planning and Analysis, Defendant denied Plaintiff's request. Defendant's letter stated that "the Wage and Hour Division withholds information that would reveal individual identities pursuant to the provisions of exemption 6 of the FOIA."

By letter dated July 11, 2005, Plaintiff appealed Defendant's denial. Plaintiff's appeal explained that unlocatable workers have an interest in having their names disclosed and that disclosure of the records would shed light on the operation of Defendant's Back wage Collection and Disbursement System.

Under 5 U.S.C. §552(a)(6)(A)(ii) and 29 CFR §70.25, Defendant had 20 working days to respond to Plaintiff's FOIA appeal. To date, Plaintiff has not received a written response to its appeal nor has it received any records pertaining to unlocatable workers owed back wages.

Plaintiff is therefore deemed to have exhausted its administrative remedies under FOIA. See 5 U.S.C. §552(a)(6)(C)(i).

Plaintiff has a statutory right to the records it seeks, and there is no legal basis for Defendant's failure to disclose them to Plaintiff.

CLAIMS FOR RELIEF

WHEREFORE, Plaintiff requests that this Court:

A) Declare that Defendant's failure to disclose the records requested by Plaintiff pertaining to unlocatable workers owed back-wage benefits under federal back-wage settlements is unlawful;

B) Order Defendant to make all the requested records available to Plaintiff;

C) Award Plaintiff its costs and reasonable attorneys' fees pursuant to 5 U.S.C. §552(a)(4)(E); and

D) Grant such other and further relief as this Court may deem just and proper.

Respectfully submitted,
Signature
Adina H. Rosenbaum
(DC Bar No. 490928)
Brian Wolfman
(DC Bar No. 427491)
Public Citizen Litigation Group
1600 20th Street, N.W.
Washington, D.C. 20009
(202) 588-1000
(202) 588-7795 (fax)

January 18, 2006
Attorneys for Plaintiff

A Brief to an Appellate Court (1)

IN THE

COURT of APPEALS of INDIANA

CAUSE No. 85A02-0604-CR-338

KELLY A WATKINNS SPAULDING, Appellant (Defendant below), v. STATE OF INDIANA Appellee (Plaintiff below).	Appeal from the Wabash Circuit Court, Cause No. 85 C01-0407-FD-78 Hon. Robert McCallen III, Judge

BRIEF OF APPELLEE

STEPHEN R. CARTER
Attorney General of Indiana
Atty. No. 0004150-64

GARY DAMON SECREST
Deputy Attorney General
Atty. No. 0002259-49

Falian Zhang
Law Clerk
Office of Attorney General
Indiana Government Center
South, Fifth Floor
302 West Washington Street
Indianapolis, IN 46204-2770
Telephone: (317) 232-6315

Attorneys for Appellee

TABLE OF CONTENTS

Table of Authorities ··
Statement of the Issues ···
Statement of the Case ···
Statement of the Facts
Summary of the Argument ···
Argument
 The evidence is sufficient to sustain Defendant's conviction for Neglect of a Dependent, a Class D Felony. The Defendant abandoned her son without running water, sufficient food, or necessary support ····················
Standard of Review ···
Discussion ··
Conclusion ··
Certificate of Service ···

Table of Authorities

Cases

Gross v. State, 817 N. E. 2d 306 (Ind. Ct. App. 2004) ·················
Harrison v. State, 644 N. E. 2d 888 (Ind. Ct. App. 1994) ·············
Richetts v. State, 597 N. E. 2d 597 (Ind. Ct. App. 1992) ··············
Trice v. Stat, 693 N. E. 2d 649 (Ind. Ct. App. 1998) ···················
Weis v. Stat, 825 N. E. 2d 896 (Ind. Ct. App. 2005) ···················

Statutes

IC 35-46-1-4 ···

Other Authorities

The Six Edition of *Black's Law Dictionary* ································
Webster's Ninth New Collegiate Dictionary ·······························

IN THE
COURT of APPEALS of INDIANA

CAUSE No. 85A02-0604-CR-338

KELLY A WATKINNS SPAULDING, Appellant (Defendant below),	Appeal from the Wabash Circuit Court,
v.	Cause No. 85 C01-0407-FD-78
STATE OF INDIANA Appellee (Plaintiff below)	Hon. Robert McCallen III, Judge

BRIEF OF APPELLEE
STATEMENT OF THE ISSUE

Whether the evidence is sufficient to sustain Defendant's conviction for Neglect of a Defendant, her son.

STATEMENT OF THE CASE

On July 23, 2004, defendant was charged with Neglect of a Dependant, a Class D Felony. The case proceeded to a jury trial on December 13, 2005 which resulted in a verdict convicting Defendant of the charged offense (App. 97).

A sentencing hearing was held on January 11, 2006, at the conclusion of which the court sentenced Defendant to a term of one and one-half years at the Indiana Department of Correction, with one year to be suspended and served on probation (App. 100—101).

A Notice of Appeal was filed on January 13, 2006 (App. 111—112).

The Notice of Completion of Clerk's record was filed on February 10, 2006. (App. 113—114).

The Notice of Completion of the Transcript was filed on March 28, 2006. (App. 115—116).

The Brief of Appellant was filed on May 4, 2006, pursuant to an extension granted on May 4, 2006, with personal service on the Attorney General.

STATEMENT OF THE FACTS

In the summer of 2004, Defendant and her son Andrew Olinger ("Andrew") were living in a house in LaFontaine in Wabash County (Tr. 26). During that period, Defendant twice left Andrew at home alone and for a total three weeks (Tr. 32) and did not tell Andrew her whereabouts. *Id*. Andrew was sixteen (16) years old at the time (Tr. 22).

Defendant left for two weeks for the first time (Tr. 32), shut off the water (Tr. 33), left no money, and very little food and drink. (Tr. 28). During these two weeks, she did not call or bring in anything for Andrew to eat. (Tr. 32). Andrew has to go get a shower and use the restroom at a friend's house or his grandmother's house. (Tr. 29—30). There was no food in the house for a few days. (Tr. 54)

The second time, Defendant left for one week (Tr. 33), and Andrew was put in the same situation as before. Andrew's grandmother finally discovered Andrew's predicament and brought him food and brought to live with her. (Tr. 34). Defendant served different jails sentences in this country and Huntington County (Tr. 119).

Andrew felt psychologically depressed then he was left alone. (Tr. 42). Andrew also testified that there were periods of time that he was hungry, and that he lost five to ten pounds during the three-week-long period when he was alone at home. (Tr. 35)

SUMMARY OF THE ARGUMENT

There is sufficient evidence to prove beyond a reasonable doubt that Andrew was placed in a situation that endangered his life or health; he was abandoned and deprived of necessary support. The evidence introduced at trial was therefore sufficient to support Defendant's conviction for Neglect of a Dependant, a Class D Felony.

ARGUMENT

The evidence is sufficient to sustain Defendant's conviction for Neglect of a Dependant, a Class D Felony. The Defendant abandoned her son without running water, sufficient food, or necessary support.

STANDARD OF REVIEW

When reviewing the sufficiency of the evidence, the court will neither reweigh the evidence nor judge the credibility of the witnesses. *Trice v. State*, 693 N. E. 2d 649 (Ind. Ct. App. 1998). The Court will consider the evidence most favorable to the judgment together with all reasonable interferences to be drawn therefrom. *Id.* The Court will affirm a conviction if it is supported by substantial evidence of probative value. *Weis v. State*, 825 N. E. 2d 896, 904 (Ind. Ct. App. 2005).

DISCUSSION

Defendant's argument is that the State failed to present sufficient evidence that her conduct threatened either Andrew's health or life. IC 35—46—1—4 provides in relevant part:

IND. CODE SECTION 35—46—1—4

(a) A person having the care of a dependent, whether assumed voluntarily or because of a legal obligation, who knowingly or intentionally:

(1) places the dependent in a situation that may endanger his life or health;

(2) abandons or cruelly confines the dependent;

(3) deprives the dependent of necessary support; or

. . .

Commits neglect of a Dependent, a Class D Felony.

Dependent was charged with neglect by each specification in Subsections (a) (1) through (a) (3). Anyone of which, is alone sufficient to convict and sustain that conviction. Defendant must defect each mechanism of neglect in order to prevail upon his sufficiency challenge.

(a) (1) *Endangering Life or Health*

When constructing a statute, words and phrases must be given their plain, ordinary and usual meaning, unless a contrary purpose is clearly shown by the statute itself. *Harrison v. State*, 644 N. E. 2d 888, 890 (Ind. Ct. App. 1994). Although penal statutes must be strictly constructed against the State, a statute should not be overly narrowed so as to exclude cases fairly covered by it and should not be interpreted so as to give efficient operation to the legislature's expressed intent. *Id*. The Six Edition of *Black's Law Dictionary* defines health as the "state of being hale, sound, or whole in body, mind or soul, well being." *Webster's Ninth New Collegiate Dictionary* defines health as the "condition of being sound in body, mind, or spirit." The references in these definitions to "body" and "mind" lead to the conclusion that the ordinary meaning of health is not limited to one's physical state, but included an individual's psychological, mental and emotional status. Additionally, the purpose of the neglect statute is to protect a dependent from the failure to those entrusted with his care to take the action necessary to safeguard their dependents' "health". If the neglect statute is narrowly read to protect dependents only from *physical* harm, a care giver would suffer no consequence for failing to protect a child from dangers and offenses such as sexual abuse that do not result in bruises, scrapes or other physical injuries. "Under the neglect statute, 'health is not limited to one's physical state, but includes an individual's psychological, mental and emotional status.'" *Gross v. State*, 817 N. E. 2d 306 (Ind. Ct. App. 2004) (quoting Harrison, 644 N. E. 2d at 890). The plain language of the statute and decisions of the Court support the inclusion of mental and psychological harm within the definition of "health." As well, it could not have been the legislature's intent to leave such severe consequence of neglect beyond the reach of the law.

Although Andrew denied having any "health" problems during the time in question (Tr. 53), he did lose five to ten pounds (Tr. 35) and he missed meals because there was no food in his home (Tr. 41). Andrew also testified that he felt depressed because his mother left him alone for several weeks without telling him where she had gone (Tr. 42), with very little food and drink at home, and no water service. He was required to visit his neighbor and grandmother's houses for *basic necessities* of hygiene and care. (Tr. 29, 40) The evidence demonstrated physical and psychological suffering caused by Defendant's abandonment on two occasions. Andrew's life or health was subjected to an actual and appreciable danger.

(a)(2) *Abandonment*

The trial court instructed the jury that "abandon" means to desert the child with the intention of casting off all parental obligations. (App. 79) This definition does not necessarily require an element of "finality" to the decision. Any period of time when a parent casts off all parental obligations is abandonment.

Defendant had certain responsibilities to care for her child. However, Defendant left Andrew home alone twice for a total of three weeks. (Tr. 32). During this time Defendant made no provision for her child and evinced no interest in him. She did not entrust him to anyone's care during her absence. Defendant cast off all parental obligations during his three week period of time. An interpretation as Defendant urges would effectively permit the abandonment of children and other dependents for long periods of time — even years — and no neglect by abandonment would occur provided the parent reappears sometimes before the dependent's majority, emancipation or death.

(a)(3) *Deprivation of Necessary Support*

This Court has held that necessary support is considered to be that which is "essential, indispensable or absolutely required food, clothing, shelter or medical care without which the dependent's life or health is at risk or endangered." *Richetts v. State*, 597 N. E. 2d 597, 601 (Ind. Ct. App. 1992).

Andrew testified that there was absolutely no food at home for days. (Tr. 54). Andrew lost weight during this time, not because he wanted to but because he was hungry. (Tr. 35) He had no change of clean clothing. His grandmother provided him with clean clothing when Andrew took a shower at her house. (Tr. 41) There was no water service, which is "essential, indispensable or absolutely required," especially during the summer months. It is beyond a reasonable doubt that Andrew was deprived of necessary support.

The State sufficiently proved that Defendant neglected her son by endangering his health or life, abandonment and deprivation of necessary support.

CONCLUSION

For the foregoing reasons, the State of Indiana respectfully urges the Court to affirm the judgment of the trial court.

Respectfully submitted,

Steve Carter
Attorney General of Indiana
Atty. Number 4150-64

_____

Gary Damon Secrest
　　Deputy Attorney General
Atty. Number 2259-49

Falian Zhang
Law Clerk

Certificate of Service

I do solemnly affirm under the penalties for perjury that on June 5, 2006, I served upon the opposing counsel in the above-entitled cause two copies of the Brief of Appellee by depositing the same in the United States mail first-class postage prepaid, addressed as follows:

Craig Persinger
215 S. Adams St., Suite 202
P. O. Box 113
Marion, IN 46952

_____

Gary Damon Secrest
Deputy Attorney General

Office of Attorney General
Indiana Government Center South, Fifth Floor
302 West Washington Street
Indianapolis, Indiana 46204-2770
Telephone: (317) 232-6315

A Brief to an Appellate Court (2)

IN THE

COURT of APPEALS of INDIANA

CAUSE No. 49A04-0604-JV-186

M.O.,	Appeal from the Marison Superior
Appellant (Defendant below),	Court, Juvenile Division, Room 3,
v.	Case No. 49D09-0512-JD-005278
STATE OF INDIANA,	49D09-0512-JD-002785
Appellee (Plaintiff below).	Hon. Geoffrey Gaither, Magistrate.

BRIEF OF APPELLEE

STEPHEN R. CARTER
Attorney General of Indiana
Atty. No. 0004150-64

GARY DAMON SECREST
Deputy Attorney General
Atty. No. 0002259-49
Office of Attorney General
Indiana Government Center
South, Fifth Floor
302 West Washington Street
Indianapolis, IN 46204-2770
Telephone: (317) 232-6315

Attorneys for Appellee

TABLE OF CONTENTS

Table of Authorities ···
Statement of the Issues ···
Statement of the Case ···
Statement of the Facts
Summary of the Argument ··
Argument
     The evidence is sufficient to prove beyond a reasonable doubt about that Juvenile hit the victim and caused bodily injury ·······················
Standard of Review ··
Discussion ··
Conclusion ···
Certificate of Service ··

Table of Authorities

Cases

Smith v. State, 809 N. E. 2d 938 (Ind. Ct. App. 2004) ·················

Statutes

IC 35-42-2-1 ··

IN THE

COURT of APPEALS of INDIANA

CAUSE No. 49A04-0604-JV-186

M.O., *Appellant (Defendant below)*,	Appeal from the Marison Superior Court, Juvenile Division, Room 3,

v.	Case No. 49D09-0512-JD-005278
STATE OF INDIANA,	49D09-0512-JD-002785
Appellee (Plaintiff below).	Hon. Geoffrey Gaither, Magistrate.

BRIEF OF APPELLEE

STATEMENT OF THE ISSUE

Whether the evidence is sufficient to prove beyond a reasonable doubt that Juvenile committed a battery resulting in bodily injury

STATEMENT OF THE CASE

This Juvenile action was initiated on December 8, 2005, when the state alleged that Juvenile committed an act which would be battery, as a Class A Misdemenor (Ind. Code §35-42-2-1), if committed by an adult. (App. 10) Juvenile was on probation at the time of the offense, and was therefore also alleged to have violated his probation in the other cases. (App. 63) An initial hearing was held on December 12, 2005. (Tr. 1) The denial hearing was held on January 25, 2006, and the trial court entered a true finding on the delinquency allegation and a true finding on the Violation of Probation allegation. (Tr. 43) The disposition hearing was held on March 1, 2006, and Juvenile was placed on probation for the new allegation, and continued on probation for the violation. (App. 38)

A Notice of Appeal was filed on March 10, 2006. (App. 1)

The Notice of Completion of the Clerk's Record was filed on April 18, 2006.

The Notice of Completion of the Transcript was filed on June 13, 2006.

The Brief of Appellant was filed on July 12, 2006, with personal service on the Attorney General.

STATEMENT OF THE FACTS

Juvenile, fifteen (15) years old and the victim both were students of Emma Donnan Middle School in Indianapolis. (Tr. 31) On the afternoon of

December 8, 2005, Juvenile got on the bus while the victim was already sitting in the front of the bus. (Tr. 12) The victim went to the back of the bus where Juvenile was sitting to ask why he called her names. *Id*. But Juvenile responded with calling the victim a "black bitch" and a "nigger" again. *Id*. Juvenile started fighting by hitting the victim on her face which was painful. When the fight was stopped by others, the victim's nose was bleeding. *Id*.

SUMMARY OF THE ARGUMENT

The trial court properly dealt with the evidence. There is sufficient evidence to prove beyond a reasonable doubt that Juvenile hit the victim and caused victim's nose bleeding thereby establishing Battery, Class A Misdemeanor.

ARGUMENT

The evidence is sufficient to prove beyond a reasonable doubt that Juvenile hit the victim and caused bodily injure.

STANDARD OF REVIEW

When reviewing a claim of sufficiency of the evidence, the Court will neither reweigh the evidence nor judge the credibility of the witness. *Smith v. State*, 809 N. E. 2d 938 (Ind. Ct. App. 2004). Rather, the Court will consider the evidence and reasonable inferences drawn therefrom that support the verdict and will affirm the conviction if there is probative evidence from which a reasonable person could have found the defendant guilty beyond a reasonable doubt. *Id*.

DISCUSSION

Juvenile's argument is that the State failed to present sufficient evidence to prove beyond a reasonable doubt that the victim was hit by Juvenile first and caused bodily injury.

The victim testified that Juvenile hit her first and punched her in the face, which caused her bodily injury:

Q: Physical things happen between you guys?

A: He pushed me and I pushed him back.

Q: Okay. And then what happened?

A: He hit me right here on the side of my face.

Q: What did he hit you with?

A: His hand.

Q: Was his hand open or closed?

A: Open.

Q: And did you feel any pain?

A: Yes.

Q: Did you have any sort of injury from that?

A: My nose was bleeding. (Tr: 12—13)

Q: And are you claiming that — are you claiming today that you did not hit Michael first?

A: I didn't hit him in his face.

Q: You hit him in his face?

A: I didn't.

Q: You're claiming that you didn't hit him at all?

A: I pushed him. That's all about it. (Tr. 15)

The other witness is an independent, non-biased witness who has no reason to lie and he was doing his civic duty as a bus driver at that time he saw this incident. This driver testified that he saw Juvenile hitting the victim and victim's nose was bleeding.

Q: But you saw her nose bleeding?

A: I saw him hitting her, yes. (Tr. 25)

The State sufficiently proved beyond a reasonable doubt that Juvenile attacked the victim and caused bodily injury. The evidence is sufficient to prove that Juvenile is guilty of Battery as a Class A Misdemeanor.

CONCLUSION

For the foregoing reasons, the State of Indiana respectfully urges the Court to affirm the judgment of the trial court.

Respectfully submitted,

Steve Carter
Attorney General of Indiana
Atty. Number 4150-64

_____
Gary Damon Secrest
　　　Deputy Attorney General
Atty. Number 2259-49

Falian Zhang
Law Clerk

Certificate of Service

  I do solemnly affirm under the penalties for perjury that on June 5, 2006, I served upon the opposing counsel in the above-entitled cause two copies of the Brief of Appellee by depositing the same in the United States mail first-class postage prepaid, addressed as follows:

Patricia Caress McMath
5255 E. 73 rd Court
Indianapolis, IN 46250

_____
Gary Damon Secrest
Deputy Attorney General

Office of Attorney General
Indiana Government Center South, Fifth Floor
302 West Washington Street
Indianapolis, Indiana 46204-2770
Telephone: (317) 232-6315

A Brief to an Appellate Court (3)[1]

No. COA04-1219   TWENTY-EIGHTH DISTRICT

NORTH CAROLINA COURT OF APPEALS

STATE OF NORTH CAROLINA v. CHRISTOPHER ERIC MILLER, Defendant.	From Pamlico

DEFENDANT-APPELLANT'S BRIEF,
FILED PURSUANT TO ANDERS V. CALIFORNIA

INDEX

Table of Authorities and Cases ....
Questions Presented ....
Statement of the Case ....
Statement of the Facts ....
Statement of the Grounds for Appellate Review ....
Argument ....
Request for Review Pursuant to Anders v. California ....
Conclusion ....
Index to Appendix ....
Certificate of Service ....

TABLE OF AUTHORITIES AND CASES

CASES

Anders v. California, 386 U.S. 738, 87 S.Ct. 1396, 18 L. Ed. 2d
   493 (1967) ....
State v. Kinch, 314 N.C. 99, 331 S.E.2d 665 (1985) ....

---

[1] http://www.ncids.org/Brief%20Bank/Briefs/Miller,%20Christopher.doc

STATUTES

N. C. Gen. Stat. §14-7.6 (2004) ·············
N. C. Gen. Stat. §15A-1022 (2004) ·············
N. C. Gen. Stat. §15A-1340.14 (2004) ·············
N. C. Gen. Stat. §§14-7.1, et seq. (2004) ·············
N. C. Gen. Stat. §§15A-1023 (2004) ·············

No. COA04-1219	TWENTY-EIGHTH DISTRICT
NORTH CAROLINA COURT OF APPEALS	
STATE OF NORTH CAROLINA	
v.	From Pamlico
CHRISTOPHER ERIC MILLER, Defendant.	

QUESTIONS PRESENTED

1. Whether the sentence imposed results from an incorrect finding of the defendant's prior record level, because the court used two of the felonies used to support his Habitual Felon status to calculate his prior record level.

2. Whether Defendant's plea was involuntary and not entered knowingly when the Plea Transcript that he executed incorrectly showed each of the Obtaining Property by False Pretenses at a lower of class of Felony and a maximum term of imprisonment that was half the actually applicable maximum. The trial judge corrected the plea transcript and advised Defendant of the changes in open court. Defendant was not given time to reflect or consider the effect of these changes.

STATEMENT OF THE CASE

On January 7, 2004, in Buncombe County Superior Court, the Honorable E. Penn Dameron, Jr. presiding, Defendant-Appellant Christopher Eric Miller pleaded guilty on Bills of Information to the following charges:

CASE NUMBER	CHARGE
03-CRS-60869	Obtaining Property by False Pretenses
03-CRS-61665	Felony Breaking or Entering and Larceny after B&E
03-CRS-61666	Obtaining Property by False Pretenses
03-CRS-61874	Obtaining Property by False Pretenses
03-CRS-61875	Obtaining Property by False Pretenses
03-CRS-61876	Obtaining Property by False Pretenses
03-CRS-61877	Obtaining Property by False Pretenses
03-CRS-61878	Obtaining Property by False Pretenses
03-CRS-62042	Felony Larceny
03-CRS-62043	Felony Larceny
03-CRS-62044	Obtaining Property by False Pretenses
03-CRS-62045	Felony Breaking or Entering and Larceny after B&E
03-CRS-62295	Obtaining Property by False Pretenses
03-CRS-62894	Obtaining Property by False Pretenses
03-CRS-62895	Obtaining Property by False Pretenses
03-CRS-62896	Obtaining Property by False Pretenses
03-CRS-62950	Obtaining Property by False Pretenses
03-CRS-19335	Habitual Felon
03-CRS-19334	Habitual Felon
03-CRS-19333	Habitual Felon
03-CRS-19332	Habitual Felon

Sentencing occurred on January 7, 2004, immediately after the guilty plea and pursuant to the plea agreement. Judge Dameron found Mr. Miller's prior record level was V and that mitigating factors outweighed aggravating. He sentenced Mr. Miller to serve a minimum of 90 months and maximum of 117 months in the North Carolina Department of Corrections. In addition, he ordered restitution of $12,300.77. Mr. Miller filed written pro se Notice of Appeal on January 9, 2004.

The Record on Appeal was settled by agreement between counsel for the State and counsel for Defendant. The Record was filed in the Court of Appeals on September 10, 2004 and docketed on September 20, 2004. The Clerk mailed the printed Record on Appeal on September 28, 2004

STATEMENT OF THE FACTS

Defendant-Appellant was charge with thirteen counts of Felony Obtaining Property by False Pretence, four charges of Felony Larceny, two counts of Felony Breaking or Entering, and four counts of Habitual Felon status. He pleaded guilty pursuant to a Plea Agreement with the State. The terms of the Agreement were that upon his guilty plea, the State would agree to consolidate all charges into one count of Habitual Felon, to be served concurrently with any revoked probation and that the state would dismiss other charges pending in Buncombe County District Court. (R. pp. 3—39 and 41—43.)

Defendant stipulated to the factual basis for the plea, allowing the State to summarize rather than present evidence in that regard. The State's summary tended to show the following. The false pretense charges arose from checks on a closed account written by Mr. Miller during the course of his former business as a contractor. The details of those specific counts are set forth in the Transcript, a copy of which is attached as an Appendix to this Brief, p. 9, line 9 — p. 12, line 18. The Habitual Felon count was based upon prior convictions of Felony Larceny, Felony Possession with Intent to Sell or Deliver Marijuana, and Forgery. (T. p. 9, line 9—p. 12.) The defendant, through counsel, stipulated to his prior record level of 18 points.

STATEMENT OF THE GROUNDS FOR APPELLATE REVIEW

Mr. Miller pleaded guilty and was sentenced to the bottom of the presumptive range. The only grounds under which he is entitled to appeal as a matter of right is provided by N. C. Gen. Stat. 15A-1444 (2003), which states:

> [a] defendant who has ... entered a plea of guilty ... is entitled to appeal as a matter of right the issue of whether his or her sentence is supported by evidence introduced at the trial and sentencing hearing only if the minimum sentence of imprisonment does not fall within the presumptive range for the defendant's prior record or conviction level and class of offense.
>
> Id.

ARGUMENT

Request for Review Pursuant to Anders v. California

The undersigned, court-appointed counsel has conducted a thorough examination of this case, including the Superior Court record, relevant cases, and statutes. After conscientious examination, however, she finds the appeal to be wholly frivolous. Counsel is unable to identify an issue with sufficient merit to support a meaningful argument for relief on appeal. Counsel therefore respectfully requests the Court to fully examine the record on appeal for possible prejudicial error and to determine whether counsel overlooked any issue, in accord with Anders v. California, 386 U.S. 738, 87 S. Ct. 1396, 18 L. Ed. 2d 493 (1967) and State v. Kinch, 314 N.C. 99, 331 S.E. 2d 665 (1985).

Counsel sent a copy of this brief with a cover letter to Defendant by first class mail. The cover letter advises Defendant of his right to file supplemental arguments on his own behalf and provides him with the address of the court. A copy of the letter is attached in the Appendix to this Brief. Counsel respectfully asks the Court grant Defendant sufficient time "to raise any points that [he] chooses in support of this appeal." Id. at 744.

In accordance with Anders, supra, counsel submits this brief to provide what assistance she can to the Court reviewing this matter for possible error. Counsel directs the court's attention to the following issues that might arguably support the appeal.

1. The sentence imposed results from an incorrect finding of the defendant's prior record level, because the court used two of the felonies used to support his Habitual Felon status to calculate his prior record level.

Assignment of Error No. 1, R. pp. 44—45 and 51—53.

N. C. Gen. Stat. 15A-1444 (2003) gives a Defendant the right to appeal from a guilty plea on "the issue of whether his or her sentence is supported by evidence introduced at the trial and sentencing hearing only if the minimum sentence of imprisonment does not fall within the presumptive range for the defendant's prior record or conviction level and class of offense." Counsel directs this court's attention to the following to assist it in determining whether Mr. Miller's sentence falls within the presumptive range:

1) Offense classification for Habitual Felon, N. C. Gen. Stat. §14-7.6 (2004);

2) With regard to offenses used to calculate prior record level, Prior Record Level Worksheet at R. pp. 44—45;

3) With regard to the calculation of prior record level points, N. C. Gen. Stat. §15A-1340.14 (2004);

4) With regard to Habitual Felon status in general, N. C. Gen. Stat. §§14-7.1, et seq. (2004).

2. Other areas of possible error.

Finally, pursuant to Anders and Kinch, counsel directs the court's attention to the issue of whether the court complied with the statutes related guilty plea procedures in Superior Court. See N. C. Gen. Stat. §§15A-1022 and 1023 (2004).

CONCLUSION

Wherefore, in accordance with Anders, supra, the undersigned counsel respectfully requests this court to review the entire record in this matter for possible error. Further, counsel prays the court grant Defendant an adequate opportunity to prepare and present any written arguments he wishes to make on his own behalf in light of counsel's inability to find a non-frivolous argument in this appeal.

Respectfully submitted, this the _____ day of October 2004.

Leslie C. Rawls
Attorney for Appellant

PO Box 38325
Charlotte, NC 28278
704-583-1279
LeslieRawls@Carolina.rr.com

INDEX TO APPENDIX

Transcript of Proceedings on January 7, 2003 ....
Letter from counsel to Defendant ....

CERTIFICATE OF SERVICE

I hereby certify that I served the foregoing Defendant-Appellant's brief all parties to this action by depositing a copy of the document in the United States Mail, properly wrapped with postage attached, addressed to:

For the State:
Jill F. Cramer
Assistant Attorney General
NC Dept. of Justice
9001 Mail Service Center
Raleigh, NC 27699-9001

This the _____ day of _____ 2005.

References

1. Alan L. Dworsky, *The Little Book on Legal Writing* (2d ed., Fred B. Rothman & Co. 1992).
2. Diana Hacker, *A Writer's Reference* (2d ed., St. Martin's Press 1992).
3. James W. Martin, *Foundations of Legal Research & Writing* (2d ed., Thomson West, 2002).
4. John C. Dernbach, Richard V. Singleton II, Cathleen S. Wharton, Joan M. Ruhtenberg, *Legal Writing & Legal Method* (2d ed., Fred B. Rothman Publications 2000).
5. Mark E. Wojcik, *Introduction to Legal English* (2d ed., International Law Institute 2001).
6. Nancy L. Schultz, *Legal Writing and other Lawyering Skills* (3d ed., Matthew Bender & Co. 1998).
7. Richard C. Wydick, *Plain English for Lawyers* (4th ed., Carolina Academic Press 1998).
8. 张法连. 英美法律术语辞典[Z]. 上海：上海外语教育出版社，2014
9. 张法连. 大学法律英语教程[M]. 北京：外语教学与研究出版社，2014
10. 中国政法大学法律英语教学与测试研究中心课题组. 法律英语专业教学大纲[M]. 北京：高等教育出版社，2013